D. W. WINNICOTT
THINKING ABOUT
CHILDREN

Edited by

Ray Shepherd
Jennifer Johns
Helen Taylor Robinson

Bibliography compiled by

Harry Karnac

A Merloyd Lawrence Book

DA CAPO PRESS
A MEMBER OF THE PERSEUS BOOKS GROUP

Library of Congress Cataloging-in-Publication Data

Winnicott, D. W. (Donald Woods), 1896-1971.
 Thinking about children / D.W. Winnicott : edited by Ray Shepherd, Jennifer Johns,
and Helen Taylor Robinson.
   p. cm.
 "A Merloyd Lawrence book."
 Includes bibliographical references and index.
 ISBN 0-201-40700-0
 ISBN 0-201-32794-5 (pbk.)
 1. Child mental health. 2. Child psychology. 3.Child analysis.
 I. Shepherd, Ray. II. Johns, Jennifer. III. Robinson, Helen Taylor. IV. Title.
 RJ499.W493 1996
 618.92'89—dc20
                                                              96-11007
                                                              CIP

Copyright © 1996 by The Winnicott Trust
by arrangement with Mark Paterson
Bibliography © 1996 Harry Karnac
Frontispiece portrait © Lotte Meitner-Graf

Published in the U.K. by H. Karnac Books Limited.

Da Capo press is a member of the Perseus Books Group
Cover design by Suzanne Heiser
Text design by Eric A. King
Set in 10-point Palatino by Communication Crafts

10 9 8 7 6 5 4
First printing, June 1996
First paperback printing, December 1997

Visit us on the World Wide Web at www.dacapopress.com

D. W. Winnicott (centre), with Clare Winnicott and Dr William H. Gillespie, former President of the British Psycho-Analytic Society and of the International Psychoanalytical Association

This book is dedicated to the memory
of Clare Winnicott, founder of The Winnicott Trust,
whose work in the early stages made it possible

CONTENTS

PART SEVEN
Psychosomatic problems

PART EIGHT
Autism and schizophrenia

PART NINE
Professional care
of the growing child

ACKNOWLEDGEMENTS

The initial selection of published and unpublished papers for the present volume of Donald Winnicott's work was made by Clare Winnicott, Madeleine Davis, and Ray Shepherd.

The Editors are grateful to Harry Karnac for generously allowing us to include his comprehensive bibliography of Winnicott's published works. This, we believe, will be of value to anyone interested in the great variety of subjects that Winnicott wrote about, as well as those concerned with the development of his thought.

We also wish to thank our publishers, Cesare Sacerdoti and his assistant Graham Sleight of Karnac Books, and Merloyd Lawrence on behalf of Addison-Wesley Publishing Company and Merloyd Lawrence Books, for their attention to detail and their close and helpful support during the production of this book.

Our agents, Mark Paterson, and in particular his associate, Mary Swinney, have offered unfailing help.

Our thanks go also to Ann Glynn, who was responsible for typing the book; and to Eric and Klara King of Communication Crafts, who helped in the final preparation of the book for publication.

Finally, for their help in establishing sources and references for some of the papers we would like to thank

Geoffrey Davenport, Librarian of the Royal College of Physicians; Jill Duncan, Librarian of the British Psycho-Analytical Society; Catherine Teale and Robert Greenwood at the Library of the Royal Society of Medicine; Margaret Walker, Librarian of the Tavistock Centre and Institute of Human Relations; and the staff of the British Medical Association Library.

PREFACE

The topics of the papers in this volume range from earliest infancy to adolescence, but they are held together by the author's own theory of child development. For Winnicott, facts were the reality. He wrote in the simplest vernacular; he wrote as he spoke, simply, and in order to relate. This makes these papers accessible to parents and the general reader, as well as to professionals concerned with children. A number of the papers in this collection have never previously been published; the rest are works that are otherwise difficult to access since they appeared in journals or in books that are no longer in print.

For nearly fifty years Winnicott was deeply engaged in paediatrics, child psychology, child psychiatry, and psychoanalysis. He held office as President of the Paediatric Section of the Royal Society of Medicine and was awarded the James Spence Gold Medal for Paediatrics in 1968. He was also Chairman of the Medical Section of the British Psychological Society and was twice elected President of the British Psycho-Analytical Society. All this was in recognition of an originality founded in great common sense and also of his understanding of children and their families, in their whole setting and at their particular stage of development. A striking feature of Winnicott's work was his great power of observation and description so that what he writes has an air

of extraordinary familiarity—one feels that one has known what
he reports all along.

Winnicott held that the innate potential for growth in a baby
(and he was aware of the damage to innate potential, or the
restrictions of potential in the baby, too) expressed itself in spontaneous gestures. If the mother responds appropriately to these
gestures, the quality of adaptation provides a growing nucleus of
experience in the baby, which results in a sense of wholeness,
strength, and confidence that he calls the "true self". The growing strength of the "true self" enables the infant to cope with
more frustration and relative failure on the part of the mother,
without loss of liveliness. If a mother is unable to meet her baby's
gestures appropriately, the baby develops a capacity to adapt to
and comply with the mother's "impingements"—that is, with the
mother's initiatives and demands—and the baby's spontaneity is
gradually lost. Winnicott called such a defensive development
the "false self". The greater the "mis-fit" between mother and
baby, the greater the distortion and stunting of the baby's personality.

Stressing that the decisive phase in the infant's development
is the achievement of a unitary self capable of objectivity and
creative activity, Winnicott described transitional stages between
initial subjectivity and growing objectivity in the infant based on
the development of the self through the growing capacity for
symbolization and cultural experience.

These are the barest bones of some of Winnicott's main
contributions to the theory of child development. On the basis of
his theory he was able to make contributions to a wide range
of problems of concern to those trying to help children and their
families. Winnicott maintained a central role for both innate and
internal, as well as external, influences on child development.
Therefore, he emphasized the role of trauma and deprivation as
well as that of intra-psychic conflict in the formation of psychopathology. He attributed health and creativity to the quality of
early care-taking, primarily by the mother and supported by the
father. This gives hope to those trying to help, such that when
ill-health and breakdown occur, the regressive disintegration of
the personality is not seen as irreparable. Not just re-growth, but
new growth is possible in Winnicott's theories.

* * *

The Editors have followed the policy adopted for all the hitherto published works of Donald Winnicott: namely, to make few changes to the writings that Winnicott left, in order to preserve the characteristics of Winnicott's style, which often shows the development of thought—or the process of forming thought—in full flow. Also, many of the papers in this volume were originally presented as speeches or lectures (a full list of the original sources appears on pp. 287–289); these papers, too, have been left as they would have been presented, rather than being changed to a less informal style.

The Editors wish to draw particular attention to four subgroupings of papers whose subject matter belongs together. These are (a) two transcripts of talks (chapters 3 and 4) about the earliest stages of development written in 1948, by which time Winnicott was expressing his theory of early infant life with great clarity; (b) three papers (chapters 16 to 18) on a still much-neglected subject—adoption—in all its ramifications for the welfare of the child and for the natural and the adoptive parents, both as it affects early development and in later repercussions if adopted children seek out their natural parents; (c) two papers on childhood schizophrenia, one specifically on aetiology, written in 1966 and 1967 (chapters 25 and 26), which represent a natural continuity of Winnicott's thinking to a radical conclusion (these papers are described in greater detail in the Introduction); (d) papers concerned with the complementary and interlocking roles of those professions responsible for the care of children as they grow up—namely, chapter 12 and chapters 29 to 31, which date from 1967–1970 and arose from Winnicott's long working connections with colleagues in allied professions as well as his period of office as President of the Association of Child Psychology and Psychiatry.

INTRODUCTION

Winnicott started his life's work—the observation and study of children—as a medical practitioner and, in particular, as a paediatrician. He began his vocation with children in a medical framework, the paediatric hospital setting. Becoming interested in Freud's writings and in his own psyche, he undertook analysis with James Strachey in 1923, followed by a second analysis with Joan Riviere in 1933, and trained as a psychoanalyst. He practised as an analyst until his death in 1971, while at the same time continuing to work with children in the medical framework, at Paddington Green Children's hospital, where he actively applied to his work the understanding gained from his training in and practice of psychoanalysis.

The process of psychoanalytic observation and study was founded by Freud, first on the basis of the observations he made from his own self-analysis and later based on the analysis of adult men and women, and then, briefly, and only by proxy, on experience gained from working with a child ("Little Hans"). His inferences about the human psyche, in infancy, childhood, and adult life, thus drew on his experiences with adult patients in the setting of his consulting rooms in Vienna, where he practised, privately, as a doctor, seeing adult patients frequently, and intensively, sometimes every day. Later, Melanie Klein and others adapted the psychoanalytic method for the treatment of children. Working with small numbers of children, again seen intensively, Klein drew conclusions about the psyche that she could apply from child psychoanalysis to the understanding of adults and in later years to the so-called psychoses in adults. Her research, and the source of her thinking and writing, like Freud's, both grew from and remained within a two-person (analyst and patient) clinical setting.

In his short talk entitled "The Bearing of Emotional Development on Feeding Problems" (Chapter 5 of this volume), delivered in 1967 to a Symposium on Environmental Health in Infancy held at the Royal Society of Medicine, Donald Winnicott emphasizes the extent of what he owes to his medical training and continuing experience.

> As you probably know, I started off as a paediatrician and gradually changed over into being a psychoanalyst and a child psychiatrist, and the fact that I was originally a physically minded doctor has greatly influenced my work. I do happen to have a very big volume of experience, which simply arises out of the fact that I have been in active practice for forty-five years, and in that time one does accumulate a lot of data.

This acknowledged debt to medical science and also to a setting in which psychoanalytic investigation could be continuously tested and applied put Winnicott in a position that might be described as having the aim of both understanding children's behaviour and trying to search for its causes. From this position Winnicott was comfortable in speaking about data, and it is possible that this continuation of "active practice", as Winnicott puts it, in order both to develop and to modify psychoanalytic ideas may have great significance for the future of psychoanalysis as a model or theory of mind that can be studied and researched.

Winnicott maintained his paediatric work, and the medical setting in which he had trained, alongside his development as a practitioner of psychoanalysis. He stayed in touch with the field which afforded him sustained clinical contact with the child (and in particular the child who is brought by the parent, usually the mother, to see the doctor when ill), and he used this experience for prolonged psychoanalytic study of infancy as it develops into adulthood. This allowed him nearly half a century of case study and clinical observation, and access to some 60,000 or so inter-actions with patients (a volume of observation comparable with that of his admired predecessor and strong influence, Charles Darwin, in *On the Origin of Species*).

Winnicott established this practice of clinical observation, both in the children's hospital setting of Paddington Green Chil-dren's Hospital and also in the setting created during the turmoil of the war years—the hostels for evacuated children, many of whom were deprived and delinquent, to which he was a Govern-ment-appointed Consultant, and where he came to know and collaborate with his future wife, Clare Britton. This observation continued in the setting of his own consulting-rooms where analysis of children and adults could appropriately be offered or where analytic assessment or short-term psychotherapeutic help might be given. He recorded the results of these researches in the many volumes of papers, lectures, notes, talks, broadcasts, and letters that comprise his work. This invaluable documentation of data is what he speaks of as "accumulating".

The combination of the concentrated focus upon individuals by means of the psychoanalytic method, together with the obser-vation of large numbers of mothers and children passing through his hospital and private practice work, also allows the singular and highly unusual contribution of Winnicott to the broader fields of study of the human psyche. This concentrate of psychoanalytic reading of his material, together with the range, difference, distinctness, and dissimilarity that he observed in hundreds of individuals coming for treatment, enabled him to make his most significant and distinct contributions to psycho-analytic theory.

Psychoanalysis began as a particular kind of observation, and by inference and deduction Freud, as a scientist, hypothesized his theories of mind. The methodology he laid down in the setting of the consulting room, where it was felt that such observation and deduction could continue, and the increase of clinical experience from more analysts in such settings, led to Freud's hope that a body of data could be established reflecting accurately the nature of this work. This hope has borne fruit and has validated his method of research; it was the foundation on which Winnicott, adding his wide experience and the fruits of his own observations, was able to build further.

In "Towards an Objective Study of Human Nature" (chapter 1), Winnicott, speaking to the senior pupils of St Paul's School, London, says:

> Intuitive understanding of human nature must often prove unreliable as a guide in the more general field of social living. It might enable a doctor to be brilliantly understanding of a patient who was a thief, but unless the psychology of delinquency is studied as a science, intuitive understanding will not prevent doctors as well as other people from doing and saying all sorts of useless things when decisions have to be taken in a practical way, as, for instance, in a juvenile court.

Winnicott continues in the same paper to elaborate this point further:

> Perhaps you are beginning to see that there is some point in making the study of human nature a science, a process characterized by observation of facts, by the building of theory and the testing of it, and by the modification of theory according to the discovery of new facts. Can you see one essential way in which science and intuition contrast with each other? True intuition can reach to a whole truth in a flash (just as faulty intuition can reach to error), whereas in a science the whole truth is never reached. What is important in science is a construction of a satisfactory road towards the truth. That is why a scientific training is so important for everybody; it enables you and me to test our own little bits of the world satisfactorily.

Winnicott is clear that for himself as a scientist it is the reliability of evidence in a given setting that must be established. The construction of a satisfactory road towards truth, the importance of a scientific training, and the attempt at objectivity characterize the formulations that have already made Winnicott a leading figure in the science of the psyche; that science, in his case, being largely derived from the particular contributions made by psychoanalysis, as against the many other disciplines that enable us to think about and study the psyche.

This decision to specialize and to remain a specialist in paediatrics, together with the choice Winnicott made to undertake psychoanalysis and to study and write about paediatrics and psychoanalysis as they came together in his own understanding, can be said to have led inevitably to the particular specialization that he made his own. This specialization was the observation and study of the infant and its mother, in a diversity of forms, and what this allowed him to deduce about the psyche, infant and mature.

The distinction, methodologically, from Freud and others, was the decision to continue to study the infant and its mother, in situ, as a *"psychic unity"*, a decision that grew out of the unique investigatory position afforded to the paediatrician/psychoanalyst. This was the opportunity to be in a position to observe the succession of mothers and babies (in some cases, very small babies, in the first weeks of life) that would pass before the doctor, and to use that as potential data pertaining to *the infant–mother constellation* rather than the infant and its mother purely as two distinct beings.

As we have said, Freud inferred his theories about the infant psyche and its development by way of what his adult patients chose to tell him. He did not study children or their mothers systematically except by these means. Neither Freud nor Klein chose to study the infant and its mother *together*, in the analytic setting. All inferences about object relations, infant and mother, were made either without the presence of the living data in the form of the mother, or without the presence of that data in the form of the child. What the actual infant did with the actual mother was something that Winnicott, through the particular use of his trainings in both paediatrics and psychoanalysis, could uniquely come to observe and document in some detail. Like Freud, who observed Charcot's hysterics, Winnicott could subject these observations to the understanding he also derived from psychoanalysis. In this way he could use his observations of infant and mother together and try to test out, according to his psychoanalytic thinking, in what ways his observations held true. "It enables you and me to test our own little bits of the world satisfactorily" (Chapter 1).

Furthermore, it can be argued that only by virtue of the process of repetition and replication entailed in the collection of data was it possible to attend to significant changes occurring in the infant in specific, perhaps minutely different, "settings" (Winnicott's 1941 study, "The Observation of Infants in a Set Situation", which appeared in *Collected Papers: Through Paediatrics to Psycho-Analysis*, 1958, is a highly creative early example), and thus to come towards the construction of a psychoanalytic theory of Object Relations. Without sufficient and repeated opportunities to test the infant and mother *as a psychic unity*, and the consequent opportunity to observe and record significant changes, recognition of an evolving pattern might not have occurred. The fruits of this great contribution to the study of the psyche are already familiar in the published collections of his works, including "Transitional Objects and Transitional Phenomena", 1953, and the later conceptualization of a cluster of ideas around the construct he termed "the use of an object" in the second half of the 1960s, in " The Use of an Object and Relating through Identifications", 1969 (both of these works appear in *Playing and Reality*, 1971).

It can also be argued that the same repetition and assessment of data or information pertaining to the infant and mother as a psychic unity, and the noting of minute and particular significant differences in this psychic unity, was precisely what allowed the inference that the actual "setting"—that is, the environment in whatsoever forms it could be observed—made a scientifically significant contribution to the nature of the data collected. This complex interplay of infant and environment—infant and/or aspect of infant with mother and/or aspect of mother—was, to Winnicott's clinical eye, not an abstract formulation but something to be observed and examined, and from which deductions could be made by virtue of the scientific model he was using.

This is the research model that Winnicott was excited by, and undertook to increase the fund of knowledge of, in his many years of continuous work, and the Editors of this present collection of his psychoanalytic thinking about children wish to emphasize it as having special significance for the development of his theories. In preparing this collection of Winnicott's papers, addressed to different audiences and describing disparate and diffuse kinds of evidence and data, the Editors were struck by the familiar areas of interest in the infant–mother matrix that are in evidence at the very start of Winnicott's working life, and which continued to preoccupy him in yet more intriguing forms, until its close. In-between lie forty years of experience and twenty published volumes of writing testifying to this preoccupation.

In a paper from *The Child and the Family* entitled "The Only Child", written as early as 1928, Winnicott says:

> The majority of mothers and of those who form the world that the child meets from birth onwards act on intuition. It is possible to think and then act, to act and think afterwards, and to act without thinking at all. *The most important influence on a child's life is the sum of the unthought-out actions and reactions of the mother, and of the other relations and friends; it is not the one or two thought-out actions that have the main effects.* [emphasis added]

The third sentence in this paragraph is a hypothesis about the child and the mother, and there is no scientific evidence to support it, although it can be seen to derive from Freud's theories of the existence of unconscious fantasy in infant and adult human relations. But here it is, itself, an intuition, yet to be validated or disproved. It is a formulation capable of scientific research—no more. As the chapter unfolds, this hypothesis is placed at the centre of Winnicott's thinking about one clinical case, one clinical example among many that he sees. Winnicott describes a boy of 5½, his mother, his father, and the arrival of a baby sister, based on a clinical interaction, primarily with the boy, but also with the boy's mother. He states the evidence from the mother that represents his central hypothesis. Although this boy had changed dramatically for the worse in terms of his behaviour since the arrival of his baby sister, "The mother said that she was quite certain the change could *not* be due to the advent of the sister because he [the boy] was simply devoted to her [his baby sister]." This is an example of the mother's unthought-out actions and reactions, and Winnicott regards the effect it has on this boy as central to his thinking about this case. As he affirms, "We found ourselves born into a world in which the coexistence of love and hatred towards one object was considered impossible. We could not imagine ourselves not showing love, and the easiest way out was to become unaware of hatred." The mother's *lack of awareness* of the boy's hatred, as well as or alongside his love, leads to certain consequences for the boy that makes him, "psychologically speaking", "an only child". This is further described in the way the boy, on meeting with Winnicott alone, goes on to show Winnicott—by bringing a dream, through the use of drawings, and through the dialogue and the behaviour that emerges between the two—that the arrival of the baby sister has come too late. "In other words, emotionally he [the boy] will not accept the truth." This has consequences that Winnicott hypothesizes again in terms of the boy's adult emotional life. This formulation, which Winnicott also calls a truth, only in so far as it is derived from his own thinking and understanding of the case, has as yet no scientific validity; it has no claim as such, and is on the way to such scientific validity only if it is scientifically studied and researched.

Some forty clinical years later—and subsequent to Winnicott's major writings on the infant and mother, this specialization that he continued to write and think about in great detail—the above hypothesis, articulated in 1928, *reappears* at the centre of a formulation of quite a different kind, as part of a piece of thinking and writing also included in this new collection. This formulation, which takes shape in a document entitled "The Aetiology of Infantile Schizophrenia in Terms of Adaptive Failure" (chapter 26) was intended as a contribution for a study day on "Psychosis in Infancy", held in France in October 1967. It appears that Winnicott was unable to attend, but we believe that the paper was read in his absence; until its inclusion in this selection of Winnicott's writings it had not been published.

It is clear from at least three other papers, one of which is included here for the first time also (chapter 25, "Autism", delivered to the Society for Autistic Children, in Leicester, in 1966), that Winnicott was preoccupied in his thinking in the mid- to late 1960s with the infant and mother as a psychic unity in the area of infantile psychoses, infantile schizophrenia, and autism.

Two important papers, "The Psychology of Madness: A Contribution from Psycho-Analysis", 1965, and "The Concept of Clinical Regression Compared with That of Defence Organisation", 1967 (both already published in *Psychoanalytic Explorations*, 1989), together with "Autism", in the present volume, are preparatory, in our view, to the thinking in his paper on the aetiology of infantile schizophrenia (chapter 26).

The hypothesis or postulate derived from observation that "The most important influence on a child's life is the sum of the unthought-out actions and reactions of the mother, and of the other relations and friends; it is not the one or two thought-out actions that have the main effects" appears, in a recognizable, yet different, form in "The Aetiology of Infantile Schizophrenia in Terms of Adaptive Failure" as Note H of the paper, and we would like to draw attention to it in some detail.

Note H can only be understood in the full context of the document as a whole—that is, the entire formulation given in this summary of Winnicott's ideas at this point in time—and it is stressed by the Editors that a wider reading of Winnicott's thinking on the infant and mother as a psychic unity in health and otherwise would have to be taken as the full context for understanding this Note. Furthermore, it is one of a set of Notes constituting a cluster of significant ideas with regard to schizophrenia. The Notes (hypotheses) are formulated as a contribution to a scientific meeting in which he attempts to address the neuropsychological causes of schizophrenia in the infant, and in which he is fully aware that his own psychoanalytically orientated thinking, backed by a breadth of medical practice and experience, may hold little sway with the research of medical science coming from other directions towards the schizophrenias. That this is a neuropsychological statement or set of statements has to be emphasized, in that Note H itself, taken by itself, without the surrounding set of Notes, can be seen as psychological, rather than neurological. It is the accompanying formulations that complete the full picture. Nevertheless, from the point of view of the development of an early hypothesis made in 1928 about the child and the mother, there is a significant thread of continuity of thinking, now re-formulated after many opportunities to look at mother–infant coupling in health and in ill-health. Hence, it has the potential to be constructed and tested along the lines of a research model or project.

Winnicott places what he has to say in the following familiar context:

> Much of what I give here is to be found in the writings of others, but my own view developed in the course of my work as a paediatrician in the 1920s and 1930s, and became reformulated in the 1940s when I began to have my own way of stating the essential stages of the intertwined physical and emotional development of the human infant.

The reformulation Winnicott refers to here belongs to the period following his psychoanalytic training, which added to his medical and scientific training in the 1920s and 1930s. Here is confirmation that Winnicott's thinking on the schizophrenias has grown out of the medical/scientific and the psychoanalytic model—not one, not the other, but both.

After the necessary preliminary remarks in the first part of this document, essential to a full understanding of what he can now go on to postulate, Winnicott offers a cluster of nine ideas, (Notes A to I) that for him constitute the relevant ideas for a further study of infantile schizophrenia, which he gives reasons for designating as such, rather than the more accepted present-day term "autism". Again, we need to remember that this is not a scientific body of evidence, it is a cluster of significant ideas, or hypotheses, of which science, if it chooses, can make use. There is only the clinical evidence that Winnicott cites elsewhere, principally in chapter 25, "Autism" (repeated clinical interactions with many so-called "autistic" cases in his clinical practice), that can be said to support these ideas, together with all the body of thinking he has contributed to the study of the infant and mother as a psychic unity.

Note G is relevant before coming to Note H, and we quote both in full.

> (G) From my point of view, the essential feature (from amongst the vast sum of features) is *the mother's* (or substitute mother's) *capacity to adapt to the infant's needs through her healthy ability to identify with the baby* (without, of course, losing her

own identity). With such a capacity she can, for instance, hold her baby, and without it she cannot hold her baby except in a way that disturbs the baby's personal living process.

(H) It seems necessary to add to this the concept of the mother's *unconscious* (repressed) hate of the child. Parents naturally love and hate their babies, in varying degrees. This does not do damage. At all ages, and in earliest infancy especially, the effect of the repressed death wish towards the baby is harmful, and it is beyond the baby's capacity to deal with this. At a later stage than this one that concerns us here one can see a child all the time making effort *in order to arrive at the starting post*—that is, to counteract the parents' unconscious wish (covered by reaction formations) that the child should be dead. At the earlier stages that relate to the subject of autism, the baby can only show the *distortion* that results from his or her having been cared for by someone whose positive actions are all reaction formations; direct or spontaneous free and adaptive movements would all reveal the (repressed) death wish.

Such ideas call for courage on the part of those who discuss them, and yet without these ideas there is no hope, in my opinion, that any body of scientists will move towards an understanding of the aetiology of autism.

Note G may be said to represent Winnicott's own significant contributions towards the theory of Object · Relations, well known from all his previously published volumes—that is, his observation of the significant contribution that the mother can make to the emotional health and well-being of her infant: the provision of maternal preoccupation, reliability, and adaptation, particularly in terms of adequate empathic identification with her infant's needs. *The Maturational Processes and the Facilitating Environment* (1965) contains, among other collections of papers, much of Winnicott's work establishing and documenting clinical material to support this thinking.

Note H, in the opinion of the Editors, formulates some of what Winnicott has already expressed previously in relation to the mother's unconscious or repressed hatred of her infant, in "Hate in the Countertransference", 1947 (in *Collected Papers: Through Paediatrics to Psychoanalysis*), but here it is formulated in terms of another earlier idea, "the lost memory of unthinkable anxiety", stated in "Ego Integration in Child Development", 1962 (also in *The Maturational Processes and the Facilitating Environment*) and elsewhere, and they come together to arrive at a new position. This new position is that of the infant meeting with a failure of adaptation on the part of the mother towards it (a repudiation of the infant or a failure to identify empathically with it), before the infant has formed sufficient self or ego to sustain the failure and to conceptualize it in any other form than by the extraordinary sets of behaviours that comprise infantile schizophrenia/autism—that is, the characteristic "invulnerability" that marks such infants. Winnicott describes the infant in this state of extreme immaturity defending against the mother's active unconscious and repressed *hatred* of her child manifest in its denial. The mother is conceived of as wishing her baby dead but, more particularly, representing this wish by reverse behaviours. (This formulation of the death-wish by mother towards baby should be distinguished from the formulation of the Death Instinct as formulated by Freud and developed by Klein.) This, Winnicott hypothesizes, leaves the infant attempting to defend itself yet unable to do so except by means of distorted behaviours, these behaviours representing the mother's own distortions or reaction formations towards her infant. Winnicott also affirms that the coincidental brain damage or neurological damage that may or may not accompany such manifestations in such infants is also a significant factor (see Chapter 26) and one that may contribute significantly to the mother's hatred of that child.[1]

---

[1]For additional material elsewhere in Winnicott's writings on his theories of the importance of a mother's conscious and unconscious hatred for her baby in its positive and negative aspects with regard to the effect this may have on the baby's development, the Editors would like to draw attention at this point to two references because of their direct relevance to Winnicott's hypothesis here: *Therapeutic Consultations in Child Psychiatry* (1971, Case 1, pp. 12–27, in particular the interview with the mother, pp. 25–27), and "Hate in the Countertransference", 1947, in *Through Paediatrics to Psycho-Analysis* (1975, pp. 194–203). Related material can be found in the following: "A Note on Normality and Anxiety", in *Clinical Notes on Disorders of Childhood* (1931, pp. 98–121); "Aggression and its Roots", 1939, in *Deprivation and Delinquency* (1984, pp. 84–89, especially p. 87); "The Deprived Child and How He Can Be Compensated for Loss of Family Life", 1950, in *The Family and Individual Development* (1965, pp. 132–145, especially pp. 140);

As we understand it, such hypotheses, formulated in this way four years before Winnicott died, make a potentially significant contribution to the understanding of the psyche in so far as it concerns the schizophrenias, and they differ from other formulations, psychoanalytic in orientation, by virtue of this combination of clinical experience, medical and psychoanalytic training in tandem, and the wish to make a contribution to the scientific enquiry and development of such ideas along orthodox research lines—that is, the presentation of potential data for such research.

One of the difficulties of the conscious/unconscious paradigm as Freud formulated it is that, in creating the separate definitions (of conscious and unconscious), we inevitably tend to formulate a division between these two areas rather than see one area moving through, within, and all around the other continually. Despite an essential unity and continuity, there are differences between these two states of mind, and the act of extracting one from the other redefines them terminologically as if they were separate. In studying the infant and the mother at the inception of life, Winnicott quite rightly thought to catch the archetypal matrix of conscious and unconscious (the baby) as it

---

"For Stepparents", 1955, in *Talking to Parents* (1993, pp. 7–13, especially p. 11); "The Contribution of Midwifery to Psycho-Analysis", 1957, in *The Family and Individual Development* (1965, pp. 106–113, especially pp. 111–112); "Classification: Is There a Psycho-Analytic Contribution to Psychiatric Classification?", 1959/1964, in *The Maturational Processes and the Facilitating Environment* (1965, pp. 124–139); *Human Nature* (1988, especially pp. 114–115 and in particular the final paragraph on p. 115).

In addition to the reference material already present in Winnicott's writings, the Editors would like to draw attention to a hypothesis with regard to the eruption of hate, so called, at the birth of the infant, and directed primarily by the mother towards her child. This hypothesis is with regard to the arrival of the infant into the pre-existing matrix of mother and father as a couple, now creating a new oedipal triangle or constellation of relations. Any failure or difficulty within the mother relating to her own original oedipal constellation would now be potentially vulnerable to this new arrangement, which awakens dormant difficulties and activates new forces of love and hate, both conscious and unconscious. The potential for unconscious hate here is, of course, determined by factors in addition to these, but the constitution of the new oedipal triangle overlying the old can also be included as relevant, in both mother and, inevitably, father. It has, as a hypothesis, relevance to the conditions of post-natal depression and puerperal psychosis.

meets a new archetypal matrix of conscious and unconscious (the mother) at birth. He also was happy to leave the gap between mother and baby, each having their own area of reality intact, and suggested that this transitional area, far from being a void for all mothers and babies, a distance, was in fact an area of play, creativity, shared distance, and another meaning of the word "play", which is the kind associated with string or rope, the room for ("the play in a piece of rope that allows for . . ."), the expandability, the ability to manoeuvre, and so on.

Winnicott thought that mothers could tell us a lot about babies, meaning that they could tell us a lot about that paradigm, Conscious/Unconscious, in a very intense and heightened moment of experience—childbirth—and its continuing manifestation—mother/baby interaction in health and illness. So he watched, studied, and observed children and their mothers, at these heightened moments, to glean what he could of this. The interest of the papers that we have gathered together here is the fruit of that watching, established in the studies, presentations, notes, contributions, lectures, talks, which he then directed at new audiences, listeners, each time.

It is hoped, from the data—and the varied and distinct thinking that emerges from it in this present volume, in particular perhaps in the understanding that Winnicott brings to schizophrenia, though not solely in this area—that interest and perhaps future research will follow, and that Donald Winnicott's special gifts in this area—his conscious and unconscious thinking about children—will continue to be recognized and valued.

Ray Shepherd
Jennifer Johns
Helen Taylor Robinson

Part one

OBSERVATION, INTUITION, AND EMPATHY

1

Towards an objective study
of human nature

[1945]

You have invited me to speak to you on the subject of the
background of psychology, its basic assumptions and discoveries. In order not to get lost in so large a subject, I
must speak of the small part of it which comes my way; or, shall
I say, I must be allowed to look at the whole from my particular
angle.

I shall not be able to do what I ought to do, which is to take
into consideration the fact that you yourselves who are listening
to me come to the subject each from your own direction. Some of
you think easily in terms of scientific experiment, others are used
to being taught the facts, in so far as they are known, of history
or geography; and among you there are some with strong intuitive bent, who like to approach any new subject subjectively at
first, having ideas which you are unwilling to develop until you
have stated them and recognized them as your own. I cannot
cater for all this, so I shall go at it my own way.

I want to put before you the view that psychology simply
means the study of human nature, and that it is a science, just as
physics, physiology, and biology are sciences. This is my view,

I wish to thank my colleague Mr. Masud Khan for advice leading to modifi-
cations of the original lecture. D.W.W.

and my life's work is based on this assumption, for I think you ought to know at the outset that I am not only a doctor but also a psychoanalyst.

Psychoanalysis has only recently become recognized as a serious subject. As a word it has now passed into common speech, and, as usual when this happens, it has come to mean something different when used popularly from what it means technically. If you were to ask a doctor just what part psychoanalysis is playing now in the general medical field, and in the whole study of human nature, you would be unlikely to get correct information. The tendency to examine the psychological factors of every case that can be found in medicine today is extremely new, and it will take a generation more before the work that has already been done by psychoanalysis will be fully applied in ordinary medical practice. Some of you will become doctors, and a few will probably wish to practise in that part of doctoring which particularly involves the study of the mind, and then you will need, in addition to the ordinary medical training, a training in the psychoanalytic technique; but you can be helped by such training even if you plan to do that most difficult of all medical jobs—to be a good family general practitioner.

Psychology makes no claim to priority in regard to the understanding of human nature, except in one respect: that is to say, in the making of this study a science. For instance, it is possible that everything that can be discovered by psychoanalysis can be shown to have been understood by Shakespeare, taking Shakespeare as a good example of someone with intuitive understanding, based, of course, on observation as well as on feeling or empathy. Each step forward that we make in the science of psychology enables us to see more in Shakespeare's plays, just as it enables us to talk less foolishly about human nature. Talk we must, and psychology as a science justifies itself, in my opinion, if it enables us to talk less foolishly.

Also, it is not suggested that no psychological healing took place before psychoanalysis came on the field. Good doctors have always been good psychologists in so far as they could feel the patient's position in his relation to external reality and also in his relation to his private inner world. But doctors, when they talk about human nature, say silly things just as other people do. Intuitive understanding of human nature must often prove unreliable as a guide in the more general field of social living. It might enable a doctor to be brilliantly understanding of a patient who was a thief, but unless the psychology of delinquency is studied as a science, intuitive understanding will not prevent doctors as well as other people from doing and saying all sorts of useless things when decisions have to be taken in a practical way, as, for instance, in a juvenile court.

The doctor's long and arduous training does nothing to qualify him in psychology, and does much to disqualify him; it keeps him so busy from the age of 18 to 25 that he finds he is middle-aged before he has the leisure in which to discover himself. It takes him years of medical practice, and a struggle to find time to live his own life, before he can catch up on his fellow creatures, many of whom have lived a lot by the time they are 25.

Perhaps you are beginning to see that there is some point in making the study of human nature a science, a process characterized by observation of facts, by the building of theory and the testing of it, and by modification of theory according to the discovery of new facts. Can you see the one essential way in which science and intuition contrast with each other? True intuition can reach to a whole truth in a flash (just as faulty intuition can reach to error), whereas in a science the whole truth is never reached. What is important in science is a construction of a satisfactory road towards the truth. That is why a scientific training is so important for everybody; it enables you and me to test our own little bits of the world satisfactorily. Our feelings and our imaginings may get out of hand and may take us anywhere, this moment enabling us to dream we are able to fly and the next moment allowing us to feel infinitely unsupported, so that we fall and fall, and there is no bottom, except waking, which means a return to science, to the well-tested and welcome external reality.

Have you ever thought of science just in this way? If, in a subject that is being approached through the scientific method, there is a gap in our knowledge, we just record it as a gap in knowledge, a stimulus to research, but the intuitive person's gaps are unknown quantities with somewhat terrifying potential. The physicists say that there is an element that we have not yet discovered. No one gets in a panic; later on the new element is found, and it fits into the scheme of things. When the drug "M&B"* was discovered, no one knew why it acted in the way it did act, but no one suggested that its action was anything to do with magic; the biochemists simply felt stimulated by the fact of their ignorance, and they gradually found out more and more, but they still do not know all they want to know about it. In psychology there are many huge gaps in our knowledge. But, since psychology is a science, we do not even mind when the intuitive people say of something we have discovered, "We have always known that"; for they do not mention at the same time all the weird things they also knew, wrongly. The scientific approach to the phenomena of human nature enables us to be ignorant without being frightened, and without, therefore, having to invent all sorts of weird theories to explain away the gaps in knowledge.

You and I started as scientists when we were very young, in fact as soon as we were born. We started life as scientists provided we had good-enough mothering in the very early stages, so that we did not get pushed into a muddle. We were then at the mercy of our imaginings, and, as soon as we could perceive external reality, every real thing happening to us was welcome as depending on something external to ourselves, and therefore dependable, because of being something we could get to know. Even things that made us angry, like being kept waiting when we were hungry, had a value for us. External reality helped us to stand the magic quality of our ideas, which at that time were very primitive because we had so little experience of real things, and so we had nothing to dream about, only (one might say) feelings to feel. These magical primitive feelings can be indeed very alarming as well as wonderful, as we see from the study of those people who have not succeeded in coming to terms with them, and who are insane. Many people develop a scientific interest in external reality to get away from the intuitive and the subjective approach to life. I suppose Western culture, on the whole, tends towards an exclusion of *feelings* by scientific *think-*

---

*An anti-microbial drug introduced in 1938, subsequently superseded by antibiotic drugs starting with penicillin.

ing, whereas in Eastern culture the scientific method is relatively despised. In the best of our Western culture we enjoy a scientific method of approach to external reality—whilst at the same time we preserve in music, painting, and poetry, and in religion, the recognition of the importance of the creative and intuitive approach to life, as well as the magic of primitive feeling and spontaneous instinctual expression.

Well, if we agree to all that, why not settle down to the scientific study of human nature? Why has psychology come at the end of the sciences, following biology, which, I suppose, could be said, in one sense, to have followed physics? (Of course, I know they co-exist today.)

Obviously the more closely connected a science is with life, the more difficult it is for a scientific approach to seem adequate. I remember my excitement in my own schooldays before the First World War when I first met Darwin's *Origin of Species*. I could not leave off reading it.

> Then felt I like some watcher of the skies
> When a new planet swims into his ken;
> Or like stout Cortez . . .
>
> (Keats, "On First Looking into
> Chapman's Homer")

At the time I did not quite know why it was so important to me, but I see now that the main thing was that it showed that living things could be examined scientifically, with the corollary that gaps in knowledge and understanding need not scare me. For me this new idea meant a great lessening of tension and consequently a release of energy for work and play.

I feel sure that, if I were at school now, I should find the same value in the corresponding book that would put psychology on the map as a science, but I think there is no book exactly corresponding to the *Origin of Species*. No doubt the latter would be said now to contain many fallacies and misstatements, but the same could even more strongly be said of any one book dealing with psychology. Freud's *Introductory Lectures* might be cited. There have been such tremendous advances, many of them Freud's own, since Freud wrote this pioneer work, that a psychoanalyst might well hesitate before recommending even that one book, except to be read along with many others, and read with full knowledge that Freud was starting a new science. Freud's works, read in chronological order, give a good picture of the way his ideas developed. He not only started a new science, but he also carried it a long way; and it is now being carried further by those who have continued to use his methods, and to develop them in their own ways.

Now let me say something about the difficulties inherent in the science of psychology. I shall begin by quoting what I said just now. I said that a scientific training was important because it enabled us to test our own little bit of the world satisfactorily. When it comes to psychology these words "our own little bit of the world" mean not only the phenomena of other people's human nature but also our own. In this respect psychology is distinct from other sciences and must always remain so. With our minds we are examining the very minds we are using, and with our feelings we are examining our feelings. It is like trying to examine a microscope under its own high power. No wonder psychology came last in the sequence of sciences. Many people hold the view that psychology can never be a science because of this difficulty, and the impasse of (so-called) academic psychology illustrates the dilemma, but Freud went ahead in spite of this, and some of us think that he had already established psychology as a science at the beginning of this century. In *The Interpretation of Dreams* you will see how he showed that what most people regard as an insuperable barrier to psychology as a science could actually be turned to use in furthering scientific investigation. He realized that if he were to claim that he could use his patients' dreams, believing in the significance of every detail recorded by the dreamer, he must show willingness and ability to examine his own dreams. Most of what Freud said about dreams was original and brilliantly constructive and has stood the test of time. *The Psychopathology of Everyday Life* was another book in which he started to put before the public the possibility of a science of psychology, and there was a steady stream of scientific work from this great man. I was unaware when I was at school that these books were already written, and I doubt if I was ready for them then.

I now come to the main difficulty of psychology as a science, and there Freud made his most important discovery. In no other science is there a twist corresponding to that produced in psychology by the existence of the unconscious. The word "unconscious" can, of course, mean the sort of thing that happens when you get a crack on the head and pass out. Psychologically the word had other meanings, and it has been used for a very long time to describe unawareness. For instance, one cannot, at any one moment in time, be aware of everything that one could theoretically be aware of. In painting, an artist may reach feelings of which he was unaware before he started, and which may come from so deep in his nature that he is hard put to it to acknowledge responsibility for his picture.

Freud was not daunted by the well-known fact that there are depths to our natures which we cannot easily plumb. He discovered and established by scientific method that there is a special variety of unconscious, which he named *the repressed unconscious;* here the trouble is not the depth of the thing of which the individual is unaware, but the fact that what is unconscious cannot be remembered because of its being associated with painful feeling or some other intolerable emotion. Energy has to be all the time employed in maintaining the repression, and it can easily be seen that if there is a great deal of an individual's personality that is repressed, there is relatively little energy left for a direct participation in life. The first reason why people can get practical help from psychoanalytic treatment is that in so far as it is successful, it enables the patient to release painful material from repression, with the consequence that the patient has all that energy which formerly was used in the service of repression for the enjoyment of life and for constructive being.

Freud invented and developed a method, an instrument of scientific research into human nature which has turned out to be, at the same time, a method of treatment. Briefly described, psychoanalysis is: that the psychoanalyst prepares stable and simplified conditions in which the individual who undergoes psychoanalysis can let his mind work freely. Sooner or later he will be found to be approaching the difficult part of himself, showing in his relation to the analyst that he is wanting to relive even the episodes and types of emotional experience which for him are associated with so much pain that he is not able to reach them on his own. Thus growth that was held up can take place.

In the simplest possible example, a person who is being analysed is able to correct a past experience, or an imaginary experience, by reliving it in simplified conditions in which the pain can be tolerated because of its being spread over a period of time, taken, so to speak, in small doses, in a controlled emotional environment. As you can well imagine, in actual practice there is seldom anything as uncomplicated as this, but the main thing can legitimately be described in this way.

In a psychoanalytic treatment the analyst and the person being analysed are working together on a problem on equal terms. This makes the psychoanalytic method applicable to the treatment of many people who would not allow themselves to be totally in the power of another individual, even for a short period, as in treatment by hypnotism, even though by hypnotism it might be easier for a doctor to effect removal of symptoms. Freud's invention, psychoanalysis, was more important than a mere treatment, for its aim was not primarily the removal of symptoms; its aim was a scientific one: to approach a little bit of truth for the sake of truth itself. Undoubtedly, one of the early good effects of the process is an indirect one, due to the fact that the person being analysed begins to feel that emotional phenomena can be examined scientifically, so that all the enormous gaps in his understanding of himself become just so many things not yet understood, instead of sources of anxiety and invitations for the construction of false theories and philosophies.

You will readily see that one important consequence of all this is that psychoanalysis rescues logic from the death to which it was fast sinking after a brilliant start. We can see now what was wrong with logic, and why it lacked social usefulness when it should have been able to make human behaviour more calculable and so strengthen the roots of society. It quickly got as far as it could ever get without taking into account the unconscious, the part of the personality of which the individual cannot become aware, and against awareness of which he must defend himself with all his power and skill.

Through psychoanalysis, insight is being gained into the causes of much that is unhealthy in persons and in society. At the same time through psychoanalysis there has come about an increased understanding of the development of man's conscience, and also of his constructive or sublimatory potential, looked at as a compromise between instinctual drives and the demands of a mature and personal conscience. The compromise enables the individual to harness instinctual energy in a way that does not violate his relation to the social structure.

Incidentally, when investigation into neurosis is made it is always found that the blockage holding up emotional development has its origin in early childhood. It is at about the years of 2, 3, and 4, when the most intense interpersonal relationships are being experienced, that the most severe anxiety is roused. Anxiety leads to a setting up of defences in the individual and it is these organized defences that appear as neurotic illness or character disturbances. At this time, when the child is 2, 3, or 4 years old, the individual is not yet an independent unit; at this age in a child the ego can be said to be in the process of building up a personal Superego for the management and employment of the Id (instincts). Loving human beings and a stable environment are particularly necessary during this period, and the people around are used by the growing child as ideals, and as strict persons, during the process of the construction in the individual of the more personal Superego, with its own ideas about control and licence. This is a statement in psychoanalytic terms; the terms of course are not essential, but they are useful symbols for theoretical construction and for discussion.

The more and more profound disorders that are usually known as the psychoses have their origin earlier and earlier in infancy, in the period in which the personality is not yet integrated into a unit, and when the capacity for communication with external reality is tenuous and not yet established.

Thus psychoanalysis turns out to be a fine new instrument by which human beings may study themselves and their interpersonal relationships; but it does remain an instrument of scientific research or a therapy, and it never makes a direct philosophical or a religious contribution. Freud took pains to point this out, and those who come to psychoanalysis for the first time will do well to be quite clear about the limitations of its aims and aspirations.

There is one thing that could be added. People often ask whether psychoanalysis makes life easy. Quite naturally they would suspect anything which made such a claim. Psychoanalysis, apart from its being a painful process in itself, does not alter the fact that life is difficult. The best that can happen is that the person who is being analysed gradually comes to feel less and less at the mercy of unknown forces both within and without, and more and more able to deal in his or her own peculiar way with the difficulties inherent in human nature, in personal growth, and in the gradual achievement of a mature and constructive relationship to society.

2

"Yes, but how
do we know it's true?"

[1950]

Students who are for the first time meeting instruction of
a psychological nature rather regularly pass through two
stages. In the first stage, they learn what is being taught
about psychology just as they learn the other things. In the second stage, they begin to wonder—yes but is it true, is it real, how
do we know? In the second stage, the psychological teaching
begins to separate out from the other as something that can't just
be learnt. It has to be felt as real, or else it is irritating and even
maddening.

It is not difficult to see that there must be a difference between
the effects of one kind of teaching and another. For instance, you
are being instructed in administration. You read the Child Care
and Protection Act, and trace the social development that led up
to the Curtis Report.[1] Or you find out about the workings of
Juvenile Courts, the use made of probation officers, and so on.
You form your own ideas from reading and from actual visits to
the Courts.

Contrast this with what happens when you learn psychology.
The old academic psychology has died a natural death, and this is

_____

[1] Home Office Report of the Care of Children Committee. London: His Majesty's Stationery Office, 1946.

13

a loss to you because you could have learnt it just as you learned about Acts of Parliament and about the procedure of courts, without trouble but without value. Psychology is now a matter of *feelings*, of *live people*, of *emotions* and *instincts*, and also it deals with the unconscious, and conflicts in the unconscious that cause symptoms because they are not available to consciousness.

Do you see? Whereas most types of teaching take you out of yourself, psychology, the psychology that matters, tends to throw you back into yourself. For we are all human beings ourselves, and if we learn about another we learn about ourselves. We can try to be objective and we can make every effort to learn about people without developing morbid introspection, but this requires effort, and you notice this effort, and you feel disturbed; this psychology is not going to behave itself properly as the other subjects in the curriculum do.

Indeed, psychology is not going to help eventually in the same way as the other subjects help, and the result of what you learn will always be the recognition that the care of human beings is more complex than you thought. You can be taught how to proceed in a Juvenile Court case, but you cannot be taught how to cope with a child who is unhappy in a foster-home. In the latter case, you can only be given more and more insight into the factors involved, so that in coping with the trouble you can do what you feel like doing with more and more understanding of the reasons.

Here I have introduced a new idea, and I want to follow it up.

When you learn ordinary things you make no contribution from your own person, you just learn what is taught. The past tense of "je suis" is "j'étais"; the way to address a magistrate is "yer 'onor" (or whatever it is), and that's that. When you learn psychology, however, you never learn anything cut and dried. There is no instruction that can be carried out as such. In the end it will always *be you acting as you feel*. The only thing is that you can be enriched by knowing of other situations similar to the one you find yourself in, and also you can be enabled to have the power to see more and more clearly what you are doing and why.

Let me give a homely illustration. A friend of yours goes into a mild depression. She rings you up and you agree to go round to her flat, but you don't know what to do. You first take a book on psychiatry and look up "depression", and after a brief glance at the clinical description you rush on to the paragraph on treatment. You get no help. You are bewildered. "Keep the patient from suicide" is not applicable, because your friend is not so ill as all that.

Psychology has so far not helped you much.

Let us say, however, that your friend had the good sense to have 'flu or sciatica. She is alone in her flat and you are feeling unwell yourself, and so you fly round and you do all the necessaries. You know exactly what to do. You serve an appropriate meal, you make the bed comfortable, slipping in a hot-water bottle, you go around and get the rations, and when you leave you put some water or milk within easy reach, and tell your friend exactly at what time tomorrow she may expect you.

To do this, you certainly did not have to consult a psychiatry textbook.

The fact is that you knew exactly what to do for a friend with a mild depression. It was easy because in this case the patient had a physical complaint that made it all seem sensible. (She probably had a depression too; most people are ready with a depression if only they can find someone to cherish them, and why waste the opportunity provided by the 'flu, and your response?)

Psychology does not try to teach you what to do when your friend needs your help. It can do a lot, however, towards enabling you to be more sure of yourself, to understand what is going on, to grow on experiences, to see where mistakes might have been made, to prevent distress and disasters.

Take another example. It is possible to talk to mothers about the management of their children and to give instructions based on our knowledge. In the matter of physical health and the prevention of disease, there is plenty of room for instruction, and this corresponds with what I have referred to as your gaining instruction in such things as the Children's Act.[2] When it comes

---

[2]The Children's Act, 1948. London: His Majesty's Stationery Office, 1948.

to telling mothers about mothering, however, psychological instruction can easily be harmful. Mothers either turn a deaf ear or else they get muddled, and feel hopeless, and the extreme is expressed in the cartoon of the parent smacking her child's bottom with one hand and holding in the other a book on child psychology which she is feverishly reading with the aid of strong glasses.

To talk to mothers usefully, I think it is necessary to discover and strengthen what comes naturally to them. This will be enough for many, perhaps for the majority. Some will want to go further and learn more about what they do and why they do it. Mothers who have actually done their job well can stand very deep instruction indeed, because they are not afraid to discover what tremendous forces were at work, and what a lot depended on just that being done just that way, just then. They know they did not do what they did by chance, or by cleverness, but by deeply rooted intuitive or instinctive feeling, strengthened by the self-confidence that belongs to health.

The reason why I am going into all this about mothering is that I think it is relevant.

The trouble is that you are being taught dynamic *psychology at a time when you are not in fact dealing with children*, or with people for that matter. For the time being, although you are experienced men and women, you are *in statu pupillari*, you are divorced from just those things that make you feel confident in your power to draw on intuition.

Perhaps you have been teachers, or you have actually been parents, or you have had charge of people in an office or a factory. Every day you found yourselves surprising yourselves, acting or not acting in a way that exactly fitted the situation, as much as Hamlet's speech "To be or not to be" fits into the exposition of the theme of the play exactly. When you were so placed you could have stood a great deal of digging down into the psychology of your fellow human beings and of yourselves.

Here, in the temporary state of being learners, you can easily develop that lack of self-confidence that makes dynamic psychology seem dangerous. Telling an expectant mother that "her baby can never make a satisfactory contact with the world unless she knows how to introduce external reality to her infant in small doses" may alarm her, and even make her have a miscarriage, for she becomes alarmed at her own lack of conscious knowledge. Yet, if left to it, she will do just this thing perfectly, simply because of her devotion to her baby.

Similarly, if I tell you that a baby's whole future depends on your knowing that a certain foster-mother has an unconscious revenge feeling against her own mother that renders her unfit for the job of fostering, you may recoil. How can you ever know these things? If, however, you were on the job, you would be finding yourselves suspicious here, and doubtful there, and you would be asking to have a chance to discuss the hidden aspects of the case.

And now, what about the teaching that tremendous forces are at work in the infant from the word "go!"; that the foundations of the mental health of the adult are laid down in infancy and childhood, that the little boy of 2, 3, 4 years has instincts that make him in his dreams just like an adult, so that he is (in that sense) a sexual rival of his father; that infants who are bandied about from one minder to another do not develop a capacity to believe in the effectiveness of their own love impulses—what about all this kind of thing that you will meet during the year's course? You see, if you believe all these things, you are believing that these things were true of you, and yet you obviously can't get at these same things by remembering. Also, if these things are true things, you and I and all who have come through in a satisfactory way at all owe a debt to someone. Someone saw us through the early stages. In fact we couldn't have done without the care we received at the start. We were dependent, and as we think further and further back so we must admit we were more and more dependent, and at the time of birth and for a few months the degree of this dependence is alarming to contemplate. It must remain alarming to everyone always.

No wonder it is difficult to learn about psychology.

What is the answer? One thing is to go slow.

Another is to get relief from the fact that some of what is taught is bound to be wrong, although psychology can teach a good deal about human nature that is true as far as it goes. Also, whenever you can, travel from experiences you have had, from things you have done, towards the insight that psychology may be able to provide; the reverse direction from psychology to experience is no good at all.

Lastly, here is a half-way house. You can lodge there while you are growing. I refer to intelligence tests. These valuable tests have one foot in the academic psychology of the past, and therefore they are restful. Fortunately, they also have a foot in the dynamic psychology of the present, and therefore, if you go in for I.Q. estimations thoroughly, you will eventually find yourselves in the deep waters of feeling and unconscious conflicts. However, testing for I.Q. provides a very neutral territory and can be recommended interim.

Part two

EARLY
INFANT DEVELOPMENT

3

Primary introduction
to external reality:
the early stages

[1948]

W e seem to have made a start in regard to the study
of the development of the human being, and we are
gradually, I hope, getting earlier in our study of the
child and development. You may have the idea that a human
being starts early and that development is in one long line in
which there is no gap. Any gap means ill-health, and health really means things have gone on at their own pace and completed
themselves and got as far as they could reasonably be expected
to at the right time.

I was thinking how to illustrate why I am not talking about
all the psychoanalytic theory of development. Partly it is because
much is well known and you can read it, and partly because it
does not affect your actual work. It is a bit more difficult to talk
about normal psychology, and I was thinking of an illustration.
Take the fact that certain people are preoccupied with ideas of
beating. It comes into their lives a great deal, and some children
have a preoccupation with such ideas mixed with masturbation.
We have to be able to talk of these things in order to talk about
punishment. A woman who has been bothered by these particular things eventually comes to psychoanalysis, an ill person who
wants to do something about it. A great deal of work is done

patiently over a long time. In the course of treatment these fantasies turn out to be where this patient has kept something from infancy which could not be integrated into her personality: the aggressive part of her relationship to the mother, to the breasts, and to the mother's body at the very beginning. These very aggressive excitement fantasies come along and destroy the quiet relationship to the mother's body. To make it clearer, this patient, in reliving these things in the specialized setting of analysis, found that she could not tolerate in her infancy the direct attack on something so beautiful that she felt was part of herself, the body she was in contact with, and nearly lost everything, but just held something, because, when frustrated, she could feel all the hate and destructiveness towards frustrating things—the buttons, fastenings, and delays. So two things were separated off, one the loving and the complying and the other the taking, taking of what was given. This eventually turned into the excitement about the beating etc., as when the infant is free and finding his mother's body and having instinctual tension and is suddenly overtaken by an overwhelming desire to have a go at it ruthlessly.

This is a difficult situation inherent in the development of every child which the child has to come to terms with, with the help of the mother and her loving experiences with the infant. A person's life can be disturbed for years and years from difficulties starting in these early times. Therefore, I have made a special point of the development of the capacity for concern, of the very big problems that it raises to do with the child's development of a sense of guilt, which is a big step forward.

We now come on to some of the earlier stages. I have said that a sort of psychoanalytic understanding is not what you want when looking after children in school and helping a child to continue his process of coping with his guilt feelings. There you are coming into it not so much by an intellectual understanding of his problem as by being an important person in his life. He has feelings of different kinds, and you are there and continue to exist and give him the chance to feel pleased and sorry and, if he wants, to have the opportunity to make up for the hurt he feels he has done. There is much more in it than is covered by the words "you continue to exist over a period of time in a child's life". You don't have to know all that is going on in the child. You know a great deal is going on and if you continue to exist he will be able to come through. It is not just that you continue to live. He gets to know you and to allow for you as a human being. Not in a good temper on Monday mornings, but nevertheless on Friday everything is all right. There is one thing implied in all this, which is that what starts in infancy is never finished then. With every child it is going on all the time, consolidating positions, which can always be lost and gained again. So if we can state something to do with infancy, we are talking about something which continues all the time. If we show why it is important for an infant to enjoy his bath, we are also showing why it is important that children bathe in the sea and why it is important to provide baths for them and to let them swim and dive and there should be soap for them etc. later on. It is not something new but something which joins on to the importance of bathing at the beginning. And if we have the idea of the importance for the infant to be seen naked, we also see it is important for children to be seen naked. Very often people rely on the doctor to see them. I was once horrified by a psychologist saying why he had taken up psychology: because, as he said, "I can't bear children's bodies". One of the difficulties about child guidance for me as a paediatrician is that I like seeing children's bodies and should lose this as a psychiatrist: and I should be handing over the children to a friend to examine. But also I should not like to be only examining their bodies and have nothing to do with their feelings and ideas. Therefore it suits me to have the child there, examining him all over. This is an advantage. For some children it is really important that one person sees the body and the psychology as one thing. It is very funny that sometimes as psychiatrists we want a grown-up patient examined by a doctor, and perhaps they don't get properly examined and come back. I remember a case of a hypochondriacal person. He always came with a report that the doctors could find nothing wrong. All perfect. But he could not get a doctor to undress him and see him as a whole person including his genitals. As these had not been examined, he was convinced all the trouble was there. As someone once said, "At any rate osteopaths undress you"! It is important for people to be seen.

All this is really an apologia because I am talking about infantile needs and getting to earlier infancy when I am actually talking to persons who are dealing with children. Now for some more primitive things in human development, more the things you take for granted—for instance, that you the teacher comes on time or are always three minutes late and that you don't teach your children in the dark. If you started teaching children in the dark they would not know where you were, you would get all mixed up with the hallucinations. You could not introduce reality to them in the dark. It would be so complicated. If they were blind, then you could have special techniques to deal with the darkness. If we liked, we could look into all the things you do, into how important they all are, when we are talking in terms of the earlier stages of infant development.

Let us simplify the matter of primitive development and say there are three things which can be separated out. One is making contact with reality. Another is feeling that you live in your body, and the other is the integration of the personality. These things overlap, but give us tags to hang on to. Let us take the integration of the personality. I have spoken to you about the stage being arrived at at which a child can make a circle and say this is a person and mother is another person, a similar one. He can begin to know the inside world and the outside world and that there is something at the edge and this is himself. This line between inner and outer can also be very weak and hardly discernible, and at the beginning one could say there are all sorts of different things which Glover calls "ego nuclei":[1] all sorts of things which the child can use "I" about and it is only a little bit of "I" such as a toe seen, a finger moving, a hungry impulse, or the feeling of warmth from a hot-water bottle. This includes anything that impinges on the child and that the child is aware of, not at first separated out externally from the self, but only very gradually becoming separate. All these bits and pieces go to make the human being. How important it is at such a stage that

---

[1]This refers to a paper by Edward Glover: "The Birth of the Ego. A Psychoanalytic Approach to the Classification of Mental Disorder". In *Journal of Mental Science* (October 1932); reprinted in *On the Early Development of the Mind* (London: Imago, 1956 [later Allen & Unwin].)

the mother has the child in her mind as a whole person, because the child can then afford to be in pieces. No doubt, sometimes when babies are very hungry, all out in an attack, they come together and flow into something which becomes almost like a whole. Or, if they are very angry, things gather up into the anger and no doubt the bits come together.

In the quiet moments there is no line between inner or outer but just lots of things separated out, sky seen through trees, something to do with mother's eyes all going in and out, wandering around. There is a lack of any need for integration.

This is an extremely valuable thing to be able to retain: we miss something without it. It has something to do with being calm, restful, relaxed, and feeling one with people and things when no excitement is around.

For the world to flow in and out without hungry taking and angry giving, infants need very satisfactory management at the beginning and then they are able to manage this as well as the actually more exciting experiences. On the other hand, some children have not managed this, such as the patient I was telling you about. The aggressive attack was kept separate and developed into an organized beating fantasy. On the other hand, those who have a wonderful life built up on a quiet basis can identify with nature and people in a quiet way.

The integration of the personality is something which becomes an achievement through two sets of things. One is the times of keen feeling of one kind or another which makes the infant gather together and become one person, angry or hungry. The other is the management of the child. I try to think of it as what the mother does when she picks up her baby. She does not take him by the toe. She may make a little noise to give him time, folds him round, and somehow gathers him together. She does not assume he is an acrobat. She shows that she knows what is going on. Let us jump to a patient who throughout childhood had great difficulty in establishing her identity.

She had to hide her identity from her powerful-minded father. She drew a picture of her father when he suddenly called her name. She drew a very meek little girl looking very good and absolutely nothing was there, but little bits of herself were rushing round trying to get there in time, bits from the dog where she had placed most of herself all rushing trying to catch up before she got to her father but they never did, and she was an ineffective bit of flesh. Anyway, she parked herself out in little boxes, behind things. (She was the patient up in the box at the top of a tree sometimes.)

This is to illustrate that we are not dealing with things only at the beginning, but we are saying that when you call a child, two children, in your classroom, one is there, but the other you have to take as the infant all over the place who you have to collect into himself, to be there, and to be there at the right time. You can't be certain that one is better than the other. They are different types.

When you deal with children it is much like managing a baby. When collecting a child of 6, he may be a child specializing in being part of nature—a poet. He finds his life as an interchange with the world. He can't come immediately you call, he will be confused unless you really make him integrate and then he will suddenly come together. Therefore, you have two things making a child come together: one instinctual experience, and the other your management. You are giving children all sorts of satisfactions in giving them something with which to pull themselves together from within. You make what you are teaching interesting, and also you manage them in such a way as to keep the class-room somehow related to their bodies. I think architecture comes in here. I was helped one day by an architect. I said "Why is it, although I did not know I liked the old Regent Street, I feel quite different about the new one?" He said: "In the old Regent Street the proportions wherever you looked were similar to the proportions of the human being and therefore people felt they extended easily into the buildings, but the present buildings have no relation to the human being at all except by chance, therefore people feel like robots. They have to find other ways of getting into contact."

[An intervention occurs here of which there is no record. Later a question was asked about the building the lecture was given in—part of Senate House, London University.] Everybody has their own right to an opinion about the building we are in.

It may be that some people love this building and I would hate to hurt their feelings, but when it comes to children it is different. Did you know that in the old days Dr. Susan Isaacs had a nursery school here? I don't know what the children felt about the proportions, but I don't think it is the thing to ask little children to come into this huge building. By temperature, air, etc. you are managing children and creating conditions which they can identify with as human beings. I think many big buildings have no proportion to people; the building tends to be a sort of place where there are innumerable bits and you are one of the bits.

This subject is much like the subject of the child feeling he lives in his body because here there are two things, the child having experiences in which the whole body is involved, kicking, running around, eating, getting to know himself, as the place where he lives, and also the management from the outside. Don't take it for granted that people live in their bodies quite easily. Anyone, if very tired, could easily find themselves not exactly where they are, and as I have said before about Lawrence of Arabia, after five days on the camel he said he was about five yards up on the camel's right ear. This is how you get absent from your body and not know, therefore, where you begin and end. There is the complication that we have all had differences within ourselves. Take the example of the man who has lost a leg. It is all right when he is not tired, but if tired the memories of the other leg come back. In the same way, we are all very different, all sorts of differences inside ourselves, and if a person is very much reliving a childhood experience the body feels heavy and he doesn't know what to do with it. In this photo you see the child who left her body and did not come back for three years. She had never had a good contact with reality. She had a good brain but did not make use of it. Her head drooped and eventually she went away. She was the most flabby creature, except where she lived—in her eyelids and in her jaws. She was fed through the nose. Her eyelids were always closed, but it was possible to see that she sometimes opened them enough to see what was going on. At present she is coming round, walks, says things, and even laughs at jokes. This is an extreme case of what you can often find in normal children. A child has a bilious attack and becomes like death, flabby and absent. You put him to bed. It is very frightening, and just as suddenly he has recovered and is playing on his scooter. As long as we know, we shall not get alarmed but be able to allow for these things.

4

Environmental needs; the early stages; total dependence and essential independence

[1948]

You have been listening to me now for a number of lectures. In what we have dealt with I have, as it were, tried to put up a building. I think that building (outside) is what lectures look like at the moment. I want to consider children in different phases of development. I was thinking we could compare the different phases now, taking the word morality. For children who have reached a certain stage, that of whole human beings, I would say morality is a matter of compromise. They have their own ideas of what they think is right and wrong, but you know they can see that the other person has a point of view, so, very often, the word compromise comes in. In the stage a bit earlier, morality seems to be represented by reparation in respect of guilt; this is the sense of guilt which is tolerable if something is being done about it. When we come to these more primitive things, morality has become a terrific and terrible thing. There is no compromise; it is life or death. If somebody has failed to complete something in these earlier stages then nothing can be done, they can't accept compromise, they may prefer to spend their lives in a mental hospital rather than give in. We can understand what that means when we take extreme cases in ourselves, or in children who are managing to have times when they must stand up for something, their own integrity, their own individuality, their own rights as individual human beings. At any rate, it seems to me there is something very fierce in the morality of the infant, and in all that which is in us which belongs to infancy, and to earlier infantile development.

I want to speak now about the introduction of external reality to the human infant, and I don't want to be misunderstood if I talk about a mother and her new-born infant when I say I know what happens in the case of a new-born infant. I would say that an infant comes into the world, and no doubt a great deal goes on which we are not talking about, but, at a certain moment, he begins to become interested in some outward thing; there is an outward turning of the personality towards something. He begins to get hungry. He is ready to accept something outside himself and he has no idea of what that is going to be, but here is that line towards something, the mother. Then there is the mother with her breast and she has got something to offer, too, and it seems so easy, if one has not thought it out. The baby looks, sees and feels whatever is there, and that stimulates the baby, who stimulates the breast, and all that is physiological, and it is quite true but not quite enough. We have to see that here we have a very tricky situation, one which makes me tremble when I think how doctors and nurses interfere so easily. Here is the baby's capacity to hallucinate something and here is the mother who has what she knows is good but the baby does not yet know, and the mother has to manage to place herself here so that what the baby is willing to find is actually herself. In that case we could say that she manages to give the baby the illusion that what he actually gets and takes and finds is what he created out of his own feelings, his own power to hallucinate. This, of course, is a matter of a living experience. The mother makes all sorts of arrangements about how to manage her contact with the baby. But it is a matter which goes on, and, in the ordinary case, the mother has many times placed herself in the right direction for the infant and he has come, gradually, to have material from the real experience to hallucinate with, so that he is managing to see the actual nipple and experience the details of the smell and the breast and everything, and gradually by a painful and long process he is able to imagine what is actually likely to come. It is something which is done, and when it is successfully done it has

given the infant the basis for mental health which it is very difficult for the infant to lose. But it is never entirely successful, and
we will now look and see what happens in the case of failure.

The words "illusion" and "reality" come into the writings of
psychologists and philosophers, but it is something one can
pinch, an idea. We may say they are talking about something
like this, but we say to them, you are liable to miss out the basis
of this thing, the experience between the mother and the infant
at the beginning. This is not a theoretical concept. If we have no
difficulties here, we owe something to someone. This is the external factor. It seems that one can say there is some degree of
failure which must be very common, and then, sometimes, one
has a complete failure.

Here is a splitting of the personality at a very early level,
which is one of the meanings of the word schizophrenia. Here a
child has two relations to external reality. In one there is compliance, the actual *taking* on a compliant basis, and then a purely
imaginary experience with an imagined reality. In the extreme
case, there is very little contact taking place, the child has nothing
to imagine with except what is in himself, which is just a matter
of something rather like thumb-sucking or rocking movements,
something very poverty-stricken. On the other hand, *enough* of
real contact and illusion can have taken place for an infant to
have built up a world which has quite a lot in it that we could
recognize has come from our shared reality. And in a case where
this has become an important feature because of breakdown later
on, and a child has gone back to a split, you can often have a child
in a world which is extremely rich, and rich with things which we
know about in our reality-shared world.

When you see children, you can see two relations to external
reality. One seems sometimes to be very satisfactory in the sense
that the child is, on the food basis, taking everything or, on the
teaching basis, accepting everything and behaving well, but you
feel all the time there is something lacking and you are not surprised to find, later on, a breakdown to this relationship which is
not to external reality but to an inner world. I want to refer to a
child who had been asleep for three years, who had really lived
in this world for a long period of time and had regressed and
retired into her world. When you meet a child who retires for

minutes, weeks, or years, you will be interested to try and guess what in this inner-world experience there is of the external world that we know about.

If we talk about Shakespeare and being able to get into one's inner world, we can see that Shakespeare's inner world was as rich as the world we live in. Whatever came from him was something which could have been based on very acute observation of human beings in the real world. All that he felt and knew had gone in, and when he was able to bring it out we can recognize it and check up on it. We can look to Shakespeare to keep a sense of proportion on it. But if we take a musician, like Beethoven, we shall find, too, that all the human emotions and feelings and relationships are represented here, not in persons, but in terms of "to and fro" of forces of spontaneity, without human beings being brought into it. But if you look at the "turning in" activities of children in your care, some of them you will feel not too worried about because they have an inner world which is rich and has a relation to the external world, and their life is rich. But with another child, you feel their inner world is very poverty-stricken, is so much cut off, that you recognize this as illness. Take two children, both preoccupied. One you do not worry about because you know he is full of richness, but the other you worry about because you know he is ill, his preoccupation has no richness. There has never been anyone at the beginning to give enough for this child to have an illusion about reality. Reality has remained something which can never be accepted in a whole way.

On another occasion I was bold enough to talk about the infancy of Juliet. It so happens that Shakespeare took the trouble to say a great deal about Juliet's infancy.[1] Perhaps this is not off the subject. The question is whether Shakespeare can be talked of in that way at all. Desmond McCarthy in the *Sunday Times* was very cross with a psychologist for having written a book on Hamlet. "How could there be a childhood of somebody who had never lived?" He said the reason why Shakespeare made Hamlet have a conflict was because the play had to last two hours! But I do think that when we take somebody like Shakespeare, any

---

[1] *Romeo and Juliet*, Act 1 scene 3.

little detail of the conversation has something to do with the main themes of his play. I don't believe he put the bit in about Juliet's infancy because on the first night he knew some midwives were coming. He tells us Juliet's mother was about 13 and the nurse 14, and the nurse's child died and she wet-nursed Juliet. He thereby gives us to understand that the nurse had a great deal of sweetness in her and knew the difference between wet-nursing someone else's child and her own. And Juliet had something like an adopted child's difficulties. The nurse could not wean her until she was nearly 3 and then only because Juliet had a rather fresh conversation with the nurse's husband the day before. The husband had made remarks when the child fell down. And when she weaned the child, she did it, not in the ordinary way, but by bitter aloes. She weaned the child in this indirect way. It seems to me Shakespeare was trying to show why Juliet had to have the split in her nature. The compliance to her mother and everybody is all right for this other thing, the extreme of romanticism, whereby the impossible is going to happen. She is going to have all the feelings of love in relation to somebody who is coming along, something which is actually doomed to end in death and actually by poisoning. A great deal is made of the poisoning being a breast experience, being good because it is bad. All this is Shakespeare's understanding of the need to go back to infancy to explain the later developments in a person's type of life. But the rich inner world of a person like Shakespeare makes bridges between the inner and outer worlds. He was describing somebody without any bridges between the inner world and external reality.

In coming to the business of guilt feelings and reparation, I said what a tremendous amount you as teachers provide when it comes to reparation in respect of guilt by being a person or a set-up in which a child can find, in course of time, the love and the aggression and the guilt and the opportunity to give. When you mention primitive things, you are talking about processes that are going on all the time. You do a great deal for a child because you can't just fit in for every child. You let him have some things, and not have others, but by being more or less there and reliable you give him an opportunity to experience his love and hate. No child completes these experiences; they are going on in your school work, using you to reinforce the good start they have had.

In the case of treating patients, we get these things illustrated many times. I have told you before about this patient I am going to describe.

> For a long period this patient had no relation to me at all unless I turned up on the doorstep and was there inside the door as the patient came and rang the bell. I had to be there actually at the moment when this patient came, in a very, very real way. For quite a number of months I had to put aside everything for twenty minutes beforehand, because, if I did, the patient could come and we had a good session, but if anything went wrong there was no relationship. An ill person this, to illustrate the extreme. This patient came and she took two years to break down and be as ill as she had to be. When she came she was still apparently well. She had formed a very good relation to everybody and was called the little friend of all the world and everyone said, "well, if anyone is sane, you are". And then she broke down in the end by having a physical illness which turned out to be produced by herself in a certain way, but all this took a long time. In the beginning she had missed it. She had been one of twins and she had been handed over to other people. So I had to provide something which she had never had.

So with an ordinary patient or child, you are dealing with people who have had a good early position and you can slip in to that position and reinforce it into a position which other people have created, guiding and expanding and widening their growth. But if there has been failure at the start, you would have to be like doctors doing a difficult job and this would be impossible.

Question: "Is it then important that you stay in a school for a number of years?"

D.W.W. That is an interesting question. You get to know the children, it is wasted if you leave. There are always casualties when teacher leaves, and a sigh of relief from one or two. And then with these things there are phases the children have to go through. You will find that certain ones are using you at certain times for certain purposes. Some have finished with you for the time being. I think a lot of troubles are there whenever you leave. On the other hand that brings up the whole subject of whether you take your class on with you or not. Children who are adolescent are like small children, with instincts, tremendously important instincts carrying them away, and then there is something special about this need to find people to reinforce whatever is there in their experience.

A typical case would be a boy of 17 recently who was in difficulties. He told his school he must see a psychologist. It upset the school, but his parents found me. He was dumb when he came and nothing happened at all, and so I said, "I will see you again some time". And then, one day a telephone message came to say, "Can I see you tomorrow?" I knew I had got to say "Yes". In that situation you have either to fail or do the right thing. Then I had to rearrange all my plans. I had to be like the mother with the tiny baby. Then he came, and we had an extremely rich hour and a half, did a tremendous lot of work which had a big effect. He took everything into his own hands, left school, got work in London in order to have a long treatment. It all depended on my doing everything at that moment.

There must be moments like this for you, and other moments when you will feel it silly to give up things to meet the child's immediate need.

But if you look round you can see when children are depressed—they can't put it on. When they are ill you know that if you try to make contact with them you can't. You have to let them feel the urge and then be there for it.

Although you are employed to take the responsibility for the children, having a relationship to a child is much more difficult. Take being a doctor at a clinic. It seems as if the community is trying to find out whether he will be allowed to do this difficult thing, to be a good doctor. It is odd that the doctors are putting up any response at all. Why should they be expected to ask to be allowed to be called up in the middle of the night? They may perhaps hope to get something very important out of it, but if it is challenged they will give it up. The same with mothers. They will not choose to do the difficult thing, the responsibility for the infant's feeding and bringing up, if they are going to hand over to the state. The same with teachers; it is not all teachers who come to courses like this which makes their work more difficult. Perhaps some could think it will make work very easy, but in practice it either makes no difference or, as time goes on, you find yourself taking personal responsibility. Doing things. Living experiences with children in your care. Thinking things out, risking things which otherwise you would have let go or done by rule of thumb. By coming to this course, it means that you have thought these things out. If psychology is dynamic and making a difference, in a way it is making it more of a strain and making it much more difficult. The difficulty about psychology is that if you get off the academic rails, talking about feelings, this can't be done without disturbing oneself. This is why it would not be a good idea to force all teachers to come to psychology lectures, because it would reduce anger and hate and make people less good. Nor would it be good to make all mothers go to lectures on the psychology of infancy. And if you said to all artists, poets, "you must come to a thing on psychology", you would come across terrific feelings, because the best artists loathe psychology.

Part three

THE FAMILY

5

The bearing of
emotional development
on feeding problems

[1967]

Y ou are here to consider certain problems of infancy, and
        you bring to the meeting, each one in a special way, an
        experience of the management of infants based on the
theory of their growth and development and on distortions of
development due to physical factors. My lecture must needs be
to some extent out of step with the other lectures because I wish
to talk about the difficulties that do not depend on physical illness. To simplify my subject I must assume that the baby is well
in a physical sense. I think you will not mind my drawing attention to the non-physical aspects of baby care, since in your
practice you are all the time dealing with these problems and
your interest does necessarily extend outside the field of actual
physical illness.

My problem here is a matter of presentation. As you probably know, I started off as a paediatrician and gradually changed
over into being a psychoanalyst and a child psychiatrist, and the
fact that I was originally a physically minded doctor has greatly
influenced my work. I do happen to have a very big volume of
experience which simply arises out of the fact that I have been in
active practice for forty-five years, and in that time one does
accumulate quite a lot of data.

In half an hour, I can do little more than point towards the highly complex theory of the emotional development of the human individual as a person. What I must do, however, for my own sake, is to convey some of the strength of feeling which I have accumulated in these forty-five years.

It is strange, but the training of doctors and nurses on the physical side undoubtedly drains away something from their interest in infants as human beings. When I myself started, I was conscious of an inability in myself to carry my natural capacity for empathy with children back to include empathy with babies. I was fully aware of this as a deficiency, and it was a great relief to me when gradually I became able to feel myself into the infant–mother or infant–parent relationship. I think that many who are trained on the physical side do have the same sort of block that I had myself, and they have to do a great deal of work on themselves in order to become able to stand in a baby's shoes. I am aware that this is a rather funny figure of speech since babies are not born with shoes on, but I think you will understand my meaning.

It is important for the paediatrician to know about human affairs, as they are at the beginning of the life of a new individual since when they talk to parents they must be able to know about the parent's important function. The doctor comes in when there is illness, but the parents have their importance all the time, apart from illness in the child. It is a terrible complication for a mother and for parents when the doctor that they call in with such confidence if the child has pneumonia is blind to all that they do in adaptation to the baby's needs when the child had not got an illness.

For example, the vast majority of difficulties in infant feeding have nothing to do with infection or with the biochemical unsuitability of the milk. They have to do with the immense problem that every mother has in adapting to the needs of a new baby. She has to do this on her own because no two babies are alike, and in any case no two mothers are alike and one mother is never the same with each child. The mother cannot learn how to do what is needed of her, either from books or from nurses or from doctors. She may have learned a great deal from having been an infant and also from watching parents with babies and from taking part in the care of siblings, and most of all she has learned a very great deal of vital importance when playing at mothers and fathers at a tender age.

It is true that some mothers are able to get help of a limited kind from books, but it must be remembered that if a mother goes to a book or to someone for advice and tries to learn what she has to do, we already wonder whether she is fitted for the job. She has to know about it from a deeper level and not necessarily from that part of the mind which has words for everything. The main things that a mother does with the baby cannot be done through words. This is very obvious, but it is also a very easy thing to forget. In my long experience I have had a chance to know many doctors and nurses and teachers who thought they could tell mothers what to do and who spent a lot of their time giving parents instruction, and then I have watched them when they became mothers and fathers and have had long talks with them about their difficulties, and I have found that they have had to forget all they thought they knew and in fact had been teaching. Quite frequently, they found that what they knew in this way interfered so much at the beginning that they were not able to be natural with their own first child. Gradually they managed to shed this useless layer of knowledge that is intertwined with words and settled down to involvement with this one baby.

The fact is that, to be a mother or to be maternal (I am to include the man), there has to be a high degree of identification with the infant although of course the mother retains her adult status while making this identification.

6

Sleep refusal in children

[1968]

I t is noteworthy that Henoch in his lectures on children's diseases,[1] did not index sleeplessness, except in so far as this is included in pavor nocturnus. His observations on the whole field of what we now call paediatrics were comprehensive and exact, and one can only assume that in his day (the period 1874–85), when 5,368 (70%) out of 7,815 (under 2 years) and 1,420 (23%) out of 6,165 (over 2 years) children in his clinic died, there was so big a problem on the physical side that a mere matter of sleeplessness seemed trivial. Yet, as we know today, a child's sleep disturbance may cause considerable distress to parents and to children.

Now that we are free to look at the emotional difficulties and disorders even of healthy or normal children, we can profitably study sleep disturbances, including those that come under the heading of sleep refusal, when it can be rightly said that the child *deliberately* keeps awake.

The problem here is rather like that of school refusal, where likewise there is a degree of wilful and deliberate action. In each case, of course, the motivation is *unconscious*, and it is the re-

---

[1] E. Henoch, *Lectures on Children's Diseases. Vol. 1* (London: The New Sydenham Society, 1889).

pressed elements in the child's and in the parents' psychological make-up that determine the intractable nature of the disorder.

The whole subject of sleep disturbance would be too big for discussion here, but narrowed down to sleep refusal it is perhaps possible to point out one or two features without doing violence to the vast thing called human nature.

The key to the sleep disturbances is anxiety. The child dreams intolerable dreams which bring about the relief of an awakening, or else there is a fear of sleep because of the dreams that threaten. Or very frightening physical sensations accompany the sleeping state or the twilight phase before sleep, sensations which are in fact body-memories of past experiences, perhaps dating from infancy and specific failures of the holding that goes with good-enough nurture. Or there are very real problems that belong to the transition from the waking to the dreaming state, problems that are commonly solved by the use of a familiar personal object or technique (such as thumb-sucking, and its elaborations) which carry the child over this dangerous moment when the time-gap may so easily be filled with hallucinatory phenomena.

All these things belong to human nature itself, to the tasks accomplished in the emotional development of the individual through the drive forward by inherited integrative and other growth tendencies made possible by good-enough environmental provision. These matters are highly complex, and they have been stated in many different ways, and there is a big measure of agreement among various workers in regard to the main trends and the main details.

Obviously excitement, local and general, associated with instinctual drives, contribute to the acute nature of some sleep disorders, such as the common nightmare.

The term sleep refusal may perhaps be used to draw attention to a special form of sleep disturbance, as, for instance, when a child will not go to bed, or will not "try to go to sleep", or will sleep only among the noises of the family life or with the mother lying alongside, or will wake at the time when the parents go to bed.

In this type of disturbance it will be noted that the mother or the parents together are involved, and in some cases it is just this that provides the clue to (at least a partial) understanding of the aetiology.

It may as well be stated, although this information is of re-markably little use, that in these cases it is often an unconscious element in the parental attitude that is causing the trouble. For instance, the child may have no difficulty about going to sleep when staying a few days with an aunt. At any rate, in some of these cases the main trouble is a failure of nurture—a weak spot in that complex thing, the good-enough facilitating environment. This good-enough environment combines strength with adap-tive management in a way suited not only to the child at the phase of his or her development, but also as he or she is on any one particular day or night. Also, the human beings who are this facilitating environment have their own private lives, their moods, their phases of tiredness or exasperation, their weak-nesses.

They also have their own difficulties, which may involve re-pressed material in their own personal defence organizations. In illustration, let me build up out of the imagination. Here is a married couple with two or three children. They do not want more children, and their sexual life is not any longer so smooth that they can easily admit a discussion as to contraceptive meas-ures. In any case either one or the other is liable to get caught up in instinct arousal, and things can easily happen before there is time for careful deliberation.

How convenient, then, if one of the children tends to need special attention just when the parents are likely to come to-gether. With no conscious organization it can happen that the child has come to fit into an assigned role—that of contraceptive.

This can become a painful affair, for the parents become estranged, the child may easily fail to enjoy his or her position of controller of the household or "controller of the world" or find it irksome. And, added to all this, sleeplessness at night leads to irritability in the day, and a host of secondary symptoms.

It will be seen from this that the administration of sleeping draughts to such children is doomed to failure, and ought not to be started. Also, there is no point in the doctor coming in with a heavy hand, metaphorically or otherwise, since the child is unaware of what he or she is doing in the direction of providing a solution for the parents' life-problem of which even the parents are not aware or are only partially aware.

Also, there is nothing more cruel than criticism or castigation of the parents, and it can even be unwise to give advice. What should the doctor say, except "change your natures", "know what you don't know about yourselves", "think of yourselves only", although you know that you must take into consideration many other factors, such as adaptation to each child's needs and compliance with immediate social standards.

Let us not forget that the doctor is just as likely to be involved in difficulties of this kind as are his patients.

It may be best to do nothing and to tolerate the awfulness over a phase. However, one can say that what is needed is *case-work*: that is, a structured social worker's professional involvement, maintained over a length of time, with the development of that confidence which brings with it the rewards of new insights.

One can build up from imagination and from experience not only the difficult case, but also a gradual evolution of increased awareness in all concerned, and of a consequent new freedom on the part of the parents to find a way of management that meets all the requirements to some extent, and perhaps enough.

Doctors like cures. But in this work they must be contented with watching personal and social evolution.

7

The effect of loss on the young

[1968]

It is strange but true that people do need to be reminded that FEELINGS matter. Our feelings are so much a part of us, and yet when it comes to the feelings of others we easily clock off, and pretend that all is well. It is difficult enough with positive feelings of love and trust, and we are shy to assert our beliefs. When the feelings are negative, or associated with hate and fear and suspicion, we are careful, and tend to deny what we really know is true. Worst is the tendency we can find in ourselves to deny the fact of sadness or grief in others, to pretend to ourselves that things are all right really.

Perhaps we can be forgiven. We carry round with us, each one of us to some degree, much sadness and confusion and even hopelessness, and we can only manage to get up in the morning and do our work on the basis of putting serious things aside. So when we meet someone else's grief we soon come to the end of a phase of morbid collusion, and then we feel all right and expect the other person to feel all right too.

It is as if the game of soldiers is over. All the dead people and animals among the toys that were lying flat are stood up again, and the world is repopulated with live creatures.

But life is not a game, and for the bereaved the loss is permanent even when there is a recovery, and from when a sense of the dead person's aliveness re-emerges, so that the period of mourning can be said to be over, except perhaps for anniversaries, ᴏɪ when some special feature brings a reminder that there is suddenly no opportunity for sharing.

It is especially easy for us to belittle the effect of loss on the young. Young people are so distractible, and life comes bubbling up whether they like it or not. But loss of parent, or friend, or pet, or special toy, may take away the whole point of living, so that what we mistake for life is the child's enemy, a liveliness that deceives everyone except the child. The child knows that the liveliness has to be paid for.

Or perhaps the child is given no time to pay for this real underlying ɡ ʿ ɪnd hopelessness, so that a false personality is built up, one that is jocular and shallow and infinitely distractible. Then the complaint is that the child never settles to any one thing, or goes from one relationship to another without a capacity to make friends.

These things can go very deep, and can be difficult to cure; nevertheless it is worth our while to see that we do not contribute to the child's uncomfortable state by refusing to allow the child the real grief and hopelessness, and even self-destructive ideas that belong directly to the severe loss that has been sustained.

When we find a ch'' nhappy and withdrawn we can surely do more by a sympat, ' holding operation than by jogging the child into a state of false liveliness and forgetfulness. If we stand by and wait and wait we shall often be rewarded by real changes in the child that indicate a natural tendency to recover from loss, and from the sense of guilt that the child feels even when it can truly be said that the child did not contribute to the tragic happening.

8

Out of the mouths of adolescents

[1966]

There is this adolescence, and there are these adolescents . . .
Out of the new books on adolescents I would take this as one worth reading.[1] It gives a very good account of boys' and girls' thinking and feeling, and it hands on something of their Damon Runyanesque verbalizing capacity. "When in trouble I expect to tak punishment liker man." "Its wrong to intimate before marriage." "Its wrong to have intercourse with a girl but its lovely."

The Eppels, working together, used a good method for capturing the conscious reactions of 250 young workers of 15 to 18 years attending day-release classes in London. In the main part of the investigation the children were asked to complete sentences, the first few words being given, like:

A good friend . . .
My greatest wish . . .
The older generation . . .
Young people . . .
It isn't fair . . .

---

[1] E. M. Eppel & M. Eppel, *Adolescents and Morality* (London: Routledge & Kegan Paul).

48

The completed sentences make good reading, and the authors classify the remarks in a way that is simple and yet quite brilliant in giving the reader help in the evaluation of the material.

The reader has been introduced in the first part of the book to the expectations of samples of magistrates, probation officers, and youth leaders who were asked to give answers to questions designed to elicit general views on morals, the differences between the generations, and the major influences on morals.

Here, too, the replies are usefully classified.

The Eppels include other types of investigation, filling out the picture of the moral beliefs of these young workers, and their ideas of what good behaviour means and their views on life generally. The total presentation provides a valuable glimpse into the conscious thinking and available feeling of these young people whom the reader is glad to have met. People whose work takes them into contact with the anti-social aspects of the adolescent scene could find here a natural correction in that the boys and girls of this investigation appear as persons, as individuals becoming autonomous, as total personalities with a morality that belongs to the individual, to the age of late adolescence, and to the near-adult state.

One stimulus was: *The person I would most like to be.* The reactions contain everything, but I liked the boy who wrote: "I am quite happy being myself (or almost) though I would like to make less blunders"; and another who wrote: "I would like to stay as I am, a big handsome, broad shoulder, muscular male. A person who is cool, calm, collective at the worst of times; and always looks on the best sides of things (THAT'S WHAT I LIKE TO THINK)".

A few more quotations may be helpful, but I confess I like the answers best when the spelling is individual:

"Its wrong to go on the wrong side of the law but sometimes it is neseery."

"The older generation is mixed between old fogies and decent understanding adults who remember they were young once."

"The older generation have gone through a rough time . . . that subconshusly they think we are have it easy."

One further point is that the threat of the bomb has the effect of strengthening the adolescents' recurring feeling that perhaps it isn't worthwhile to try:

"I would try to make a peaceful world for the next generation."

"I would get rid of the bomb and live a quiet life."

"I'd give up a lot to know that if you give birth to a child they will live to die a natural death and not by an atom bomb."

9

The delinquent and habitual offender

[early 1940s]

This observation on the psychology of anti-social behaviour can only be understood properly if the author can be given credit for a willingness to study internal factors. What I have to say concerns the external factors and their importance in the aetiology of anti-social illness, but there can be no question but that I consider the important thing in the understanding of any human being is the internal development of that being.

The reason why I wish to talk about the external factor in this setting is simply this, that it is so very important. Although I do not see eye to eye with Bowlby in regard to details, I do find that his paper read before the Psycho-Analytic Society says something that I had already learnt from clinical material before hearing his paper.[1] He says that "in over half of a series of cases there had been a separation lasting more than six months of the child from the mother in the first five years of the child's life". My way of putting it is that "to be unwanted, to be bandied from one person to another in the first months of life, predisposes to

---

[1] J. Bowlby, "Forty-four Juvenile Thieves: Their Characters and Home-life." *International Journal of Psycho-Analysis, 25* (1944): 1–57, 207–228. (Published under same title, London: Tindall & Cox, 1946.)

anti-social illness". However our views coincide to the extent that I want to emphasize one of his points.

It is true that separation of a child from its mother before the child can keep its mother alive in his mind must be bad for any child and might lead to any sort of disorder, according to the psychology of the child at the time of the separation

Yet I must say that clinical material observed over a space of twenty years has led me to believe that anti-social illness is more an illness of normal children disturbed by environment whereas (for instance) manic-depressive illness is more an internal illness of children that is unrelated aetiologically to gross environmental events.

I know that this must break down if examined too closely, but I believe there is value to be got from this statement as it stands.

It is clear that whereas the study of manic-depressive disease is obviously to be done best by psychoanalysis of patients with the illness, study of delinquency cannot successfully be made by psychoanalysis of delinquents. Psychoanalysis of delinquents is a highly dangerous job, and if delinquents are one day to be cured by psychoanalysis this will be done because of the psychoanalysis of normals and of manic-depressives, and also because of the study of the external aetiological factors found through case histories.

I want to say of a delinquent that he is a potential revolutionary, and that in war he is at his best. In war he wins V.C.s, and in peace he may be able to sublimate his difficulties into the perfectly social act of revolutionary activity. I say social, but of course the social order for which he is working is a future, new one, an ideal one.

It could be said that the anti-social person is the arch-complainer. He has always an idea of what should be, and people soon fail to reach the standard. Actually, there is no more delightful person than the typical delinquent boy, during the period when he has idealized you, and before you have failed him.

And what does he expect of you? He expects you to be glad to be stolen from, to want to be tired out by him, to love him to make a mess anywhere, and to be always present to control his show of strength, so that he need not protect himself or others. In short, he is still looking for the ideal mother of infancy that he never found. But he believes in her, that's the trouble.

A normal child, in comparison, has really had the experience of an infant's mother, and he is capable of that much content- ment. He believes in contentment, having experienced it, and tries to recapture it in his life. He is, therefore, not necessarily idealist and Left wing, and indeed he is the despair of revolu- tionary organizations.

It will be seen that this matter of the break-up of the family life can easily become a issue. One has only to remember the horror of communist Russia's disturbance of family life that was strongly expressed in the first years of the revolution. Probably Russia has to live down this generation before she can be stable, for the revolutionary character must be anti-social, unless there is a revolution to take part in.

It is likely that the political Left wing openly despises family life, but I think danger comes from the Right wing: the very people who protested most loudly against the break-up of the family in Russia are liable, according to my view, to use this present unusual circumstance to actually break up family life in England. This would be a return of the repressed, an inversion of morality such as one expects to find in war-time, but which one nevertheless wishes to prevent.

If I were asked how best we could sow seeds which would eventually germinate into revolution, I would prescribe a whole- sale break-up of the family such as is contemplated under the evacuation schemes. This may or may not be sense, but I cannot get away from my clinical experience of the relation of not being wanted at the start of life to the subsequent anti-social tendency.

10

A clinical approach
to family problems:
the family

[1959]

The family is a localized element in a society, an element that is orientated to the task of dealing with the arrival of a new individual.

The nature of the family naturally varies with the pattern of the society. At one extreme we think of father and mother and child, and at the other we remember the families described in anthropological writings in which the actual parents are so integrated into the society structure that it looks as if aunts and uncles and grandparents and perhaps priests are more important than the actual father and mother.

Behind the idea of the family is a recognition of the individual small child's initial need of a simplified version of society, one which can be used for the purposes of essential emotional growth, until development brings about in the child a capacity for using a wider circle, and indeed an ever-widening circle. *Maturity* can be described as the growth of the individual in relation to society appropriate to the age of the child, and resulting eventually in the individual's capacity to identify with society without too great a sacrifice of individual impulse. Naturally, maturity does not lead us all to world citizenship. Perhaps we always have a few Gilbert Murrays[1] in our midst, some unrecognized, but, on the whole, we accept as mature the capacity of an individual to identify (without loss of personal identity) with a sub-group—a nation, a race, a political party, an ideology, a religion, or a persecuted minority.

We do not expect maturity in these terms till the individual has passed through adolescence and has begun to think in terms of establishing a family, with of course the co-operation of a partner.

You, although you are senior persons, are this year once again members of the most exciting of all groups: you are students. You contribute to society by your potential. I am sorry this happy state of affairs will, undoubtedly, end.

Societies vary in their conscious support of the family as the unit known to be of the right size and kind for meeting the need of the child as he emerges out of a two-body relationship to the mother and develops a capacity for making a three-body relationship. (I return later to the theme of the father's role in relation to the infant–mother partnership.)

Parents, I suppose, know much more about their children's needs than society does, because the parents are immediately involved. Society is remote, and needs to be kept constantly informed as to what it does and why.

For instance, ten years ago our country knew enough about deprived children to support the Children's Act[2] (1948) and this means that there was a general willingness to foot the bill.

The Government Paper on Children in Hospital (1959) is perhaps a good example on the positive side, reminding society of the value to society of the family.[3]

I do not think, personally, that we do so much by proving the value of the family scientifically, as by the provision and the

[1]Professor Gilbert Murray, 1866–1957: British classical scholar of renown whose poetic translations of Ancient Greek drama received great interest at this time.

[2]London: His Majesty's Stationery Office, 1948.

[3]GB Ministry of Health. Central Services Council. "The Welfare of Children in Hospital." Report of the Committee (Chairman Sir Harry Platt). London: His Majesty's Stationery Office, 1959.

keeping open of channels of communication between (in this instance) parents, who know, and society, that needs to be kept informed.

And parents need to be informed too, about their own value both to the children and to society; here you and I come in because of our professional position. It is not a matter of propaganda but a matter of putting into words that parents can understand the things that they feel and do and refrain from doing, thus providing information that they need about their function.

There are ill parents, psychiatrically ill, and my job will be to refer to these illnesses, but our work is done on the basis that the vast majority of people are well enough in the area in which they choose to operate, and parents, on the whole, do well as parents, and can make great use of help, if this is given at the right time, and in the right way.

A rough outline of the dynamics of family life will include those factors in parents tending to form and maintain the family structure and those tending to disrupt it. The same factors are found in children, and then there is society's contribution, both positive and negative.

We shall need to study the family at its inception, covering the toddler age, the latency period interweaving with school, the early stages of puberty, puberty itself, and finally adolescence, early and late. This will involve us in a study of the infant—mother relationship, because of the reappearance of infantile dependence at all stages.

We shall consider the family as affected by the type of parent and by illness in the parents.

Eventually, of course, we shall arrive at the individual child, since an understanding of the emotional development of the individual forms the basis for all other branches of dynamic psychology, even social psychology.

The study of the individual will lead us to the unconscious and to instincts, and to intrapsychic conflict.

[Winnicott went on to describe a particular child's difficulties and the part played by the mother and father. Unfortunately, he did not write this down.]

Part four

STARTING SCHOOL

11

Mental hygiene of the pre-school child

[1936]

Y ou have done me the honour of asking me to speak to you about the pre-school child. I hope that I have found something out of my own experience and study to interest you, even perhaps to be of practical value to you; but I confess to feeling diffident about my ability to give what is required of me. You are asking me to deal with something that the great Shakespeare himself shirked. Fools, they say, step in where angels fear to tread. Fortunately Shakespeare is no angel, so perhaps I may avoid being thought a fool for attempting to introduce a new act into the seven ages of man that we act on the world-stage.

You remember

"All the world's a stage . . .
"First the infant . . .
"Then the school boy . . . !"

It cannot be denied that Shakespeare fought shy of the pre-school child, and of all the problems of the nursery school. He might have said

First the infant, mewling and puking in its nurse's arms,
And then the pre-school child whose mental hygiene will tax
the twentieth-century brain,

but I have no doubt that the difficulty of setting this to blank verse was too much for his muse. Try to make "pre-school child" fit into blank verse, and you will understand.

Or else, in the sixteenth century the toddler age was a kind of tweeny, ignored by the poets and philosophers as the tweeny was, lost between the cook and the housemaid. Nowadays the tweeny has become cook plus housemaid, and so has gained recognition; and the toddler years are also coming into their own.

Three distinct approaches to the study of the toddler are possible; these concern the physical, the intellectual, and the emotional development respectively. Each has its importance. There is a tendency, I feel, to give the first, the physical development, more than its share of relative attention, the idea being that if you look after the body of the little child everything else about him looks after itself. This doctrine is dangerous, and has recently called forth a letter in *The Times* newspaper from Susan Isaacs, who should have been lecturing here this evening instead of me. (At the time when the lectures were arranged she was ill and did not wish to undertake out-of-London work, however pleasurable).

It may be possible to cater for the body needs of the older child and to let the problems of emotional development slide, and to get away with it. The school boy or girl, even only 6 or 8 years old, is capable of seeking and finding emotional experience according to his or her individual inner needs. But the toddler urgently needs something special in the people around if emotional development is to proceed. Also, the toddler is undergoing rapid psychological development, much more so than the older school-child, and the effects of traumata have consequently a relatively great effect at the pre-school age.

I need scarcely illustrate the needs of *physical* development and the effect of proper food, clothing, and routine on the mind as well as on the body of the little child. So much is obvious at the present time. I will, however, illustrate what I mean by the *intellectual* and the *emotional* development, because the distinction between them is sometimes missed, with harmful results. Of course the two are inter-related.

You all have stories like this one, only mine is true. Mary aged 2 years and 8 months, had her friend Bridget to tea. Afterwards she said: "Mummy, I want Bridget's mind."—"What do you mean, dear?"—"I mean I want what she thinks with; so I'll be Bridget and Bridget'll be me." This at 2 years and 8 months!

We are apt to be surprised each time we hear some story or more directly gain evidence of the intellectual capacity of a little child. There is not so much difference in intellectual capacity at the different ages; only the language and the subjects that engage attention change with the years.

Intelligence can be measured, and there are those who delight in devising new and surer means of stating intelligence in mathematical terms or geometric graphs. They are entitled to what enjoyment they can get from such work. My temperament neither fits me for this kind of study nor does it even allow me to see its full value, since I personally enjoy trying to recognize the child's feelings, and to understand the conscious and unconscious emotional conflicts with their widespread influence on the individual's life. What interests me about intellectual capacity and about skills is less the measurement of them than the variations in them secondary to difficulties in emotional development. Often, intellectual capacity which is high at the beginning of the toddler age is apparently much less by the end of that age and the start of the school age. The child has "been through" a lot in the toddler years, and intellectual attainment as well as physical skills have to become to some extent hung up as a result of the various defences set up against anxiety, depression, and violent feelings, and defences against violent fluctuations of feeling.

You will see that already I have separated the intellectual and the emotional, since I have said that the course of emotional development, even its normal course, often involves intellectual inhibitions: anxieties can also involve intellectual forcing, producing the child who *must* know, who *must* be top at school, and for whom intellectual development is more a matter of defence against feeling bad than a matter of pleasure.

It is this emotional development that most interests me. I will give an illustration of the play of feelings which I want you to distinguish from skills and achievements, asking you to forgive me if I speak too simply.

In my hospital practice I find myself dealing with a young mother, rather diffident, and feeling terribly inexperienced as she comes to consult a physician. She brings her only child, a boy of 1½ years. He has had a pain in the belly for which she consulted a general practitioner, who at first suspected appendicitis, and then said it was colic; and now the child is run down and needs a tonic. Will I please prescribe one?

I find I am unable to say there is no physical disease, and I begin to fish round to get a clue to the debility, which cannot be explained properly as a sequel of colic.

At length I get the following simple story:

Daddy, a seaman, has been home on a fortnight's leave. He and the kiddie became great friends and made up for lost time. The colic came in this fortnight, and is quite likely to have been a part of the general excitement, and certainly it gave no great trouble. But soon the time came for Daddy to return to sea; now the child fretted badly. To deal with this the mother actually *got her husband to come back home for a week more.* The child was much reassured by this, and eventually stood the father's departure fairly well, but remained somewhat sad and off food. This is what the mother called "run down after an attack of colic". I should call it a mild depression and should not call it necessarily normal. Looked at in this way, the symptoms are not those of an illness but are the visible part of a complex reaction in a developing child to a frustration. All the things that went on beneath the surface can only be guessed at. You might say the child felt guilty feelings in regard to the enjoyment of his father's attentions. He dealt with these guilt feelings fairly well until the father's departure—but then he felt this to be a punishment, and his guilt feelings increased. Really it is much more complicated. Can I put it in this way without attempting to separate conscious from unconscious? Things happen in the inner world of the child in relation both to the father's love and to his departure. The father's love leads to the setting up of a good father inside the child, but there goes with this the threat of an angry, bad, jealous mother who will separate him from this father. The anxiety feels to the child like a pain inside (what the mother calls colic). However, he manages, especially as the result of the illness, to test the external or real mother's love. She not only shows her sympathy but she actually takes him to another man—the doctor.

All goes well—the reassurance brought about by the externally real mother works; but soon father really goes. This feels to the child like a disaster. Inside him, father is dead, perhaps killed by the bad mother. The real mother recognizes that the child is being called on to deal with more than he can manage—that the reassurance that her continued love can give is insufficient to help him, and so she recalls father, quite quickly. This time the reassurance worked. The boy sees that he has felt father to be dead, but that really he wasn't. So he begins to recognize the difference between the feeling of disaster and of threat, and the externally real. If father had really died at that moment, the effect would have been bad, to some extent permanently bad. The child would have feared to let his inner world come to life, and so would have had to exert permanent control—or adopt some means of denying inner reality either by forced irresponsibility, or by delusions of persecutions in the world, or else would have had to feel almost permanently depressed, which is perhaps not compatible with life.

As it is, this healthy little child has been able to deal with the great problem, through the mother's love and understanding. Youth is on his side, for the capacity of the toddler to modify inner reality or deep fantasy by contact with external reality is characteristic of the age; and the school-child and the adult are much more fixed in this respect. This works both ways, since while the little child is open to change—that is to say, is developing—he is also much more liable than is the older child or the adult to suffer permanent damage from traumata proceeding from external reality. Hence the toddler's double need—that we should provide for him an active love relationship, besides protecting him from unnecessary shocks, frustrations, and too great stimulations.

I want you to note what the mother did. She *believed in the child's fretfulness*, to the extent of getting her husband back for a week, at great inconvenience, I may add. And she was rewarded by success.

A mother is temporarily an expert in child-feelings. People say she becomes a vegetable, but really she becomes interested in a narrowed world and so is able to believe in the intensity of the children's feelings. If she cannot narrow her world when she has little children, you will find she has more or less difficulty in believing in the little child's feelings and difficulty—in feeling how bad it is to fret when you are 2, and how terrific it is to love, and to hate, and how frightening to be afraid. I may say here that I am enunciating nothing new, but in all ages there are the few who believe in the little child's feelings, and the majority who deny or sentimentalize. Listen to this, from the year 1824:

"Let us take a view of the unnatural manner in which infants are generally treated, and the variety of needless torments they are made to undergo. The scene often commences by throwing at once the full blaze of day on their half opened eyes; or, if they make their first appearance in the night, ignorance and curiosity give them equal torment by the help of a candle held to their faces: the extreme anguish of the aching sight produces a cry of distress, which gains them the wished relief of obscurity, till the next curious person renews the torture. This scene may be repeated ten times in the first hour of a child's life, with exactly the same effects. When the painful operation of dressing commences, the covering is thoughtlessly at once taken from the child's face; a violent cry is immediately the consequence, and often continued, by a succession of disagreeable sensations, for two hours, exclusive of a little intermission of rocking, when probably the loud discord of the nurse's voice, ignorantly exerted to quiet the suffering babe's complaint, may give as much pain to the tender auditory nerve, unaccustomed to the vibration of sounds, as the unusual glare of light had before imparted to the optic nerve. Add to this, the variety of uneasy postures the infant must be placed in, to get on, and come at to fasten, a multiplicity of separate garments, with the ridiculous custom of giving a spoonful of a most nauseous mixture the first thing to be swallowed— and it will amount to an evident proof, that we have contrived to employ the first three or four hours of a child's life in giving successive torment to every sense, by light, noise, medicine, and uneasy positions.

When, after all this pain and trouble, the poor creature is what they call drest, the unnatural confinement of the limbs is a continual punishment, which can never be submitted to with ease, though it may in time be rendered by custom more familiar. Of this there needs no other proof than the visible and extreme pleasure that all children discover when stript of their encumberances, the content and satisfaction with which they stretch themselves, enjoying the freedom of voluntary motion; and the uneasiness and dislike, if not fretfulness, always conspicuous the moment the restraint begins to be renewed by putting on their shackles.

I am convinced, beyond a doubt, that to these, and other instances of our own mismanagement, is wholly owing that continual crying of infants, which, from being customary, is erroneously supposed natural to them. Was the pain of the body, inflicted at the time by this mismanagement, the only ill consequence resulting from it, that alone every feeling heart would wish to alleviate; yet this is but a trifling consideration, compared to the more injurious, and often irreparable effects, produced by the ill impression thus early made on the mind."

Now it so often happens that those whose job it is to look after children are unable to appreciate the full intensity of the feelings of their charges. For the small child the ordinary nursemaid can be better, and the mother is usually far better than the trained worker, including doctor and nurse. Fortunately there are wonderful exceptions to this, and among you there are trained workers who believe in and respect the children's feelings. But training cannot produce the good child-minder. There is no hope for the sentimental or the impatient or the callous or suspicious or "superior" worker in nursery school work. "Only those who can love need apply", the advertisement should read. Look after the toddler's body and even his belly and neglect his heart, and it were better the child should be left at home in dirt and squalor and physical want. On the other hand, and I say it immediately, if loving people are available there is a place for a nursery school round every corner, where a mother can leave her child when she is at work, or when she is at play (if she gets any play). But the mother must be able to feel that the child is still to be regarded as hers, as a human, and as an individual. Mothers, uneducated or otherwise, are very sensitive about these things. How often mothers say, as a mother said to me this week: "Rosemary is restless and a proper nuisance, but if only we could keep in time with her hands she could be quite a nice child. She shows a capacity for sustained effort and a great desire to do interesting things, but I have neither the time nor skill to keep her occupied. The nearest nursery school is a long way away, and I could not afford the bus fares."

There are, of course, hopeless mothers, whose children would be better anywhere but at home, but they are not at all common, and anyway are very difficult to help. They will as likely as not put spokes in your wheel whenever you try to help them, because fundamentally they want to do good by the child *themselves*, and, without perhaps knowing it, they are jealous of your capacity to help where they cannot. There is really no need to go about insisting on helping parents who hate being helped, especially as there is such a big need from those who are easy to help if you can once make them feel that you really understand little children.

There are many who would say to the mother of my illustration: "Don't be weak, getting your husband all the way home again from his boat because the child frets! If you behave that way the child will be spoiled. He's got to learn to bear frustration!"

Learn to bear frustration! As if we need introduce frustrations! The inevitable frustrations of experience at toddler age are surely enough, and scarcely to be borne by the most tough. It must be clearly understood that the pre-school child is dealing with as much as can be borne in the ordinary course of emotional development, and our job is to help him in his defences against the awful feelings of guilt, anxiety, and depression rather than to train him to be—to be like—to be like what? Like ourselves? I am not so convinced that you and I are in a position to dictate even to little children what is ideal. If the children love us they will try to be like the best they can see in us. Perhaps it is safer to confine our conscious efforts to helping them to avoid despair (which shows in tempers and in other ways besides sadness and depression) and not to try to mould them to a pattern which we in our finite wisdom have conceived for them. I shall return to this point later.

At the moment I want to remind you that this uninstructed mother treated her child excellently—that is with love, and with respect for the child's capacity to deal with conflicts, given time. The mother, by getting the externally real father back, enabled the boy to test his fantasies against the facts. It had seemed Daddy was dead, killed through the child's own bad feelings, but thank goodness Daddy was not dead; there must be a difference between what the child feels and what is! A time factor is involved in the recovery from depression, but gradually the child recovered from what might have been a very serious check to emotional development affecting the child's entire life. At school age the effect of the father's disappearance would have been interesting to note—at toddler age the effect was harmful.

You see from this simple story how big is your responsibility when you take up nursery school work. Please leave it alone if you feel unable to cope with this idea. Even a nagging mother is better than a correct and heartless institution. Certainly a dirty mother is better than a clean institution where cleanliness and habit-training are first principles, hung like texts on a hygienic wall, supplanting the muddy-coloured, flowered wallpaper which the child had been used to at his own home in the slums.

There is a distinct danger in starting this sort of work in poor districts. Why not start by providing nursery schools for our own children, and only when we are sure of our ground let us try to get money to extend the benefits to the children of those who live in poverty and dirt? Most children of 2, 3, and 4 are at home in not-too-clean surroundings, and may be actually frightened by austerity which you and I would call "in good taste". In many ways we can easily be subjecting children to too much strain when we put them in surroundings where to make a mess is to sin, and to smear the wall is sacrilege, and to lick the window-pane is unhygienic, and to pee on the floor is to make oneself terribly obviously an uncontrolled person.

Nursery schools are needed acutely by the modern dwellers in flats whose most valued room is the tiled bathroom; these dare not allow their children to be natural and so to gradually develop their own personal attitude towards the moralities. The children must not make a noise that can be heard above the wireless, they must not want quiet, they must not make real messes or even scribble on the wall, or just once cut the side-board with a knife. There is no backyard, not even one where they mustn't go, so they can't even easily imagine how nice it would be to sit in the dustbin. Nursery schools for such children are places where for a few hours daily children can find the extent of their own impulses, and so become more able to cope with them, and less afraid of them. No very special psychological understanding is required for this work, but a great toleration is needed, which is not too easy to find in people. Those of you who have visited Dr. M. Lowenfeld's clinic in London will have been struck by the way in which children who are simply allowed to be natural there do not constantly exceed what is possible for the clinic to put up with, but gradually the more normal ones develop their own control mechanisms, and at the same time become in many cases happier children, without having had any psychological treatment involving the analysis of the unconscious. There is plenty of room, I mean, for work with pre-school children apart from psychoanalysis—which is fortunate, since the technique called psychoanalysis takes a long while to acquire and only a few are able to spare the time to learn to do this special work.

First then, we recognize the child's intense feelings. Then we realize that the feelings are changing in kind and character as the infant grows up and the toddler approaches school age, that the child's defences against painful and depressing feelings are also developing and becoming more organized. Then we recognize the wide fluctuations of feeling and defence in the little child and so expect crises at which it is especially not good to try to educate. Then we see that there are traumata, some more or less inevitable, and others that can be avoided and that we would wish to help the child to escape; and we see also the special effect of traumata coinciding in time with crises of feeling or defence. And all the time we believe in the intensity of the child's love, hope, hate, despair, guilt feelings, reparation urges, and attempts to put right in the external world that which feels as if it has been hurt or spoiled in fantasy or in the inner reality.

Illustrating the effect of coincidence of trauma and emotional crisis is the case of Joan.

> When Joan was 4 she had fears of going in a car. She had dreams about car rides, and in her dreams her father got killed. This was not very unusual, and I expect all would have been well had she not been involved in an accident. She had tried to pull her father back from the car ride but her fears were ignored (quite naturally), and she went with the family for a car-picnic. On the way the car was in a collision. She found her father lying in the road and ran over to him and kicked him hard saying "Wake up! Wake up!" But unfortunately he was dead.

> Joan became and stayed quite powerless to move after this. She stayed put whatever you did with her, and she lost all interest in her surroundings, and hardly seemed alive except that she took food passively, and in a dazed way followed people around. You see what happens when the inner life is almost completely controlled. Any liveliness inside had become dangerous. The child felt responsible for her father's death, since his death had occurred in her fantasy world, and she had no longer the reassuring sight of him alive—inner and outer world had become as one, and she must control the world as well as her fantasy world to maintain alive what was left worth preserving. This task occupied all her energy. Treatment was successful to the extent of getting her back to school and to a fair enjoyment of life—though her intellectual powers did not regain their former standard.

This is rather a crude example, but perhaps by its crudity it illustrates my meaning clearly. It is in the same sort of way that a little child who is having a bout of night terrors or of bilious attacks is not in the best stage to suffer a change of nurse, moving house, education in manners, legal separation of the parents, and so on. External reality changes should be made if possible when the child is not under the sway of an internal crisis.

It might be imagined that once we know how to act, all will be well. It all sounds so easy: but is it?

Last week I admitted to hospital a little girl of 4, because of possible chest tuberculosis. She is a solemn little girl, and the joy of life is not in her. Possibly her removal from home will be found to have been a great trauma to emotional development. I cannot say. However, now at 4 the effect cannot be as bad as was her removal to the fever hospital at 2.

One could say how wonderful that the organization of our fever hospitals is so good that when at 2, this little girl was found to have diphtheria, she was in hospital and having serum injected within three hours of the onset of her illness! This is truly good, but is that all?

The child came out of hospital an entirely different child from what she had been—having gone in happy and trusting, she came out morose, suspicious, inhibited, dulled. It is probable that the nurses treated her nicely, for she would play at nurses with her doll, and would always seem to be a nice nurse to them. But the change in the child was brought about by the faulty technique of the ambulance nurse. This trusting little girl of 2 years was taken away *while asleep* "so as not to frighten her", and the mother was not allowed to see the child into hospital, nor during the whole three months the child was in the ward!

To a child of 2 years this treatment is entirely brutal. It is common treatment, since the delicate task of transferring the ill toddler from home to hospital environment is left to the ambulance nurse, who has no training for this special task. She may have intuitive understanding, or she may not; at any rate she has no training in psychology, and her mistakes are terrible in their consequences. I have known great personality changes due to sudden removal of fairly healthy children from home to fever hospital—on the report of a throat swab. Ill children, of course, are different, are asking for treatment, and believe in the doctor and nurses, and allow terrible operations to be done on them without turning a hair—but if the child does not feel ill, or is dealt with by faulty technique, what might have been a physical blessing turns out to be a psychological tragedy. I have chosen this particular matter of removal to fever hospital because it is easy to describe; you can perhaps see that in all sorts of ways we do not avoid brutality in the treatment of little children, not so much because we are brutal as because we cannot realize how deeply the little child feels, and how, if the child's defences fail, the results are appalling. The little child's defences are capable of dealing with almost everything life can offer provided that there is a loving background to his life and that the time factor is recognized. But lack of love or the coincidence of traumata can be permanently injurious.

I would like you to recognize clearly the tremendous forces that underlie the little child's passing symptoms. You see a child blinking. It is easy to say: "Blinking—that is a disease—let us treat it." But why not try to place the symptom in the whole picture of the child. It will be found that the blinking is essential to the child's mental health. Given his difficulties he must blink, or fail to defend against something too painful to be borne, or become confused or depressed or silly.

> Alan, aged 5½, came to me because of nervousness. He was well till at 2½ he had a fright. He witnessed a bad thunderstorm. Following this he stuttered. He got over this, but since that time he has had a new bout of symptoms with each new external strain. In fact he has gradually become sensitive to less and less of a real hurt, and recently he saw a punch ball in a window opposite—and was terrified of this, which he thought was the face of someone watching him. He has blinked a lot since this fright, also he has become afraid of many things, and compulsively makes throat noises. Moreover, he won't move off the doorstep. In the night, too, he lies awake and sweats profusely. In the morning he gets up unwillingly and unhappy.

You all know these common case histories. This boy suffers intensely—mental not physical pain—guilt feelings—depression and so on. It is in his fantasies that all the terrible things happen or threaten. He is helped by feeling they happen outside him, as then he can avoid them (phobias) and can avoid seeing what mustn't be seen (blinking). Also by lying awake he can avoid the unbearable anxiety that belongs to his dreams, *and sleep's suggestion of death.*

He is now 5, and I do not suppose he will ever get really happy or settle down to enjoy school—but he is a big responsibility for the educator, and would especially have been so to the nursery school since at the earlier age there was more chance of his seeing a good external reality in spite of his distorted inner world, and of correcting his fantasies according to facts.

The one thing that is quite useless is the *direct* treatment of his symptoms either by crude therapeutics (suggestion, persuasion, bribing) or by punitive measures. The only hope is for the boy's own emotional development to be enhanced by the provision of a background of love and through the working of time, the great healer.

* * *

There are many ways of viewing human nature, and by one of them we see that people are concerned with an inner and an outer life. The outer life is fairly obvious, though much of the motivation is obscure, and is unconscious, even deeply buried. The inner life is mostly a matter of the unconscious. There is an interplay between this inner and outer life in healthy people, so that the external world is enriched for us by our own inner world which we can readily park out on to people and things that we come in contact with; also, our inner world is modified by our contact with the externally real, so that, as time goes on, we come to be surer of ourselves in the sense of being more clear as to the distinction between the two realities. It is in infancy and at the pre-school age that this chiefly happens, though it never ceases throughout life, and psychoanalysis is a technique by which we can enable this process to come nearer to completion than occurs in the ordinary course of development. You might say that in the course of emotional development we become less superstitious—for in superstition we have no confidence in external reality since it becomes so readily invested with feelings that belong to our inner life.

One alternative to frank superstition is for us to develop, as we all do, a control of our inner people, of their feelings and activities, and this affects our self-control in our outer relationships. We do to some extent what Joan, whom I described earlier, did excessively.

An excess of control is dangerous, since it slows down, as we feel it, our vital forces and makes us feel depressed, and all that sort of thing; so we seek alternatives, and one is to place the things we consider bad in ourselves out of ourselves on to objects or people in the external world, and to fight and control them there. A homely example of this is to be seen in Germany today [1936] where the expulsion and maltreatment of the Jews is, at its best, an attempt on the part of the so-called Aryan to get something he doesn't like out of himself—he tries to see it in the Jews, imagines he has succeeded, and then feels justified in persecuting them and feels better after having persecuted them. At one time, psychoanalysis was felt to epitomize all that is worst in human nature. People saw in it all their own badnesses which they hated to own, and they felt righteous in denouncing it. A lady I know and respect got up in a drawing-room meeting and said that psychoanalysis of children was something that ought to be stopped by law, and she felt it was worse than child murder and child seduction. I found her view rather sickening, since I was training to be an analyst of children myself. The reality has turned out to be unrelated to this good lady's fantasies about it.

We all do this sort of thing—for instance, when we eagerly put down our rheumatism to germs and our pains to uric acid and our bad tempers to the English climate generally.

Now, it is easy to see that many people are eager (I speak of the unconscious feelings) to find in the child the impulses which they would hate to own in themselves; by control, training, and education of the child they hope to be able to feel better, even to feel good themselves. These people itch to deal not only with their own children, but with their relations' children, and with all the children in the city or in the whole country. You will easily distinguish these people from the natural lovers of children because they cannot see the whole child, they can only see the child's crude impulses, which they think need controlling.

But it happens that the child *is concerned with the management of his own impulses*, so that anyone who can only see these impulses is unable to see more than about half of the individual child. The fact is not that the little child has no innate control but, rather, that the child's early methods of control of crude impulses are themselves crude and vicious, and the child has often to be rescued from the too successful operation of the control mechanisms. For instance, a baby of 9 months may be terrified to find his impulse to bite, indeed to eat up his mother, and it is common for him to wean himself, or even to refuse all feeds, especially if coinciding with this fear crisis there is an externally real frustration, such as weaning, or change of minder, or special and new efforts to train to cleanliness. It becomes the business of the mother or nurse to protect the child from the physical starvation that would result from the crude operation of primitive conscience.

In the course of the emotional development of the infant and little child, one of the chief things to be observed is the growing up of the conscience, towards an ideal state (never attained) in which there is no need for a conscience because love and identification with loved, controlled real or fantasy people is enough. You will see what an advance the religious conscience is on the more primitive one, since the religious person, because of his belief in forgiveness, can do wrong, on account of which he will of course suffer remorse. The more primitive the conscience the less the possibility of wrong-doing, since any wrong-doing may be fantastically serious in its effects. In adult terms, the retention of a primitive conscience means depression at the thought of evil, and suicide at the threat of evil, whereas the religious person can envisage wrong-doing because of the possibility of repentance and forgiveness.

The child is also like the adult in being concerned with an outer and an inner world, with the appreciation of the outer by virtue of the richness of the inner, and the modification of the inner by experience of the outer. Also the child is eager to make use of the opportunity that the outer world offers for reparation, making good what has been made bad in the inner fantasy world. If we see the whole child we see all this, and we recognize that the good or the bad environment that we offer a little child is only indirectly good or bad. If we are controlled, we affect the child if the child loves us, gets to know us, is able on account of the goodness in his own inner world to see goodness in us, and if the child takes us into himself and is able to maintain us alive there. And if we are brutal we are bad for the child if the child, in dealing with brutal people in his fantasies, just now needs the reassurance that we are not brutal, our failing to correct the bad fantasy being our shortcoming. The next child may not have even noticed our brutality, being concerned with other qualities at that moment, or having many less brutal people than the other child in his inner world.

The kind of person I was describing a minute or two ago (and we are all liable to be a little guilty of these and other faults) unconsciously seeks personal happiness through the training and control of children. You remember the shattering effect of such people described in the book *Oliver Untwisted* as they make a tour of inspection of the institution after the meeting of the Board of Management. As soon as the understanding person in charge of the children had educated a committee to endure witnessing the children's individuality instead of itching to curb and control the children, a new committee would spring up making renewed demands for a nice order. Yes, even some adults are educable, and I seem to be showing something of the very urge which I am deprecating in my urge to educate the adults. Yet I may hope to be forgiven here, since you, adults, have asked me to speak to you. I want to warn you to choose your board of management as carefully as you would choose your parents, if you intend to concern yourselves with little children of pre-school age.

One more word. I have introduced you to the child's primitive conscience, not a weak one as you might expect it to be, but a crude one, from which the little child often needs protection. He may at times ask you to introduce him to your own, more developed, less cruel morality, and if you haven't one handy you may be forced into inventing one on the spur of the moment, something between your ideal of natural goodness or whatever you believe in and the intolerable punitive system that is ready made in the child. Enlightened parents are often alarmed at being asked by their child to smack him or even to tie his hands. Do not be surprised to meet these things. They must be understood in relation to the child's developing control system.

A degree of what I have just described does frequently appear and may give rise to trouble and to a false idea of the requirements of the normal child. Of this I would speak.

Children qualifying to become delinquents make continual demands, on those who mind them, for control from without. Their illness is that they cannot bear their own inner punitive system, with its cruelties and other unbearable qualities, and yet they cannot grow their conscience up. Their primitive conscience has failed to mature, and throughout their lives they will need controlling forces, eventually those of the law, if they are to remain sane. Alternatively, they develop delusions of persecution, since they cannot endure the persecutions and maltreatments that arise within themselves, in their own inner reality.

One child like this in a group of children will upset the apple-cart of your best intentions. The sweet reasonableness that you banked on is turned to futility by that boy over there who, though he looks charming, and though he easily wins your love, yet is certain to force you sooner or later into controlling him. Your immediate reaction is to feel guilty, and to wonder whether you were not after all mistaken in your cherished idea that children develop their own control in their own way given time, and love.

My parting request to you is that you harden your hearts, and get rid of the potential delinquent from your group, or, alternatively, collect together all the potential delinquents of the neighbourhood and confine your attentions to them and their special problems. It is only in this way that you can do your best work with the normal pre-school children, who are sometimes delinquent, sometimes depressed, sometimes neurotic, sometimes obstinate, sometimes confused, sometimes in a bad temper, sometimes suspicious, often beastly to each other and to you, and yet who are lovable because each is an individual with his own hopes because he has his own difficulties and his own ways of dealing with them, and because each has his own peculiar way of making use of your proffered help.

12

The teacher, the parent, and the doctor

[1936]

If you will reflect for a minute on the subject, you will see that the juxtaposition of the three types of humanity—the teacher, the parent, and the doctor—has a somewhat sinister implication. What could bring together a teacher, a parent, and a doctor? Or, to put my question another way, why should it be necessary for some hundred people to give up their holidays to the study of a relationship, evidently a precarious one, between three kinds of grown-up? The answer is, of course, that somewhere in the background there is a child. A child is the cement that binds together these stones and also a child is the earthquake that splits them asunder.

The education of a normal child (if I may be allowed to use the word normal for a moment) is a comparatively easy matter; and the normal child tends to bring the teacher and the parent together in a happy relationship, each an extension of the other's personality. Also, the normal child leaves the doctor so little to do that he remains a cipher; he may be ultimately responsible for the standard of the school food, for the regulation of exercise, the ventilation of the dormitories, and the prevention of the spread of the inevitable infectious disease, but for the normal child he may come but little into the picture as a person.

But, how few children can be called normal! Do we even want them to be? The answer must depend on the way we would define the word normal; but however we define it, and whatever we wish, we know that the misunderstandings that arise between parents and all kinds of guardians are not, by any means, all due to the personal difficulties of the parents and guardians. We know in fact that they are frequently due to the children.

A study of the difficulties in the emotional development of babies, and of children of the different age-groups, forms the best foundation for a study of the inter-relation of the parents, teachers, doctors, and all concerned in the management and education of the children.

It is not my job to study with you, here and now, the extremely complex course of emotional development of the individual, but I cannot leave out the child in pursuing my theme. For instance, see what a part the child plays in the following example of parental distrust.

A restless and highly intelligent boy of 8 who stayed during term time with someone whom I know well, and whom I know to be reliable, was fetched home at the end of last term by his mother. On the way home he told his mother how Mrs So-and-So (my friend) had refused to give him twopence a day for the bus, so that he had had to walk a long way to and from school in the middle of the day. This meanness had prevented him from having time to eat the food given him at dinner, which in any case was rather poor food, and in insufficient quantity. And so on, and so on. He told this to his mother in the nicest possible way, and it would be hard to blame her for believing him. The mother happened to have rather intense difficulties herself, being permanently apprehensive of disaster and liable to feel persecuted, and she wrote to me saying how disgusted she was with Mrs So-and-So, and how she would be quite unwilling to send her boy back to her care.

Now it happened that I knew the boy well, as he was being treated by me by the method called psychoanalysis, and I was also in close touch with my friend Mrs So-and-So. The real situation was that the boy had enjoyed being at Mrs So and-So's house, having found there a stability and a plenty that he had never known at home. Also, Mrs So-and-So is a more normal kind of person than the boy's mother, happy and not nervous. He was impressed, too, with my reliability (it is my job to be so), which he openly compared with his father's erratic habits. The school, too, was good, and he had thoroughly appreciated his term there. Moreover, he had welcomed Mrs So-and-So's firmness, which was new to him. He had been given twopence and told that it was for the bus, and when he spent it on sweets he was told that then he would have to walk, which was fair as he had sweets and pocket money from other sources.

When the boy met his mother he felt terribly bad about all this. His enjoyment of the surroundings away from home implied a serious criticism of home. He may not have felt consciously guilty, but it was this sense of guilt, deep down, that made him tell his mother that he had been ill-treated. Initially, he did not intend to put his mother against Mrs So-and-So, but I suppose that when he found he had done so, and that his mother readily believed his story, he felt he could not turn back without the sacrifice of logic, so he piled it on.

How often the desire of a child to hide from mother the fact that happiness has been found away from home has resulted in misunderstanding! The child wanted to say something very complicated, too complicated in fact to be said by a child of 8 years. It was something like this: "I do love you, in spite of the fact that in so many of the ways that love can be expressed by a mother, the school has done better than you could have done; also, towards the school my love has not been so intense, or linked with infantile experiences as my love of yourself is, and always must be, so that greed has threatened less, and hate has been less intensely roused, less unmanageable, more easily transformed into acceptable modes of expression. Conflict has been less, and I have felt happier than I have felt at home."

My 8-year-old boy wanted to say all this, but as he could not do so he made up the yarn about the frustration over twopence.

The doctor here was myself. My job was to allow the mother the grouse she wished for, for a few weeks, and then to show her its unreality, to make Mrs So-and-So laugh about the whole affair, so that she would not be hurt if she should receive a stinging letter from the mother. Fortunately, in this case, with the boy in analysis, I have the opportunity of doing more than could be done by pointing out to him his lie. I need not do this at all. In the course of the analysis, the complicated motives I have described will become clear to him, and as he becomes less guilty (in unconscious feelings) about feeling critical of mother and father and home, and more able to criticize these on externally real grounds, so the need for this kind of lying will cease without direct treatment.

I shall speak a good deal more about the complications brought about by persecutory fantasy, later on, but, at the moment, I wish to draw your attention to the question of aim. What is our aim, as doctors and teachers, and as enquirers into the truth, at a conference?

Actually the decision as to aim and motive is taken inside ourselves, and depends on the strains and stresses deep down in our own natures, but if, for the moment, I may be allowed to pretend that we have a little conscious control over our attitude towards things, and over the direction of our interests, I will give this question some thought.

To come straight to the point: are we out to blame the mother? I have so much to do with teachers and social workers and doctors who most clearly are "out to blame mother" that I am driven to ask this question of yourselves. If we have this aim, we shall have abundant opportunity for fun. Any one of you could get up and give examples of parental stupidity, double-dealing, and inexcusable ignorance. I could do some of this myself. Yet, I would point out, that, as a basis for discussion, "blaming the mother" is as barren soil to the sower.

Incidentally, teachers and doctors can be just as stupid and ignorant as anyone else, when they are parents. The truth is that the parents' strongest feelings and therefore conflicts are involved, because the parents are, and have been, the parents. The teachers and doctors start with an advantage that they have never had the intense feelings about the child that the parents have had, and the unconscious conflicts in relation to the child are correspondingly less intense and disturbing. It is only the strongest love that can breed fiercest hate and suspicion, and only those who are experiencing the strongest feelings can know what depths of guilt-feelings and depression and suspicion are latent in human nature

In fact, one of the chief functions of a teacher is to be *in loco parentis*, that is, without the maximally strong emotional tie that the real parent and child have to each other. For the tie is there, between the parents and the child, whether it shows as love or hate or both, or as indifference, and is the source of emotional strains that warp and inhibit education.

The understanding teacher, who realizes intuitively and easily that the parents' annoying ways are the inevitable accompaniments of the historically rooted emotional bonds to the child, is in a much better position to deal with emergencies than one who just feels that parents are in a class apart in their power to exhibit the meaner human qualities.

A mother feels it in her bones when a teacher can only impute a bad motive. There may be hates roused deep down in the mother in connection with her love of her child, and her jealousy of anyone who takes over the minding of her child, and the mother's chief concern may be that the hate roused should not hurt the child, love of whom has caused it. The master or mistress will be expected from time to time to have some or all of this floating hatred directed at him or herself, and will have to be able to stand it. It is not nice being hated, but doctors have to stand it, and so do teachers. Popular teachers are only popular because someone else is bearing the hatred, and are usually despised by the others, for fairly clear reasons. And it always seems to me that a popular headmaster is a contradiction in terms. If a headmaster or headmistress is popular, I suppose all the other teachers have to bear the hatred en bloc. For the floating hatred is there somewhere, make no mistake!

It often happens that the parents feel that any critical or antagonistic feelings they may have may be illogical and subjective, the result of inner personal conflicts, with the result that they

place their children unreservedly in the hands of a school authority, assuming that TEACHERS ARE PERFECT. This assumption is
unjustifiable. Parents who do not interfere because they assume
that all is well are not ideal parents, though they may have convenient qualities from the school authority's point of view.

I should like to be able to bring in the doctor here as the
person who can speak to the parent, and to the teacher, and, by
his understanding of human nature, bring each to an understanding of the other. Unfortunately, this would be an untrue
observation. Doctors (apart from specialists) have as a rule a
good intuitive understanding, which shows in their actual dealings with individuals. They often get on well with the child
patient, just as they do with the parent patient. But getting on
well with a patient is one thing, and being able to advise a parent
or elucidate a parent–teacher problem is another.

The reason for this is, as much as anything else, a result of the
doctor's method. He easily feels himself into the place of the
patient. He gets on well with the child because, for the moment,
he shares the child's interests, but chiefly because he shares the
child's antagonisms and so allows the child's persecutory fantasies a show of reality. Just as a patient with frank delusions of
persecution can be kept happy if the asylum doctor pays a tribute each day to the patient's delusional system and pretends to
believe it, so can the friendship of a child be easily bought by
anyone who can play up to the persecutory fantasies. He may
only have to become a play-ogre, or, remembering his own
schooldays, he may find himself agreeing that the science master
is a bully; or he may decide that a conspiracy of illness should be
indulged in with a note to the headmaster; "no drill till the end
of term", "homework not advisable in this case", "corporal punishment should be avoided here as Master Tom has a tendency
to weak heart" (whatever that may mean).

Infectious disease, psychologically speaking, fits into the
delusional persecutory system as a reality-tested persecution by
germs. You must have noted the improvement that certain kinds
of difficult children can show during and just after measles or
mumps, also after surgical removal or internal badness, as in
appendectomy.

In the same way, the doctor feels himself into the place of the troubled parent. He feels how awful it would be to have so difficult a child, or so unsympathetic a teacher for his child, and supports the parent's grievance, quite naturally, enabling her to get over the strain which this peeping through of the delusional persecutory fantasies puts on her.

You will see that these very real helps are far from being a true understanding in the intellectual sense. Indeed these helps are based on the common factor in the unconscious persecutory fantasies of different human beings.

The borderline of psycho-physical illness is nature's own safety device, and, thank goodness, there are always doctors ready to play into nature's hands, and to sign a child off school on account of vague unlabelled complaints, a headache, or a pain in the thigh. Frequently the parent tips the doctor the wink, and gives him to understand that a day off school would not do any harm, and the doctor, after due display of stethoscope, pronounces the verdict. The teacher sees through it all, but is glad to be relieved of the responsibility of the next day, which was destined to bring about a clash between authority and the child. The bilious attack is frequently the outward sign of an inner wave of guilt feeling of unendurable intensity. The popular modern term is "acidosis", but the only acid demonstrable is the biting and other hate phenomena that belong to the unconscious fantasy—the inner reality—which the child hates to own. The child is unconscious of the fantasy content, but feels unutterably guilty or anxious, feels as if everything inside is hopelessly bad, and does not feel relieved till vomiting or "a good turn-out" has been achieved. A child in such a state may really try to empty himself or herself.

I know a girl whose childhood was dominated by guilt feelings and (more in consciousness) by a fear of vomiting, who would as a child of 6 to 10 sit for hours on the lavatory seat in an attempt to get every particle of faeces out of her. All inside was bad to her. The concrete motions, which were capable of being expelled, stood for the intangible deep unconscious fantasy, or the inner reality, which was so much less easily eliminated. Later on, in the course of her analysis, the corresponding attempt was made to eliminate the psychically bad, the effects of the operation of hate in unconscious fantasy, and then to eliminate the hate itself, so that only the capacity to love should remain. Eventually, she became less afraid of her hate, and was able to use it as a source of energy in work and play. Analysis, if it could have been offered her at the time of her early childhood fears, would have saved her thirty years of obsessional preoccupation.

We see, then, that whereas doctors can be more or less relied on to give temporary help to their patients (that they are helpful in regard to physical disease I must take for granted) they are no better than any other class of individual at giving understanding of the *unconscious* operative forces, which determine behaviour. Doctors find it as hard, as everyone else does, to believe in unconscious fantasy and to allow for such things as an *unconscious sense of guilt* which plays such an important part in the life of most children as well as of their parents and teachers. I do not even look forward to a time when doctors will be able to serve humanity in this new way. Of course, there will be an increasing number of doctors and teachers (and parents I must add) who, through first-hand experience of psychoanalysis, and through training in the rather exacting psychoanalytic school, will be in a position to attempt a solution of individual problems, and even to give advice. But more than that cannot be hoped for. My opinion is that the present tendency is not one likely to bear wholesome fruit. It is common for doctors and teachers and parents to "know a little about psychoanalysis". This tendency cannot be a good one, since one goes towards the psychology of the unconscious because of fear of one's own unconscious, or, if you like it better, lack of confidence in one's intuitive power, and if this fear takes one towards psychology but does not take one to the analysis of the origin of fear the result must be a compromise between understanding and blindness. Something will perhaps have been seen, but in order that something else may remain hidden.

The teacher who is in a good position to deal with the parent who has read about the unconscious, is not the one who has also read a book on the subject. Rather is he the one who has a deep intuitive understanding of human nature, an experience of inner

and outer relationships, a capacity for happiness and the enjoyment of life without denial of its seriousness and difficulty. Such
a one may have chosen to deepen his understanding and develop his natural talents further by undergoing analysis himself;
that I have known, that I understand and I believe in. But what I
cannot believe in is that an increase in understanding should
come from the acquiring of a psychological jargon, or even from
the serious study of psychoanalytic literature, which is mostly
technical, and only to be accurately placed by those actually engaged in psychoanalytic practice.

It takes a good deal of natural understanding and of patience
to see what a mother really has to say when she speaks of her
child in terms of complexes and inhibitions. Yet it should not be
forgotten that usually the mother really does possess, and it is
only she who possesses, the valuable knowledge of the child's
progress from birth onwards, which makes possible an understanding of the child now (apart from analysis of the child). As a
doctor I have repeatedly come across children whose illnesses or
symptoms have been entirely mis-diagnosed because a doctor
has put down the mother as a bad witness. True, the mother has
added to her anxious or guilt-laden volubility a collection of
half-digested terms. Nevertheless, the same mother has been
found, in the end, to possess and to be able to give out the details
of the child's infancy and early years, in proper sequence, and in
a way that has eventually made diagnosis as clear as daylight.
"The child was well till weaning, when he lost zest for food, and
was late in feeding himself and in chewing" tells us a lot. "The
child was normal till he was 3, when he changed to a bad-tempered child with night terrors and certain phobias—yes it was
just then when I was big with the next child." "The child was
happy till 2½, when the new baby had a serious illness and died.
Since then he has been solemn and has not enjoyed feeding as
other children do." These early details are invaluable.

It may be a question of sending a child to school and to play
games and to enjoy life or of keeping him home in bed for half a
year as a case of possible rheumatic heart disease. Often such a
problem cannot be solved by examination of the child; yet a
carefully taken, and carefully sifted history of the case, from the
mother, may settle the diagnosis and decide the fate of the child.

If this is true of doctoring it is also true of headmastering. If headmasters and headmistresses had time, I imagine they would wish to take a detailed history of the infancy and early childhood of each new child, and would consult this history sheet each time the child came into prominence as a candidate for a prize or promotion, as a minor delinquent, as a potential prefect, as a sick-room case, as a case of obstinate moods or of outbursts of rage, and so on. In a rough way the headmaster does all this when he chooses his boys. He refuses those whom he thinks (on account of their family record, social standing, or on account of reports from other schools) unsuitable for his special type of school. When he eliminates potential delinquents, he eliminates children, a number of whom have been unwanted at the start, or who have suffered rather severe emotional traumata, seductions, and so on at a tender age.

A careful history of the first years would show in which child to expect periods of depression, during which efforts to force feeding, happiness, or play would be useless or harmful. Such a history would tell which child to expect to be timid and to get bullied, that is, which child has more than his share of persecutory fantasy to deal with, and who therefore may need protection from a rather hard teacher, one who may be entirely suitable for another type of child.

Such a carefully taken history would also give a hint as to which child should be given opportunity for the direct discharge of hate impulses (games with kicking, biting, killing, etc.) and, in contrast, which child requires more help in regard to reparation and restitution—creation or re-creation rather than recreation, a making good in the external reality of harm done by the hate-impulses in the inner reality or deep unconscious fantasies. The latter type of child, especially if talented in some art form, is often singularly little in need of direct aggressive activity and display, and indeed often finds such play irksome. (Is not this, perhaps, the more culturally advanced solution of the unconscious hate problem? But such children cannot be made so, they are so when they come to you, and they carry the capacity to suffer from depression, man's most noble illness.)

These sortings and siftings—and much more—the experienced headteacher does in the twinkling of an eye, when interviewing the new pupil and the parent. I sometimes wonder what would happen if serious notes were taken of the child's early history, carefully extracted from the mother. Perhaps the mother would become suspicious? But there is no doubt that where a doctor takes such notes from a mother when he demonstrates in this way to her, as well as to himself, the important part she has played in the drama, he has her confidence; whereas a doctor who thrusts the mother and all her stored-up special knowledge aside has to be a very good surgeon or medicine man to obtain her cooperation or to keep her good will.

I could go on for hours enumerating ways in which a doctor ought to be able to help a teacher or a parent. Unfortunately, doctors are not trained in the psychology of the unconscious, and are therefore mostly unable to help in the way I shall describe, but for simplicity's sake I ignore this point.

The children under your care differ from each other in this way and that way. Sometimes, you note differences that are extreme and you wonder where the normal ends and the abnormal begins. One child is more clever than another, but a third is always at the top of the class. In this third child, it is the fear of not being at the top, this *fear* of failure, of incurring anything but praise from the teacher, that strikes you. This child's success is a symptom; more normal children do badly sometimes. Such a child tends to overwork, and great foresight is required to guide such a child through school life. The doctor should be able to discuss with you the problems associated with this child's precarious successfulness. The doctor certainly cannot be left out, since there are illnesses (St. Vitus' Dance, for instance), to which such children seem specially liable because of the emotional strain which they cannot avoid. It is lamentable how few doctors are capable of appreciating the complex problem in psychology involved. It is so easy to say—give the child a period of enforced idleness. To start with, the child will one day have to earn a living, probably with her brain, and one term off at a critical time may prove a severe handicap in her competition with other similarly anxious children (probably they will all want to be teachers, to teach others to work too hard, as they had to do). Then there is the effect on such a child of enforced failure and enforced idleness. The anxiety behind the need for praise and success is not being treated, and in idleness such a child may suffer intensely, may show frank anxiety manifestations, or may develop some new technique for avoiding anxiety, such as obsessional thought-building, compulsive masturbation, or invalidism. Or the child may become depressed. The doctor and the teacher and the parent have a wonderful opportunity here for intelligent cooperation, in dealing with such a child.

Again, while one child is better than another at arithmetic, a third is a sufferer from an inhibition in regard to sums, a common complaint indeed, and yet as much an illness as is a sore throat.

The doctor should be able to help the teacher to decide which children should be treated by neglect, discipline, or psychoanalysis, on account of backwardness in sums. The same might be said of the inability to make friends (which can mean so little and so much), of a tendency not to keep to the rules of the game, of an obsession for ice-creams, of an inordinate need for pocket money, or the need to display wealth. The doctor should be able to understand the factors underlying a child's anxious desire to explore this or that or every avenue of sensual pleasure, and should surely be trained not only to examine the heart and lungs, but also to advise in regard to the child's need for punishment or treatment in respect of the not-done things. Of course, treatment is seldom available, but at such a conference as this, where ideals are being discussed, I need not apologize for being impractical. And who knows? One of you might, as a result of my talk, advise some young man or woman to train to psychoanalytic work, and so there would be added one more to the little band of those capable of treating a child who is psychologically ill.

There is certainly a movement in the direction I am indicating, but the severe lack of people adequately trained to treat the children who need treatment soon disheartens the doctors and teachers who have a glimmer of insight into these matters. And it helps a parent not a whit to be told her child could be treated but can't be. Of course, there are hundreds of people ready to try their hand at what is called child-guidance, to set social workers on the parents' tracks, or to determine intelligence quotients, but these can, I am sorry to say, be practically left out of account in this our quest for actual treaters of children. It is not just slum children, neglected children, but our own children, who need treatment of a highly technical and complex kind, but treatment which, though it can be learned by anyone of average intelligence and stability of character, is not available. Teachers and parents and doctors are cooperating in creating a demand for such trained helpers.

In the remaining minutes before the discussion, I will enlarge a little on the subject to which I have specially drawn your attention, the subject of the (chiefly unconscious) persecutory fantasy pattern, which gives such trouble to certain children, and which leads indirectly to so much misunderstanding between parents and teachers. I would have you remember, too, that parents and teachers and doctors have the same troubles over various kinds and degrees of these fantasies in themselves, and that nothing is more simple than for the fantasy pattern of one individual, say, a child, to evoke the complementary fantasy pattern of another with whom that child comes into contact. This is no more than saying that if there is a bully in the school, it is the waiting-to-be-bullied boy or girl who gets it in the neck. In fact, the experimental introduction of a bulliable child into a school would certainly result in the development of a bully, and, of course, in the development of protectors of the weak and supporters and admirers of the bully. To maintain an easy peace, a headteacher should be as keen to keep potentially suffering children from his school, as to keep out bullies.

The average child is not out of touch with the feelings that belong to the unconscious fantasies, and these feelings easily flow into the devouring of knowledge, into games of war and prisoners, games of strict schoolmistress and pliable children (a favourite game amongst little girls), and into the conventional set games. But when the fantasies are more terrifying to the owner, or are more deeply repressed, the feelings belonging to them are not available for indirect expression in work or play. Nor will they, later on, be available for expression in adult work. A child so handicapped may be specially attractive to the casual or sentimental observer, who is delighted to see in the child no sign of ordinary aggressiveness and hate. A doctor should be able to help the teacher and parent to distinguish between this child and the similar-looking child whose lack of hate-play is just part of his natural attachment to inner objects, to the people and things of the inner reality, and who probably has some talent enabling him to make contact with the external reality through his own special way of dealing with inner conflicts, since we, in his external reality, value him on account of his writings, his poems, his musical writing or performance, his drawings, or his paintings, etc. The types of children may be theoretically related, and one may change into the other, but whereas one type urgently needs treatment the other may be left to work out his own salvation. My point is that neither the teacher nor the parent can form a proper judgement on these problems alone, and yet in consultation, and with the aid of an understanding third person (let us call him the doctor), it is often possible to come to a very clear conclusion.

To illuminate this point, I cite the case of a girl of 11, who was very sweet and gentle, and who was brought to me because she was rather more nervous than the other children in her family. She had a sweet nature, but no one could really get near her, and she formed no deep friendships.

The schoolteacher was specially understanding. She said to me: "Now look doctor, I am myself very nervous, and I was terribly nervous in childhood, and I really understand nervous children. Children have come to me who have been afraid of everything at home, and after a few weeks with me they have gained confidence, and have been well-started on the road towards normality." (This picture she drew of herself was confirmed from other sources; she was a particularly successful teacher of nervous children.) "But", she went on, "this particular child is different from all the others; she's apparently nice and good-natured, and yet she *does not respond*. I cannot understand and I feel really upset about not being able to help her."

I was unable to make a clear diagnosis by my preliminary contact with the child, but in the course of her psychoanalysis, which was done by a friend of mine, whose name most of you know, the deep unconscious fantasies were found to contain persecutors in exceptional strength, so that the child had only just managed to keep from having delusions of (externally real) persecutions by dint of constant hard work. She had kept up an appearance of normality, but had been unable to allow the feelings of the deep fantasies to enter her enjoyment of play, or in the pursuit of learning. And if anyone was specially nice to her, this meant to her that they were setting a trap for her. Hence her "not responding". As the analysis progressed, and these persecutory ideas became analysed, they became less strong, less terrifying, and less repressed, and their energy became available for normal play and work. She became a happy, ordinary schoolgirl, with enjoyment of play and of work, capacity for normal naughtiness, and incidentally became a second mother to the latter end of her own mother's enormous family.

I saw the teacher towards the end of the treatment, and she had forgotten her feelings of a year previously. All she could say was that as the child was an entirely normal and happy child, in fact one of the most reliable in her class, she could not see what could be the use of the child's having treatment.

This case illustrates the child who needed treatment, and contrasts with the case of the school artist or poet, who only needs permission to go his own way, to feel depressed, or depressed and elated in turn, and someone competent to criticize his productions.

Children who struggle with inner persecutory fantasies may be driven by their fears to relations with other children in which they sensualize suffering and submission. They seek out and find someone driven by fear into sensualization of cruelty or mastery. They easily get into trouble and may have to be expelled, but really they are ill. Or, they may manage comparatively easily until they become involved (perhaps by accident) in some minor plot or escapade. The others who are involved in the prank are punished, and for them the world has returned to normal. But, for the children we are discussing, a reservoir of guilt-feeling has been tapped. They may fall ill with diarrhoea or a bilious attack, or may be driven by fear into attacking the person of someone in authority or into damaging some part of the school buildings. These manifestations of fear need most skilful handling.

But the teacher has a mild task in dealing with these open troubles as compared with his task in dealing with the hidden ones. Children with abnormally strong unconscious persecutory fantasies often manage life at school satisfactorily, but they take home stories of being neglected or ill-treated at school. Here the doctor may come in. Doctors are often consulted by parents who want support in dealing with cruel teachers, especially in a big town where parents feel all the time under the thumb of the law in the shape of the "school boardman".[1] The child gives the parents a good account of ill-treatment at school, and what are the parents to believe?

I have personally investigated many such cases and I have come to the following conclusion. A great number of the children's accusations are true. The fact is that the children I am describing to you bring out the worst in the teachers; they have a great inner need to find and to prove a "cruelty and suffering" relation in external reality. There they can park out their fantasies that threaten to become delusions. On further investigation, one probably finds that the teacher is quite successful with other children, and is not a cruel person on the whole; or, if the teacher is cruel, one seldom finds the child who complains is normal in this particular respect of my present thesis.

Understanding of the psychology of complaints about maltreatment by teachers and recognition of the strength of the forces at work beneath the surface often enables one to bring about temporary and even permanent changes. In some cases it is enough to make a joke about the teacher—that is, by giving the child and the parent permission to laugh at the offending monster, laughing-at being a legitimate hate-form. More severe difficulties may necessitate a change of class—that is, a partial capitulation to the child. In the worst cases, persecutions will reappear, or actual delusions will be easily proved. The teachers

---

[1]The education authority representative whose responsibility was to ensure children of school age attended school.

and doctors need not waste time thinking out the correct management of such severely ill children, who obviously need treatment.

Short of these serious complaints you will find all manner of complaints about the rules and regulations, the inhuman rigidity of the rules and conventions, and about the punishments. Sometimes it is the children who most need the relief for guilt feeling that these rules and punishments give, that complain the most. An understanding doctor has a chance, here again, to make the parent understand what is happening and so to save the teacher from disturbing vituperations.

I hope you will forgive me for having roamed rather than travelled over the country you asked me to describe to you. Certainly, I have attempted no map-making. You will easily point out to me historic sites I have not visited, and pubs whose beer I have failed to eulogize. But I hope you will have found something in my description to awaken memories of your own already vast knowledge of the territory covered by the words, "The teacher, the parent, and the doctor".

Part five

CASE STUDIES
AND OBSERVATIONS

13

A clinical example
of symptomatology
following the birth of a sibling

[ca. 1931]

A boy of 3 years was brought to hospital by his intelligent but not highly cultured mother who complained that her son suffered from a pain in the penis.

The young and rather sensitive doctor who saw her first felt rather uneasy about meeting the word penis and showed signs of relief when the mother proceeded to relate other symptoms, and when at the end he came to tell me about the case he had forgotten the detail about the penis. Fortunately I had overheard the consultation. This tendency to forget the sexual part of the life of our patients is almost universal. There are very good reasons for the amnesia, and the opposition to modern dynamic psychology has been chiefly derived from the same forces that caused this doctor to forget the chief symptom of the little patient with the intelligent mother.

The doctor allowed the mother to speak enough to get the following details: for a few months, the child had become irritable, and he had developed increased urgency and frequency of micturition and a skin rash which he continually scratched, leaving bleeding papules. Physical examination brought to light no abnormality, though it may be added that the doctor did not examine the penis. This was also normal.

The scars of scratched papular urticaria[1] were easily recognized, and some papules were present, surrounded by red skin; the child was all the time of the consultation gently scratching these spots.

The doctor diagnosed papular urticaria, having been brought up to think of this condition as a disease, and began to ask whether the child had recently had a banana, which of course he had. Also he suspected cystitis, and examined a specimen of urine; this, however, proved to be free from pus cells and organisms. He was puzzled about the extreme urgency of micturition in the absence of cystitis, for his medical training had not taught him that by far the commonest cause of increased urgency of micturition is anxiety in relation to the battle over masturbation, in fact, that it is often almost justifiable to call it normal. The curious thing is that this doctor knew from personal experience that excitement made him want to go somewhere, but he knew this with a different part of his mind from that which he was used to bring to bear on clinical problems. In other words, he was not yet a clinician.

It was my job to try to weave together the different clinical symptoms into one cloth. Experience has taught me that it is wise to allow the mother to do this job for me whenever possible, and so I simply gave this mother the opportunity to finish what she had to say. She first told more details about the penis pain. She said that she could see nothing wrong, but the boy continually put his hand to his penis, and when she asked him why he did it he always said: because it hurts. She also said that the boy had always been subject to the skin spots, but they had never given trouble till the last few months. The trouble had been a sort of compulsion to scratch them, so that they came up worse, and also the torn papules bled and became liable to infection. The urgency of micturition also was not entirely new, but had only recently become a problem. At the same time the boy had started to wet the bed.

I now asked the mother what was the age of the baby. She

<hr>

[1]See chapter 20, pp. 157–169.

said: "Three months; as a matter of fact the boy was quite well till the baby came, and it seemed that the new arrival caused him to change in the way I have described, as if the boy's nose had been put out of joint. Could that be so, doctor, though we have done everything in our power to make him realize that we don't feel different towards him."

I think the whole clinical sequence is now so clear to anyone with a knowledge of human nature that it is almost an insult to intelligence to try to put it down in writing. However, for completeness, I shall do so, and I must remind those who have forgotten their own infant and early childhood feelings that these feelings are very intense, perhaps more intense than can be experienced by adults. Very few remember the intensity of their own childhood feelings, and those who do, like some of the poets, are not likely to be reading this paper which interests itself in what is rational rather than what is intuitive.

This rather healthy little boy was at the age when an appreciation of reality means decreased happiness. He had already been exploring the auto-erotic as a way of dealing with his unhappiness.

The arrival of a new baby brought home to him suddenly a great deal of just that sort of reality which was causing him decreased happiness—namely his position of third person in relation to his parents. This is true whether he was feeling love chiefly towards father or towards mother.

Unless he is to fail to accept reality he must be less happy, and must seek to deal with this along the usual lines which nature has provided. Masturbation becomes more urgent suddenly. Here, however, we detect the first signs of abnormality, for masturbation is not a simple matter for him. Like many others, he has guilt feelings in relation to the fantasies that go with masturbation, or perhaps he is not actually feeling guilt, so that it must be said that the desire to masturbate produces anxiety. Similarly the compulsion to masturbate produces anxiety, even more intense.

The compulsion to put the hands to the penis, noted by the mother, is all we see of genital masturbation; in fact, the desire to masturbate genitally is repressed, and in order to feel rational he answers his mother's question by the reply that he feels that it hurts; this would justify his urge to touch without necessitating feeling guilty.

But what happens to the urge to masturbate when genital masturbation is not enjoyable? It surely does not cease to be, since the origin of the need is unaltered.

This boy's symptoms illustrate other manifestations of this urge. The boy easily falls back on his skin erotism, for papular urticaria is in my opinion no more than skin excitement, normal except when caught up in the whirlwind of obsessional masturbation. (Otherwise, how can it be explained that almost all babies have papular urticaria at times, especially when they are healthy? Also, mothers often say, if allowed, that excitement makes the spots more troublesome.) Skin masturbation is very common in early childhood, and is very satisfying, for the aggressiveness in the masturbation fantasies, which is the cause of their repression, finds expression in a way that does not arouse guilt, for the child himself suffers from the cruelty, especially when the tearing of the papules leads to bleeding. Skin erotism is closely allied to anal erotism.

The increased sensitiveness of the urinary tract is another expression of repression of genital erotism. The urinary tract, instead of the glans penis, becomes hyper-aesthetic, and the pleasure of micturition becomes very intense, almost painfully so. As the urge for auto-erotism is still present, the urethral experience is also compulsive and takes the child often far beyond the purely pleasurable, so that again in self-punishment the child deals with a return of the repressed aggressiveness.

It can be said, then, that this boy is as healthy as he appears to be, that he is not suffering from any disease, that he is finding life difficult. All children find life difficult in so far as they accept the facts, and perhaps we should never have known how difficult this particular child is finding life had it not been that the birth of a new baby brought about an inevitable recognition of facts.[1] This reality recognition could not be dealt with adequately

---

[1] Another way of putting this would be to say that most children are happy because of the fact that in childhood reality is disguised and distorted normally, as when we tell lies about sexual matters, keep children ignorant of family economies, guard them from family quarrels, put them to sleep in a separate cot in a separate room, and so on. *D.W.W.*

along auto-erotic channels because of guilt in connection with fantasies that accompany masturbation. The symptoms thus gave evidence of some degree of breakdown of normal mechanisms of dealing with normal difficulties.

The mother understood what I meant when I said the child was finding life difficult because of the new baby, without going into the details. She did not want medicines and was contented because I had shared with her the responsibility for the child's well-being. "That is what I thought, doctor, but I wanted to make sure I was not neglecting any organic disease."

14

Notes on a little boy

[1938]

A little boy has at last reached the age when he can go to school. He is an only child and has long wished to go to the place where the other children go, to go to work like Daddy, to learn how to count and to read.

He has had a particularly successful infancy and early childhood, and the relations between him and his home have been excellent, by which I do not mean that he has never been rude or angry or unhappy or frightened, but that his general attitude has been one of belief in the goodness of those round him.

Now he has been to school for some weeks, and he has made rapid strides, being able to stand up in front of the whole class and count to fifty.

What effect has this new experience had on his home life?

To the parents' confusion he has become really horrid at home, suspicious and easily upset. His appetite has become capricious. Moreover, when asked to show how he can count he cannot or will not count, even up to ten. His mother has discussed the change with his teacher, who is at a loss to explain how such a happy, normal pupil should be so nasty at home. She feels like having the private opinion that the mother is not very good at being a mother.

There is, however, an explanation of the phenomenon which does not involve ascribing responsibility to the mother—or to anyone, for that matter.

The fact is that it is quite within the normal range for such a child to react to going to school in the way our little boy has done. In two words, at school he finds a great happiness, he has the company of children, he gets intellectual food in plenty: and above all he experiences a relief in tension due to the fact that he has never loved and hated his teacher as he has his mother and father, and so has a much simpler relation to her than he has to them.

So when he comes home he is alarmed. Unconsciously, he feels that his mother must know he has enjoyed being away from her, and as he believes she loves him he believes he has hurt her, and this appears in consciousness as a fear of her, and a suspicion of her kindness when she is kind.

This is a passing phase, and if left to take care of itself will give rise to no permanent trouble. Too much distress on the mother's part, however, may make the little fellow feel so guilty that he will reorganize his attitude, will find he hates school, and will even complain of being ill-treated by his teacher or by the other children. In that case, he may regain happiness at home, which will then be a symptom.

The same may be observed in many children who go away to stay. Either they enjoy themselves away and are rather nasty on return, or else they come home and spin a long yarn about being fed badly, complaining that the nurses or the aunts and uncles were unkind. Such accusations, if taken seriously, can and often do, lead to serious misunderstandings between adults who, with little knowledge of what to expect, could cope with the situation easily and with no more than the exercise of a sense of humour.

15

The niffle

[undated]

A mother who had previously consulted me about a daughter asked to see me in order to discuss something in the life of her next child, a boy, Tom. Tom was 5 years 10 months old at the time.

Tom, she said was developing well until he had an accident (5¼ years) when on holiday. The holiday was in an outlying area, and it was necessary for the boy to be taken by air ambulance to a city. This was all rather a drama for a child of 5, and Tom had to leave the rest of the family on holiday and be among strangers. It was not practicable for the mother to do what she wanted to do, which was to tell the hospital that the boy must not be left alone. She sat uselessly in a hotel, and so flew back to care for the family. There was already a problem, which could have been dealt with by the mother, in that Tom was not able to go to sleep till late, perhaps 10 p.m.

The mother also knew that Tom would not be able to do without his precious wool object, a special piece, and she immediately posted it off to Tom, trying to explain to the hospital how important this could be for Tom. But the object never arrived. It seems to have got lost in the post. The object was therefore lost, irretrievably.

On the physical side, the hospital care was quickly successful, and Tom was soon back with the family, but using a splint.

When Tom was back with the family he seemed to be unaffected by the surgical procedures, but he showed signs of deprivation in terms of the loss of the wool. He was upset to a degree over this, and in reaction to this loss he started to show regressive features in his relationship to his mother. This would take the form of a resistance to being dressed, putting on a girlish voice, acting in a generally annoying way, unlike his usual self. The girlish voice particularly annoyed the mother, who is a very good mother to her family and who has exceptional understanding and tolerance of childhood symptomatology.

Tom would sum it all up, hopelessly:

"But I wish I had this little niffle. It makes me feel . . ."

Here he was unable to find words to describe the special quality of his distress.

The name of this object was probably given to it by his older sister, who had always been maternal towards him. It would seem to me to suggest words like nipple, sniffle, fluff, little, etc. etc.

After a while there came about a gradual recovery, and this took two directions.

Firstly, he began to accept substitute jerseys, and he adopted one in particular, which was his mother's. Telling me this, the mother remembered that the original one was derived from three shawls. One was special. These gradually wore down, and so the three were sewn together, but as a baby he always knew the special one, even in the dark, although the three seemed exactly alike to grown-up eyes. It was at about 6 months that Tom started using the first of these special objects, keeping it against his face when alone or going to sleep.

Once Tom said: "Some boys think they will turn into girls if they lose something like that" (the niffle). The mother had tried to say this was not true. She is sure he has never been laughed at because of the niffle. She added: "As a small child, he has been what one would call 'untroubled' till the loss of the niffle occurred."

Tom was breast-fed nine months. He had no bottle. There were no weaning problems.

Tom shows signs of being somewhat unusual, and he makes wise remarks that children sometimes do make that show they have been *thinking*. An example would be: "People are silly to say Happy New Year! on one night—it could be any day or any night." Or: "Someone said: how high? But it must come round to nought again."

Now that the crippling effects of the accident have gone, he runs around the house when he cannot get to sleep. He does not know what to do with sleeplessness, gets bored with it, and occasionally comes into the parents' room and says, quite openly: "I'm scared."

Tom has a good relationship with his father, and he plays happily with a boy who is twice his own age.

Continuing to talk about the "transitional object", the mother said that the sister's word niffle was derived chiefly from sniffle. She said that the word nipple is not likely to have been heard by either of the children at the early time when the name was given.

When Tom went to nursery school, the lady obviously did not like the niffle, because it was dirty. Mother said to her: "Don't wash it please." The lady found a compromise technique. For a while she talked about washing in group sessions, and one day Tom said: "I want to wash my niffle." So it was washed. This was clever of the lady. The mother rightly asks, however, was it too clever? At any rate, it was not traumatic and did not disturb Tom's relationships in the nursery school.

Now, however, in the regressive phase that is reactive to the loss of the niffle Tom does not want to dress or be dressed but says: "I want niffle" and he may undress himself, and put on "that silly girl's voice". This voice is squeaky and may be a baby's voice, perhaps not especially a girl's voice.

Sometimes he flings the (new) niffle around, or hits people with it, and he takes it always to nursery school. Whenever he is going away he says: "Where's my niffle?" and so sees to it that there will be no repetition of what happened when he had the accident.

The sister, who invented the word niffle, herself had a red jersey for her own use as a baby. She is fond of all young children and likes to put Tom to bed, although he becomes awkward from about 8 p.m. onwards because of the vague fear that has no word for it.

The first way the difficulty is resolving itself is therefore along lines of adoption of a substitute object, with some regressive behaviour.

The second method is quite different. It has to do with the exploitation of this capacity that he has for thinking. He reports the results of his thinking to his mother, and it was a bad moment when the mother told someone what he had said and that someone laughed. He called her stupid and was furious, and he said: "I'll not tell you in case you laugh." The mother made a comment that might give a good description of him with his thinking as a substitute for the "transitional object". She said: "Instead of being imaginative, he suggests an encyclopaedia." For this reason I have called the thinking a substitute for the object and not called it a transitional phenomenon itself.

He said: "Why do things fall down and not up?" And he does not want an answer. (Newton may have been just here.) The answer is what is his thinking around the problem. He makes use of a reflection back of the question, as from a mirror, and the father is good at this.

Three months later, when Tom was 6 years 1 month and now at school, the mother came to see me again. She said that talking over Tom's problem had seemed to help somehow.

Tom had now become a thinker, so the mother catered for this, and this helped him to stay in his bed. She could see that he is sometimes obviously scared at the time of going to sleep. But now there had been a step forward. Mother must say: "Have you got your niffle?" And he could manage.

Tom had started at a prep school, one where religion plays a rather big part. Tom, of course, has to be quite clear about every detail. "Why do we stand with our hands up?" (prayers). "When we said 'Our Father' I felt a fool." He knew exactly who his father was, and it was not the father of all the others. He must always be clear in his mind, the alternative being a muddle. Here is the clue to the quality of his unthinkable anxiety, namely mental confusion.

Tom: "Why must we say prayers?"

Dad: "To talk to God."

Tom: "What's God?"

Dad: (doing his best) "Well: 2 + 2 = 4. That's a *true* thing. Gravity is a *fact*. These things are *God*." (etc., etc.)

Tom: "Why do things grow?"

Dad: "Because they want to. Why do you grow?"

Tom: "Because I'm alive and came from mummy's tummy."

Dad: "Where did she come from?"

And so on through evolution to sex. Then they laughed because in the end they found a place where the answer was: "We don't either of us know. How did it all start? Well that's where God comes in."

Tom: "So not knowing, that's God."

To mother he said: "People don't know why there's gravity so they say God made it. That's stupid. They should say: *I don't know*."

The parents are hard put to it to keep up with him. They are puzzled themselves, as most thinking people are, but they try to give the children some foundation on which to build. So they tried to tackle the continued questions about prayers, and talked of Albert Schweitzer, and so on.

The headmaster of the school said to the parents: "Tom has an unusual mind; O God, I hope we won't spoil it." This was surely a good thing for a headmaster to have said.

The mother and I found it interesting to make a plan showing many different uses of the word God and of the concept of God, starting with idealization at one end and ending up with the facts of physics at the other. And we naturally put against these ideas that of evil. We were enjoying a free discussion. The mother then said: "He really seems to understand the evolution of ideas, not just what people think now."

With all this, Tom is a happy boy, though he can look puzzled at times. He has a drive to work which makes the teacher wonder where it will lead. But the problem cannot be solved by forcing play on him.

From this description of Tom at intervals, it will be clear to the reader that this is an exceptional family, providing a stable home, and affording opportunities for the personal growth of the children. The mother has a career waiting for her to resume when she has finished with total involvement in home matters.

Part six

ADOPTION

16

Two adopted children

[1953]

M any of my readers will be acquainted with the practical problems involved in the arrangement of adoptions, in a way that I myself can never hope to be. On the other hand, because of the nature of my work, covering as it does two decades of psychoanalytic as well as paediatric practice, I have an understanding on the theoretical side which is particularly my own. I am not going to attempt a wide survey on the subject of emotional development, which comprises such things as the finding of the self, the gradual maturation of each individual, and the changes in the way in which the external factor is important, leading up to socialization, and covering the vast area of human nature itself. Nor am I going to attempt to teach theory detail.

It is sometimes difficult, perhaps for legal reasons, to do follow-up work on adoption, but in this respect my position as a physician in private practice—and physician to what used to be called a voluntary hospital—has given me many opportunities for being consulted over long periods by parents who have adopted children. I intend to draw on this kind of experience and to do very little more than to describe two children, Peter and Margaret, adopted into a family. Nevertheless, I would emphasize that theory is always there in the background enabling me to evaluate what I or the parents have done intuitively, and to keep a sense of proportion, and also to use that wonderful therapeutic to which attention is drawn in our saying that "time is a great healer". I should mention that both parents had studied psychology and had had personal analysis.

Before starting to give my human story, I wish to give you a few pointers, and I will make a brief theoretical summary at the end.

First, if an adoption goes well, then the story is an ordinary human one, and we must be familiar with the upsets and setbacks of the ordinary human story in its infinite variations if we are to understand the problems that specially belong to adoption.

The second pointer is that, even if an adoption is successful, there is something different from usual (and I think there always must be) both for the parents and for the child. For instance, for children there is an alteration in the sense of obligation, and this can cause difficulties even at a late date. Children do not have to thank their own parents for their conception, although indeed they can blame them. They can take it that their parents experienced something very valuable to themselves in all that led up to the point at which conception occurred. With adopted children it is otherwise. You can put it in many different ways, but the fact remains that the parents who conceived them are unknown and unattainable, and to their adoptive parents their actual relationship cannot reach to the most primitive levels of their capacity for relationship. In some cases where there are troubles, this becomes so important a feature that adopted children when they grow up make it their business to do research into the subject of their own origin, and are not contented until they eventually find one or both of their real parents. This point does not emerge in the case of the two children I am going to describe, but then I am able to give only the surface phenomena. Both children are now grown-up and doing well, but if we had an intimate knowledge of either it is probable that we should find problems left over. The following extract from a letter to the adoptive mother from one of Margaret's closest friends is of interest in this connection:

"I cannot remember one single time when Margaret spoke unhappily or bitterly or puzzledly about being adopted ... I do not think Margaret has "worried" about being adopted— as such—but during the last six years or so she has worried about things and been unhappy over some, as all adolescent females do, and the fact that she was adopted may have made her more sensitive ... she belongs to you and Frank so irrevocably that she is, I think, completely incurious about the adoption part of it. Of all the people I know who are adopted, *I think* Margaret is the one who gives the strongest impression of not being so, that is to say, of not being conscious of it. I know we are both infuriating creatures at times ... we both brood over the iniquities of our parents! but fundamentally they don't really worry us."

The third point comes out rather clearly, which is that a very great deal depends on the history of the infant prior to adoption. I am so impressed with this point that I feel extremely critical of legislation and adoptive habits which involve delay; moreover, I think that when the early days and weeks of infancy have been muddled, an infant must necessarily be a burden, and adoptive parents should be fully informed. This explains why it is that adoptions arranged in an unskilled way (by doctors, for instance) often prove successful. I have dabbled in this myself. The point is that whereas parents accept naturally the burdens that result from their own relative failure in the early management of their children (and relative failure there must often be), do they so easily accept failures that are not their own, and tolerate the burdens which belong to environmental failure previous to the adoption and for which they cannot feel themselves to be responsible?

In the cases of the two children I am describing, you will see that the first child, Peter, had a good start, and most of the difficulties met with in his management were ordinary human problems. The second child, Margaret, had a bad start, and the difficulties encountered were very much of the type that could have been predicted at the time of adoption.

I am therefore dividing adoption problems into two broad categories: in one are those problems that belong quite simply to the fact of adoption and are present although they may not give rise to anxiety; in the other are the complications that result from the defective management of the infant prior to adoption. The former we can talk about in a general way and the broad principles apply to all cases. In regard to the latter, there is obviously a wide variation according to the case. By a study of the early history, if we know it, we can predict to foster-parents how much difficulty they will have to meet and the nature of the management problems which they will encounter. If when arranging an adoption we know the early history of the infant and the degree of environmental muddle which must have essentially complicated the very early stages of the child's emotional development, we are in a position to see in advance how far the adoptive parents will be called upon to provide treatment rather than ordinary child care. The problems here link up very much with the psychology of the deprived child, and when the early history has not been good enough in respect of environmental simplicity, the foster-mother is taking on not a child but a case, and in becoming a mother she becomes a therapist of a deprived child. She may succeed because the therapy she is giving is exactly the therapy that the child needs, but all along the line what she does as a mother and what the father does as a father, and what the two do together, will need to be done more deliberately, more with knowledge of what is being done, and repeatedly instead of once, on account of the fact that therapy has crept in as a complication of ordinary good management.

A further point is the obvious one that, owing to the fact that adoption so easily has to be a therapy in the sense that I have described, it is even more important that adoptive parents see their children right through, than that ordinary parents do. What I mean is that whereas the ordinary child is very much enriched by the experience of being seen through to adult status by his or her own home, with the adopted child one has to say that if the home breaks up for any cause it is not so much a matter of failure of enrichment as a matter of failure of therapy, and the result is likely to be illness in the child, especially an organization on anti-social lines.

The main purpose of what I am now going to tell you is to remind you, although you need no such reminder, that when you plant a child on parents it is not just a question of a nice little distraction for them. You are altering their whole lives. If all goes well, they will spend the next twenty-five years solving the puzzle you have set them. Of course, if things do not go well—and very often they must go badly—then you are involving them in the difficult task of disappointment and the toleration of failure.

In the case of the two children, Peter and Margaret, all did go well in the end, which means up to now.

Peter

In 1927, in the early days of legal adoption, a woman went to an Adoption Society to choose a child. This woman, who as a child had always had a big family of dolls, was now a teacher by profession, cultured and intelligent. When 40, she had married a lawyer, a man of exceptional ability, highly cultured, several years younger than herself, of slight build. At 48 years of age, having had none of her own, she decided to adopt one or two children.

At the adoption home she immediately chose one, a boy baby who was outstandingly healthy and likeable; but this baby, although illegitimate, was not available since he belonged to a woman worker in the home who personally cared for him and breast-fed him. Disappointed, the woman went away without any baby, but after a short while the mother of the chosen baby realized her incapacity for giving the boy a good home, and arrangements were made for his adoption by these same people. The boy was said to be exceptionally strong. His putative father was a commercial traveller of very fine physique. The child was 10 months when adopted, and immediately settled in and developed quite naturally, except that he was unusually powerful.

His progress was interrupted when he was just over 2 years by the fact that his father had pneumonia and his mother had flu. The local doctor said the boy must go away because of the risk of infection, and at first he went to friends near home. This was satisfactory, but he had to be moved to an aunt, where he proved tiresome, so he was sent to a welfare nurse

whom he knew. He was happy with her, but in the middle
of a meal he would stop eating, tears would roll down his
cheeks, and he would say: "Where's gone?" (Note that the
word mummy had become extinguished.) When his mother
eventually went to fetch him, he saw her but did not go to
her, so she took him and made no demands on him; he simply put his head on her shoulder and wept. At home he
showed in indirect ways what he had been through. He
heard a lamb bleat, and the mother said: "The lamb has lost
his mummy but will soon find her." He said: "I didn't cry."

I give all this to show how healthy was this child and also his
adoptive environment.

In the course of time, when he was 8 years old, Peter was sent
away to school. He was growing up to be a strong youngster,
reserved, and economical in show of affection. He found it
difficult to return to school each term and declined to be
visited there.

He never enjoyed games, and as he grew up he spent his time
in the engineering shop, and on the school farm. The parents
long wondered which would be the stronger—Peter's bent
for mechanical things, or for animals and anything growing.
He had no friends and disliked having visitors during the
holidays. At school he was considered to present a problem.
His writing was uniformly untidy, although school work
done at home was passable. The result of his Intelligence
Quotient done at school was 115, but that done more carefully at the National Institute of Industrial Psychology was
consistently 138. The school reported occasional over-confi-
dence and said that he generally combined care and decision
in a very satisfactory way, also that he was level-headed, self-
possessed, with a sense of humour. He had tremendous interest in, and energy for, his hobbies. He showed no interest in
girls at this coeducational school.

At 16, he came to me because of difficulties at school and
bad handwriting. At this age he was at his most powerful,
and the parents had to accept the fact that this highly intelli-

gent boy must not be put to academic work. I could see that this boy's wish to be an engine driver was something that could not be diverted into an engineering career, which means office work and drawing-boards. He could easily fear his own strength.

When he left school, after just managing School Certificate, the parents, strengthened by my advice, allowed him to become a mechanic. He was apprenticed to the railway workshops and at first was bored doing work he had already done at school. I was especially keen that he should come under the personal care of a man stronger than himself. Following a letter from myself, the boy was moved to the machine shop at an earlier date than he could otherwise have expected, and immediately made progress. At this time he lived with a retired foreman, and the two together did all the housework and cooking, and were devoted to each other. I think this was an important feature at this stage. We all agreed that the boy needed to plan his own life, even to details, but he needed the support that can come only from those who have a wider knowledge of affairs. Soon he had acquired a motor-cycle and was coming home for the weekends. Later he came home every night, and at that time his garden was his great hobby.

After some years he moved to a more important engineering firm in the Midlands, where he worked in the research workshops. Here he met the girl he has since married. He said nothing of this at home, but his mother suspected that something was up, because he came home less often. One day, being a man of few words, he asked in an indirect way whether he might bring his girlfriend home. The girl had had an unhappy childhood in the care of an aunt whom she did not like, and therefore the wedding was to be from Peter's home. He wanted "no church, no fuss, just like any ordinary day or I'll be miserable". And so, with the minimum of ceremony, this son of a well-known and respected lawyer was married in the registry office, with no one present except the witnesses. The newly married couple wrote, "Thank you for a very pleasant weekend", and started their honeymoon a week later.

They now lived in a caravan, the money for which Peter borrowed from his parents but meticulously repaid. He is superintending the building of his own house. There is a baby girl aged 2 years, and Peter's attitude to her is rather curious. He says: "I'll bring her up tough. I was too much looked after when I was small." It is not known where he got this idea from unless it can be said that his mother was over-anxious and sometimes frustrating. As a child, he was affectionate till he went to school. His mother gave up kissing him at this point, because it was obvious he did not want it. He never said "thank you", and this had to be tolerated, but now he is married all this has changed, and he is even openly grateful and writes long letters home.

So here now we have a strong man of 26, husband and father and qualified engineer, very much in charge of his own affairs.

You have wondered when this boy was told that he was adopted. I think it was when he was about 3. He had asked and been told about babies. Mother said: "You know, you came from someone else's inside, not mine. I took you over because your real mother couldn't look after you." He seemed to accept this easily, and a few days later, seeing a Mona Lisa copy on the wall he said, "Was that the lady I was carried in?" (His oral expression was always good.) After a few days he tried hard to make his adoptive mother say that he came out of her inside, but apart from this he has never referred to his adoption. Both parents are sure of this.

In between the two adoptions, the mother did some work for the Adoption Society, interviewing parents and watching two placings. She formed the personal opinion that parents who wanted two or more children were more deeply suitable for adopting than those who had the idea of adopting only one. Care was being taken at that time to get the right class of child for the adoptive parents. Nevertheless, in the case of Peter the social-class discrepancy did not lead to disaster, because the boy was healthy in terms of emotional development, and because of the tolerance of the parents, who accepted not only him but also his choice of wife from the workers in the engineering shop.

Margaret

Five years after adopting Peter, these same parents adopted Margaret, a baby of 11 months. Peter was only very superficially jealous, and was openly pleased. When told that she was delicate he said, "All the more reason to keep her".

Margaret was very different from Peter. I do not know how far it is generally recognized that a child can be a very disturbed person by 11 months, but Margaret was moderately disturbed. She was 4½ lb. at birth, and perhaps there had been attempts to get rid of her by drugs. The legal father and the putative father were both Petty Officers. The mother had no money. The baby had been somewhat starved and had had pneumonia. When adopted, she was delicate and timid and highly sensitive to noise. She wouldn't crawl. She needed a great deal of attention, and indeed she has all along been a year or two behind her age in physical and emotional development.

A great deal about Margaret's early management must be taken for granted, but I think it important that the first years of her life were dominated by one thing, the treatment for "lazy-eye". At 18 months she evidently had an external squint and had glasses. An excellent orthoptist was found, and the mother went at the care of the squint as if nothing else mattered. I think this was probably the basis of the child's subsequent recovery from what might otherwise have been a permanent defect of personality, based on neglect at the early stages. In terms of the eye defect, the mother cured the personality defect. In the treatment of squint, as is well known, there is an apparatus into which the child looks and sees a cage with one eye, and a bird with the other. Trying this with her mother, Margaret would say that the bird was in the cage in order to please her. She did this same exercise in the consultation room, and the orthoptist had a way of telling that the child was fibbing. The mother felt that Margaret learned the truth in this situation with the orthoptist, and there was a moment of change which was significant when she saw the bird in the cage for the first time. This cure of the eyes was curing something in the child's personality, and a period of lying and deception and shyness in the treatment preceded the cure. As the mother remarked, "The child learned truth from the orthoptist". This seeing with two eyes at once was the first victory. The struggle of the mother as therapist of this child happened to take this form. The mother and child had thus had a very close relationship on a job. Special care of the eyes started at 18 months, and from 5 to 7 years Margaret had intensive eye-training twice a day. The special care of the eyes lasted till the child was 13, when she was pronounced cured and her glasses could be discarded. When she went to boarding-school she was in the middle of her treatment, and this was a cause of trouble and made Margaret disliked by the matron, who was not interested in her treatment.

The home was in a bombed area, and there had to be many moves from one day-school to another during the war. Margaret was evacuated later to a safe place as a boarder, and one day she said to her mother, "You know, you oughtn't to have done it", referring to the evacuation. But, of course, parents could not help being unkind at that time.

At home she began to present problems as she grew older. On one occasion she stole thirty shillings from her mother, and she had ideas that children were plotting to steal her things. She began to develop a wish that plenty of money should be available, and she still feels she is a child deprived of wealth. She worried because her parents were older than those of her many friends, and the parents kept this idea conscious in her mind.

I came into the picture when Margaret was 10, and I saw her several times in personal interview. At that time she was markedly paranoid, and what I found was the expression in 10-year-old terms of the sensitivity to noise and timidity that had been a feature even when the child was 11 months old. She blushed if she thought she was being looked at; she was shy; she had vague fears at meal times; she always had a grievance—at school, she felt that the teachers were ill-tempered and overworked; she had a fear of double-decker buses; and so on. She had no zest for food, or, shall I say, she had a suspicion of food. There was compulsive masturbation. At home she maintained three constant friendships, but at boarding-school, though she craved for a bosom friend, whenever she found one there was always something undesirable.

She had been told about being adopted. At school she quickly became a disturber, even during her first days and weeks. Her friends were younger than herself. At home she must have the last word; she nagged her mother and constantly tried to put her in a temper.

Nevertheless, she was vivacious, excitable, and loveable, and very affectionate to everyone. She showed her appreciation of the problem of her management by exclaiming one day, with her arms full of dolls, "All this family do make me ache". She was richly imaginative. During an interview with me she drew rapidly and in a scatty way all over the page—figures, nudes, parts of people, odd objects; and in one case she cut a hole out of the belly of a woman. There had been a bout of drawings of nude girls at school.

At school she was said to have instability of character—a weak character and a dominant personality, with a power over others which (they complained) she used to force other children to do wrong, even against their will. She stole and hid food or books. The few existing rules and disciplines were not felt by Margaret to apply to herself. She was a masterhand at prevarication. Yet she would try to intervene on other children's behalf if they were in trouble.

I advised a term at home in spite of the bombing, and during this time Margaret learned to play the violin. She became very difficult over food, and developed a fear of being shut in anywhere. She was now able to go to school in the country, but the first term was very difficult. She was always on the point of running away, and for this she planned to steal—she always needed thirty shillings. At this point, Margaret developed a dependence on a psychiatric social worker who happened to be available locally, whom she called frequently on the telephone, and by whom she was visited every evening at a given time for some weeks. A considerable degree of dependence developed. Here was a critical period, but in this way the girl was enabled to gain confidence to stay at school, and her mother came to visit her at half-term. Gradually she developed her many positive qualities. At 13 the sequel to her earlier phobia of buses was a wish to be a bus conductress. She played her violin at a concert and was said to have a great appreciation of beauty. She played tennis with ability. Moreover, the paranoid quality in her personality seemed to be "swept away" at the time when she had pneumonia at school, and her mother, who had always had to promise to turn up if Margaret was ill, now felt that she could leave the child to be looked after at school. Margaret was able to accept being well looked after and brought round to health. Her last year at school was a happy one, and she made many friends. With her parents' strong directing help at home she was able to gain the School Certificate.

After leaving school Margaret went to be trained to work with children. The early stages of her career were precarious; she was the sort of person that gets stolen from, and she managed to get any ill-treatment and neglect that could be discovered. The parents took up every point and dealt with it on a realistic basis, and naturally some complaints were found to have justification. Margaret was on the point of giving up all the time, and in various ways the parents had to be constantly engaged in dealing with situations and tolerating anxiety. At the age of 19 she seemed to her mother to be at the 17-year-old level. She repeated during her training the sort of troubles that she had produced at school. For instance, she had to be home for a while having treatment for a severe state of round-shoulders, and at home she was exceedingly difficult to handle. She was slack, wasted her time, and was discontented. This went on for nearly six months, with constant illnesses. She became ill whenever her parents went away on holiday, but she did not let them know until their return.

At her training school she was good with children, but jealous and a tax on the staff. She developed a technique whereby the parents frequently found themselves spending a little more on her in order to lessen an awkward tension. She always needed the best, regardless of the parents' means, and would wear only clothes that were perfect. She even realized that she "made hell" at home. Nevertheless, with a push, she was always just able to succeed at times of test. Actual stealing and being stolen from ceased, and lying was replaced by a compulsion to get pity. The best thing in her life was her music. She repeatedly told her mother that she was mean, and she would boast of how her smart friends spoiled her. As before, so here, the turning-point came when she had an illness and was nursed at the training school instead of at home. This illness was probably of neurotic origin.

By now the mother was 72 and feeling the strain.

After recovery from the illness, Margaret became more intensely interested in her work with children, and was at last regarded as a promising student, although some of her former difficulties remained. Eventually she said to her mother, "It may be a consolation to you to know that now I would not leave the school for anything". At long last the mother felt rewarded for everything she had been through, since the word consolation showed that Margaret knew what a trouble she had had to be. At this time, Margaret started reading serious literature. In the end, after nearly giving up time after time, and needing constant encouragement, she passed her examinations first class and took two additional examinations, on the ground that her brother Peter said she ought to. Immediately she took a job, having carefully sorted applications and selected just the right one, and she is now looking after a child in a household in which there is enough money for some extras. She is herself an attractive young woman of 22, with a flair for dressing well, and she is a responsible and well-trained person. Here in her first job, looking after a "perfect baby", she seems to have found something corresponding to what is, I suppose, her idealized conception of her real parents. Her adoptive parents, with the means at their disposal, could not compete, which may have been fortunate.

A recent story illustrates her attitude. One day Margaret

found herself unable to tolerate the rude and disagreeable behaviour of a maid towards the mother, and reprimanded her. The maid retorted: "But you're often rude to her yourself." Margaret said: "That's different; she's my mother."

Theoretical summary

The first child, Peter, adopted at 10 months, is now 26 years. He had had an ordinary good infancy experience. He had been breast-fed by his own mother and weaned by her, and during most of this period the mother had no intention of parting with the child. He had had to deal with the disturbance due to change of environment and loss of real mother at 10 months, but by this date he had already been weaned and had become established as an individual in his own right. In Peter's case, therefore, the problems were more those that belong to ordinary child care than to adoption in particular. In my personal opinion it is best either that a child is brought through the early stages of infant care by the real mother, as in this case, or else that the adoptive parents should take the child over as early as possible in infancy, perhaps during the first few days. But it is probably rare for a child to have so good a pre-history on adoption at 10 months as Peter had.

The second child, Margaret, adopted at 11 months, and now aged 22 years, was already a disturbed child at adoption. In other words, her early infancy management was relatively muddled (although not as muddled as might have been the case). Margaret therefore started adoption with a handicap:

(a) The relative environmental failure in a general way deprived the child of that early good start in personal development which good-enough environmental provision makes possible.
(b) There was nevertheless some *organization* of an illness pattern at 11 months, indicating a certain strength of ego. The illness pattern was on a paranoid basis: that is to say there was an artificial rearrangement of objects in the sense that those that

felt bad were placed outside in the world, and those that felt good were collected together within. The adoptive parents therefore had to deal with an ill child. By steady and simplified environmental provision the parents gradually corrected the early failure, at any rate to a considerable extent. The child's illness pattern made it possible for her to express her suspicion of love in terms of substitutes—namely, money, treatments for illnesses, a claim on the mother for tolerance, or an expectation of ill-treatment. The child's capacity for love, and for being loved, appeared in various positive qualities, and in her music and her flair for dressing well. The child is now 22, and engaged in a job which involves identification with a mother caring for an infant. There are certainly troubles in store, and there is a long road between the present state of affairs and the child's ability to take on the responsibility for a family of her own. But the parents are still able to take part in this girl's development, and there is in addition the adoptive brother, who has a deep sense of responsibility for her, and who is there as an insurance in the background as the parents grow older.

The achievement in this case of the adoption of two children is the more remarkable in that the mother was 48 when she adopted Peter, and 53 when she adopted Margaret, and the father was only a few years younger.

This case description is given as a token of my respect for them in their achievement.

17

Pitfalls in adoption

[1954]

The subject of adoption is a very large one, and it cannot be covered in a short article. Preparation for work in the field of arranging adoptions requires a knowledge of the law, an understanding of the emotional development of the human being starting from a very early age, and also training in casework. Those who are preparing to become qualified to arrange adoptions do casework under supervision, and become familiar with the technique of the follow-through.

In actual fact, only about thirty percent of adoptions are arranged through the adoption societies. The rest are at present either third-party adoptions or are direct placings by the mother or are arranged in a more or less haphazard way. It often happens that a gynaecologist or a general practitioner meets during the same week a mother who is unable to keep her baby, and a family wishing for some reason or other to adopt a child; what could be more natural than for an adoption to be arranged? The child is taken into the home and the legal part follows. It must not be denied that these haphazard adoptions often work out well, and no doubt they will continue.

It is necessary to point out that a proportion of these haphazard adoptions fail, and the adoption societies, when they look at these failures, can often say, and with reason, that they could have predicted the failure; proper casework, well done by the right persons, would have enabled certain inevitable complications to have been foreseen. A distorted motive, for instance, can be detected, and, above all, the adoption societies can prevent a child being given to a neurotic woman in the erroneous belief on the part of a doctor, or some other third party, that if only the woman had a child to look after she would be well. Good casework not only prevents disasters but also organizes adoptions which would otherwise not have been possible, and it must be remembered that a failed adoption is usually disastrous for the child, so much so that it would have been better for the child had the attempt not been made.

It may be asked: is there any argument against the more professional method? The objection to the carefully arranged adoption carried through by an adoption society is that by the very fact of care being taken there is often a delay; this delay can be serious and can destroy good work. In order to make certain that a baby is healthy, observations and investigations are made, and all this takes weeks or months, so that by the time the adoptive parents have an infant in their care too much has happened already in the infant's life. In fact, there has commonly been a muddle of infant care before the infant is taken over, the result of which is that the adoptive parents find themselves landed with a psychologically complex problem as well as with an infant. Also, the emotional adjustment to the idea of adopting a baby taps very deep sources of feeling. Parents who have at last made up their minds to adopt a baby are just then ripe for the adoption, and delay of even a few months may be unhealthy. Several postponements and a delay, perhaps of months, or even years, may make the adoption no longer good, since the parents, although still willing to do what they had intended to do, have lost that special orientation towards the care of a small baby, a special orientation which at the right moment they had acquired, in a way somewhat similar (though much less intense) to that which real parents acquire naturally towards their own baby born after nine months of waiting.

From a consideration of these few observations it will already be obvious that there is no simple rule that can be followed. The student of the subject needs to read widely, and to doctors it can be said that a light-hearted arranging of an adoption implies a lack of real understanding of the factors involved. Above all, let adoptions not be arranged for the cure of adult neurosis.

The basic underlying principle is that if a baby cannot be brought up by the real parents, then the next best thing is for that baby to be taken into a family and brought up as one of the family. Moreover, a legal adoption gives the child a sense of being one of the family. The idea that a young human being can be brought up in an institution, even a good one, and automatically turn into a mature human being by growth has long been disproved. The internal tendency towards development and the very complex emotional growth of each baby require certain conditions, and these conditions are not to be stated in terms of good bodily care. A child needs to be loved, and there are reasons for this which can be put down in black and white. It is not that a human being can be made by the environment or by good nurture, and even by the loving care of parents, but that loving care is necessary for the innate processes of emotional growth.

Instead of attempting to collect together the joys and the pitfalls that belong to the adopting of children, I have chosen to give an ordinary case history. Like any other case history, this illustrates certain points, especially that ordinary bodily care is not enough. I give the case of a child adopted for good reason who developed difficulties and who is coming through them. The adoption was not ideal, but it is not useful to be looking always for the ideal. The fact is that this child, if he comes through, will be very much better off than if he had been brought up in an institution from the beginning. (The details have been altered in unimportant respects so that the case is unrecognizable.)

William, aged 4 years

The two parents brought this adopted child for consultation because of the symptom: head-banging. They have had the boy under treatment at a child guidance clinic. The mother has gained a good deal of insight through contact with a member of the staff of the clinic. The boy has attended a small group for weekly sessions. As it turned out, the parents were wanting a general review of the whole subject.

The interview was a ragged one. First, I saw all three together. An attempt to see the boy alone failed, and I saw the father with the boy constantly running in. Then the father and mother changed places, and afterwards the boy stayed with me alone. Eventually I had a fairly long talk with the mother.

The picture was of a deprived child, and at first it was difficult to see how this had come about, since the boy was adopted at 1 month (legally at 4 months), through a registered adoption society.

Family history.   There are no children of the marriage. It was at a late stage in the consultation that I discovered that there had been an abortion before marriage. In the marriage, sexual intercourse was satisfactory, but there was found to be an obstruction of the fallopian tubes so that no new pregnancy is likely to occur. There has been a great deal of guilt-feeling around all this, but the parents are now well on the way to recovery from the effect of these events. The mother does not resent giving up her professional life. In order to give the feeling of a family, these parents have taken in many children on a temporary basis, so there are nearly always children in the house, apart from William. This has helped him considerably. Now the parents have made application for a girl, and this may materialize, but there has been a very long wait, as is usual.

Past history.   Birth details unknown. Breast-fed three weeks. Bottle feeding was rapidly substituted for breast-feeding in preparation for the change to occur at 1 month. At adoption at 1 month, William was small, but doing well. There was no difficulty physically during infancy, and the boy has had little ill-health. He had a tonsillectomy at 2 years. At first it seemed that there was no disturbance of emotional development, but it gradually became evident in the consultation that neither of the parents had a rich memory of the infancy details. At the age of 2, the boy started head-banging, and this became very severe. He would sit against the wall and bang back. Then he adopted a special chair to bang back into. There is a sequence frequently observed; first, the banging, then a terrible tenseness, and then limpness, after which the boy is tired and has rings round his eyes. This compulsive behaviour has gradually become less obvious and is represented at the present time by a jigging up and down. At 2 or 3, there appeared a sensuous element in the kissing.

While the consultation was in progress, the boy was showing pictures of animals to his mother, and he seemed to have a satisfactory relationship to both parents. A restlessness was evident, however. I said to the parents: "This head-banging represents a deprivation of some sort, and I cannot see how it came about."

Additional Notes. William never sucked fingers or thumbs, and this was not due to his having been restrained. From two or earlier he had adopted objects for affectionate hugging in the usual way, but a variation on the theme of head-banging has become a technique for going to sleep. He lies and thrashes the top of his head with this arm. Usually the predominant note is a wish to do this, but the compulsive element was shown when, in a bad attack of diarrhoea and sickness, he was awake and banging badly and was restrained. He kept on saying: "I can't stop banging", and was very unhappy. Another feature was that he has never attempted to get out of his cot. There has been an apathy about his relationship to the world. Even now in the morning he never gets out of bed on his own account. Also, in the course of free play he goes off of his own accord to the chair and rocks forward and backward. If interested in some activity, however, as he may be over short periods of time, his concentration and perseverance is normal and keen, but at the slightest frustration or hurt the constructive element is lost, the play breaks down, and despair takes the place of happiness. There is a compulsive element about his needs. There has been no stealing, except, perhaps, taking a knob of sugar or a bit of cake surreptitiously. His imagination is good, but it is difficult to disentangle this from the mother's attitude, since recently she has played with him more than a mother usually does with a child, in an effort to make up for earlier deprivation, and she has encouraged imaginative play.

The clue to the problem.   It was only gradually that the parents came to tell me of their inability to form a good relationship to the baby when he came. The mother had had guilt about the abortion to contend with, and also her resentment that the child was not her own. The father unexpectedly felt a deep revulsion on first seeing the baby. In consequence of these matters the baby was well cared for physically, but over a period of time, perhaps a year, he was not actually loved; and there was certainly no initial specialized orientation on the part of the mother to the infant's needs corresponding to that which comes naturally when a mother has a baby of her own. These parents had not been able to love the child at first, and they had only come round to a full sense of responsibility and to a loving attitude gradually. The parents could not do anything about this in the early stages, and they hoped it would not matter, but the head-banging brought them to see that damage had been done. Fortunately, they have gradually become fond of the child, and are now doing everything possible to make up for their early lack of love; they seem to me to be truly loving and easily accessible for the child. William is intelligent, and he is affectionate, although with a certain lability of affect. He has common sense. His dependence on his mother at the present time is great. He never expresses any feelings about his mother at all, and both parents feel that this is due to the fact that the mother had had an inability to show her own feelings towards the child until quite recently.

With me alone the boy drew with grand, impulsive gestures. He was able to tell me what he was drawing and to see the funny side of it. Each drawing he took to show his mother. His drawings showed his capacity for impulsive action, which is becoming harnessed to the process of self-expression. He showed imagination and a sense of humour, and a certain amount of capacity to guy his own idiosyncrasies. He enjoyed the contact with me and also was willing to leave. In these respects he showed that there is much that is normal for his age in his personality development.

Comment

The adoption of this baby was arranged at a suitably early date. Casework was deficient in that the difficulties that the parents would experience were not predicted. One can say that if better adoptive parents had been available the child would not have developed illness; nevertheless, it is not at all certain that better parents would have been available, and the child can still count himself lucky that he was not left to more impersonal care. There happened to be factors belonging to the parents' personal life which made it impossible for either of them to feel love towards the infant at the beginning. They hoped to get away with it by giving specially good *physical* care, and at that time they had not sufficient insight to understand what they were doing, nor had they enough freedom from a sense of personal failure to give themselves to a study of the problems associated with adopting an infant. By the time the child had begun to develop symptoms, they had come round to being fond of him, and with a certain amount of help they were able at last to apply themselves seriously to the task which they had undertaken. They now have a "case" on their hands, and they are being forced to exaggerate this and that aspect of child-care in order to meet the boy's needs, that is to say, they are doing psychotherapy as well as enjoying the upbringing of a child. It happens that they are glad to have the opportunity to do something towards correcting the effects of their own earlier deficiency. They are succeeding in their double task, and although at the present time it is still possible to say that this boy is more liable than a normal child to develop an anti-social character, nevertheless, if the parents persevere, as they seem likely to do, they stand a good chance of having a son who will eventually contribute to their happiness. I would personally be in favour of their being now given a girl child for adoption.

An important fact in this case is the stability of the marriage of the adoptive parents, and in retrospect one can say that the degree to which they were upset at their own failure to produce a child is to some extent a measure of their own health.

In this work the ideal is not what is being sought. Any method that gives a deprived child a real and permanent home is to be welcomed. Nevertheless, in the long run it is the trained caseworker who avoids the pitfalls, and who arranges the adoptions that are successful.

18

Adopted children in adolescence

[1955]

I should be happier in addressing you today if I had some specific grievance about adoption procedure, or some bee buzzing in my bonnet, or axe to grind. As I have none of these, I must just match my own experience with yours, fully aware that you are all engaged in adoption practice, and red-hot on the actual clinical problem. In my own practice I do see adolescent adopted children and can compare their problems with those of ordinary adolescence, and with emotional problems of all ages. This perhaps gives me a rather special position.

There are certain things all of us here can take for granted. First, that adoption is a good thing, and very often successful. Second, that much trouble is saved if a child is told at an early age about being adopted, and, conversely, that many troubles arise from delay in giving information. A third thing is the value of stability and continuity in the home. This is a matter that affects all children.

I was recently asked by a probation officer to see a girl of 18. Apparently, this girl, Miriam, had said that I was the only person who had ever helped her; but the first thing she said in our interview was that she had never been happy since I told her, ten years ago, that she was an adopted child. I remem-

136

bered her, and remembered cutting across the line taken by her adopted parents and giving her this information. I was su e she needed to be told, because it was clear that she had already guessed the fact. So I had upset her whole life. Up to that moment she had been extremely happy, and then the blow fell—administered by me. Yet she thought of me when she needed help. I think this illustrates the value of the honest truth to a child—as to everyone. This morose girl of 18 told me that she is very fond of her adopted parents, and her life is ready to open out if she can only let it; but she could not get beyond the feeling of having been cheated. For a long period we sat together, with no one talking or moving much. She was not \ ʿ g time; she was thinking things out, and using my willingness to be involved in her dilemma. She said that her real father was nearly always drunk; that he had remarried, and lived in the neighbourhood. The real mother had died of cancer, and Miriam had been taken over as a baby by the woman senior to her mother at her place of work.

I invited the probation officer to visit the father, and to ask him for something belonging to the real mother for his daughter to have and to keep. He produced a photograph and a necklace. I warned the probation officer that Miriam might not allow herself to become excited about receiving these tokens, and that the ' ᵥ of giving them to her might even be a period of breakdo. . with the experiencing of grief; for Miriam is trying to find her real mother, so as to mourn her. When she was given the tokens she put them straight into her pocket, without opening the envelope. Nevertheless, there have been changes in her life since this episode, an important one being that whereas she was previously in distress, having lost her faith and yet being afraid to go to sleep without saying her prayers, she has now regained her religious life, which has always been important to her. She is still far from well but is now at work with other girls of her own age, and the present situation is satisfactory. The adoptive mother, who has had the child on and off from the age of 1 year, was told by the court not to tell her she was adopted, or to allow her to see her own father. All the time her excellent relation to her adoptive parents is undisturbed; she likes them very much and feels they are good friends. She is very much like her real mother, which helps.

These children need information, but information is not enough. They need a reliable *person* in their lives, one who is on their side in their search for truth, and who understands that they must experience the emotion appropriate to the real situation. Miriam feels *cheated*, but with help she may be able instead to be overcome with *grief*, and it is only so that she can reach her love of her own mother, and so reach to her own capacity to love. In another case the appropriate emotion might be anger, disgust, horror, or exasperation, according to the circumstances of the adoption.

A new need for factual truth appears at the onset of puberty. One cannot attempt to study any problem of adolescence without recognizing the basis of the new instinctual drive, which is biological. The boy is growing a new shape to his physical genitality, and a new excitability; the girl is experiencing menstruation, and a new uprush of feeling in personal relationships, and has to deal with the rapid development of her breasts, which she must be proud to display or ashamed to possess. Puberty forces on each child a new orientation to the world. This new thing is the more difficult because the child does not see far ahead, and does not want to look and find marriage looming up, as onlookers may so easily do. There is an adolescent phase which has value in itself, and which makes adolescents want to club together in a mixture of *defiance* and *dependence*. Adults can harm adolescents either by assuming from their behaviour that they are adults, or by ridiculing them for their infantility. This is especially true in the sphere of sex, for in the adolescent we see the infant's evaluation of touch, for instance, going side by side with sex-play that looks adult. Sex-play has its own value, and does not at first involve long-term planning in terms of a new family setting. This adolescent phase soon passes, but it is worthy of serious study as a normal phenomenon and is somewhat neglected in psychological literature.

Adopted children at adolescence are not the same as other children, however much we may wish to pretend that they are.

They tend to miss the delicate early stages of the adolescent phase, and to pass over too quickly to the adult idea of sex relationships, socialized by marriage. Alternatively, they may react from this, and overdo defiance, banding together with other defiant boys and girls of the same age in a group that becomes rather a nuisance. Adopted children find adolescence more of a strain than other children; and in my experience this is due to ignorance about their personal origin. This has several adverse effects. First, this ignorance gets mixed up with the usual mystery of intercourse, impregnation, pregnancy, and birth and interferes with the delicate nature of adolescent sex-play, making the child self-conscious and clumsy. Secondly, it may lead to over-stress of socialization processes—the various initiation rites, matriculation examinations, and so on; and when the idea of marriage begins to appear it may make for doubt whether the chosen mate will be able to stand the news when it is at last given. Lastly, when the wish for children develops, the adopted child becomes greatly concerned about heredity and the transmission of unknown genetic factors. Thus the ordinary problems which beset every adolescent become distorted; side issues become main issues.

Adopted children absolutely need to be told the facts of life. Other children can manage to pick up things here and there, and to play about with imagination and myth; adopted children need to be answered fully, and to be helped to ask the right questions. It is not enough for them to be told about the baby inside mother. They need the story of instinct complicating affectionate relationships; they need an anatomical and physical statement; and they need time to assimilate what they have been told. Troubles to do with adoption can sometimes clear up with no more than the giving of full and proper sex information.

In learning about sex, which is another way of learning about origins, adolescent children need a relationship with someone both mature and reliable. Adoptive parents may or may not be able to cope with this central problem of management. Adolescents in general need someone outside the family with whom they can see their home from a distance and criticize and evaluate it. The adopted child may find it too dangerous to use friends for this purpose—and indeed it is not uncommon for surprising things to happen to a friendship when information about adoption is given. The need arises for a professional relationship with an outsider, one who is not directly concerned with morals or behaviours or achievements, but who can be used when ideas are being explored.

Children living in their own homes get tremendous relief from the taboo on sex experience within the home; but because there is no blood tie the adopted child's sense of taboo is weakened, and also the sense of safety that belongs to relationships within the natural home.

I want for the moment to suspend the assumption that to be adopted is better than to be in a foster-home, and to compare the two techniques. A few years ago, it was true to say that the best thing for an infant whose own home was not available was adoption. The alternatives to adoption were haphazard arrangements; and the one thing children cannot deal with is fortuity. But nowadays deprived children are covered by a public service administered by the State and carried out by trained workers. The foster-child is in a relatively secure position, and is provided with a professional worker who maintains contact on behalf of the Children's Committee, and who keeps the child, as far as is good, in contact with whatever is left of the real home. To clarify this point, I suggest that there are three categories of adoption.

1. The child is taken over as early as possible in infancy, and brought up in a good home; "telling the child" is successfully negotiated; and the child is the concern of the adoptive parents, who seek advice, if necessary, through the normal channels, as they would for their own children.

2. Complex or late adoptions, where the child has had a good start. Here there are inherent problems arising out of the fact that the child has known other minders, and possibly one or both parents. Is there provision for continuous casework after this kind of adoption, so much more complex than the first?

3. Children who are already disturbed at the time of their adoption. There are many cases in this category, and parents who do not take the child over at the very beginning are likely to have to provide more than normal child care. Adoptive parents, like foster-parents, are liable to be called upon to

be whole-time psychotherapists, and they may find the task beyond them. Adolescence produces its own problems in adoptions in this category, and the professional worker comes into the picture only after breakdown.

Arrangements that suit cases in the first category may not be good for those in the third. If this is true, we ought to say so, however much we may wish to preserve the existing arrangements for the sake of the good adoptions that I have placed in this first category, which would be altered in character if social workers who had known the case in the past were to continue to visit the home.

Perhaps you solve this problem by steering all the disturbed children into foster-homes. How difficult, however, to diagnose emotional disturbances in early infancy! At a few months, or even weeks, muddled management may have produced a great degree of illness. This seems a far cry from the problems of adolescence, but it is one of the essential problems of adoption. It looks as if in fostering we acknowledge the situation and try to make the best of a bad job, whereas in adoption work we try to pretend that something quite natural is happening. Adolescence finds us out on this point. Adoptive parents, who may be unable to deal with the adolescent's very special need for help, have no one to advise them. Must the provision of skilled help always be preceded by a breakdown? The foster-child has the advantage of continuous, positive help from a professional service; and foster-parents usually value this outside help, provided it is offered tactfully.

What can a professional worker do? The adolescent needs to find out about the real world, and that important part of the real world which revolves about the general enrichment of relationships by instinct. Adopted children need this especially, because they feel insecure about their own origin. How can the professional worker come in to help adoptive parents here? This leads me to another point: what powers exist for research into the past when this is found to be desirable? Am I right in thinking that when a breakdown occurs there may be much difficulty because of the general confusion about the true details of the child's early life? Almost anything is of value if it is factual, and by the time a child gets near to a breakdown the need is so urgent that even unpleasant facts can be a relief. The trouble is *mystery*, and the consequent admixture of fantasy and fact, and the child's burden of the potential emotion of love, anger, horror, disgust, which is always in the offing but which can never be experienced. If the emotion is not experienced it can never be left behind.

Third-party placements are said to be "sometimes surprisingly successful"; is this partly due to the fact that in many of them there is some sort of continuity, and the facts are available because the adoptive parents have never taken up full possession? It is the difference between a long lease and a freehold; and the freehold element in the well-arranged adoption can sometimes stand in the way when, at puberty, the child must get at the truth, not only of sex but also of personal origin.

Obviously some parents will continue to prefer adoption, just as some children need it. The Curtis Report,[1] as we know, puts it first among ways of dealing with the deprived child. We can, however, still ask ourselves the interesting question: is it a sign of greater maturity in a married couple when they prefer to adopt or when they prefer to foster? Up to ten years ago, I should have said it was a sign of maturity to prefer to adopt; but now the answer is not so clear. When good professional services are available, and are duly recognized, it may be a sign of maturity to prefer fostering, especially when the infant is not being taken over almost at birth.

Adoptive parents have special problems themselves when their children reach puberty. For them as well as for the children it makes a difference that the incest barrier is only a legal matter, and is not based on the blood tie. Adoptive parents and step-parents share a special difficulty in that they cannot identify with their adoptive or step-children at the same deep level as with their natural children. When the children develop love affairs, adoptive parents are liable to be disturbed, even though the actual partners are boys and girls of the same age; the deeper significance is a thing of the unconscious.

No doubt many adopted children realize on reaching adolescence that if they had had the choice they would not have chosen

---

[1]See p. 13, footnote 1.

the particular parents that were allotted to them. But just as adoptive parents have to take a chance, so do adopted children. If we look at the grand total, we can say that in most cases adoption works out well; but we must recognize the truth that some adolescents find their adoptive homes intolerable. How can such children get into touch with those who can help them?

It might be thought that the break-up of an adoptive home must necessarily be disastrous; but in my experience I have not found more disturbance in adopted children so affected than in other children. As an example I would mention the case of a boy whose adoptive parents are divorced. One parent has remarried, and there has been a good deal of divorce among other people the boy relied on. He has managed very well and continues to make personal use of all those adults who have not proved directly unreliable for him. This boy was adopted in the first few days of life and had a very good infancy and early childhood. He was early informed of his adoption.

To sum up: all children reorientate to life at puberty, and adopted children at this age have a special task, and need specialized help. Adoptive parents also need help in the management of their own feelings, stirred up by the new capacities of these children who are not in fact of their own flesh and blood. There is also the subsidiary problem of the social worker's position in her search for facts, and whether she should have right of entry into the adoptive home before the child has become a patient and the adoption a case.

Questions from the audience

Question: Was there any proof that emotional disturbances in early infancy affected children later on?

D.W.W.: My impression is that when all goes well at the beginning much of what happens at that time becomes obliterated by later experiences and loses significance. But if things go wrong, then everything that has ever gone wrong becomes significant. Many children are already so disturbed at a few months old that their grown-up state is predictable. For example, there is nearly always an emotional background to powerful feeding difficulties in later childhood; and the trouble can be dated to certain periods, perhaps the introduction of solids or the change from breast to bottle, but sometimes to the very first day the mother and child were unable to make a relationship on that basis. So there are children who need psychotherapy because they had an abnormal pattern at a few weeks or months. Many of them are seen through by their own parents, who think of them as "difficult"—this seeing the child through is part of the continuous process of bringing up children, and parents like doing it. If an adopted child has been taken over at a few days, the parents can attribute anything that goes wrong to something they themselves have done; and they will try to put it right. But if they have taken a child who has already had difficulties in the early weeks or months, they are dealing with someone else's mistakes, which makes their task completely different.

Question: Could breakdown in adolescence be avoided if investigations and supervisory discussions were carried out in the early stages, so that adoptive parents could be warned about possible difficulties later on?

D.W.W.: Ideally, adoptive parents should be told, and would like to know, what difficulties lie ahead; but in practice one must know what sort of people they are, so as not to discourage them by anything that does not seem quite smooth and "normal". People work up to the idea of adoption, and the child they want is the one that comes at the moment they have reached the right phase. It is the equivalent of being pregnant—a state of sensitivity. No textbook rule can be applied at such a moment; we must know how much the parents can take. If they can take it, they should be told.

Question: Was it right to say to adopters: "Here is a child who has been unloved, whom you will take and love; but because of his early deprivation of that vital thing you may find troubles later on, perhaps at adolescence?"

D.W.W.: It would be better to suggest to the parents what they can do to help; for example, to say: "This child has been neglected, and for the next few months or years you will have to exaggerate all the affection you usually show ordinary children."

There are two sorts of care given to infants: one is concerned with such things as feeding, etc., and the other is best understood by the parents in terms of "holding the baby". If we say "This child has not been held properly; he has been let down", we mean quite literally that the ground has opened beneath him and there is no security anywhere; there is an infinite drop, which may reappear at any moment and will turn up in nightmares and in his drawings later. The adopters of such a child must not merely care for him, but exaggerate all the child-care things, so that he feels safely held. You can explain that adolescence is difficult with all children, and that parents may need help; if they do, they may come and talk things over then.

Question: Most adopters lavished all they had on the child. Might not this very fact cause trouble for themselves and the child at adolescence?

D.W.W.: We have to differentiate between gratifying desires and satisfying needs. Certain absolute needs exist, particularly at the very beginning—things like not letting the child fall, not letting his head suddenly drop sideways in the bath. To exaggerate all these essential things does not spoil a child in the way he is spoilt if whenever he asks for a sweet he is given two. But there may sometimes be reasons why one ought to spoil a child. There will be another mess to clear up after the period of spoiling, but it may be necessary to do it in order to get over its early difficulties.

Question: What about the special situation arising in adolescence when an adopted child is the natural child of one parent but not of the other, and consequently comes to realize that it is illegitimate?

D.W.W.: A constant difficulty in telling the child about the past is that it learns of its illegitimacy. The worst case is where it is the product of incest—say, the child of a brother and sister. No rule made to suit that child would suit another; it would be far better for *no one* to know anything about it at all. That sort of information would be very difficult for any child to stand up to, and I cannot recall ever giving it to a child. As for ordinary illegitimacy, I think sex information gets behind this problem: that is why these children need to know the facts of sex. If the child is already in a muddle about his origins, it is a terrible thing for him to learn of his illegitimacy; but if young people have the facts and can deal with and accept deep knowledge of anatomy, the physiology and psychology of love, marriage, and life, they can bear the fact of illegitimacy in that context. The real trouble is not whether the child was illegitimate, but whether it has had a good start in life and made a satisfactory emotional development—a child with a good start can stand the knowledge that it is illegitimate. When a child cannot stand that knowledge, his trouble is not just the illegitimacy, but the sum of all his difficulties in dealing with relationships, due to muddled early management.

Question: What should be told to the child of a married woman? Was it not bad for him to know that his mother was married and might have other children whom she had kept with her, and to feel that he had been rejected to keep his parents and brothers and sisters safe? Was it enough to tell such a child that his mother and father were not married to one another, which was in fact untrue?

D.W.W.: The question in these cases is: if you withhold or distort the truth, can you get away with it? Children have an uncanny way of getting to know the facts eventually, and if they find that the person they have trusted has misled them, that matters to them far more than what they have discovered. Facts are all right because they are facts; what is dreadful is not knowing whether something is a fact or a mystery or fantasy. A child who has been well seen through the early stages, and has made a good emotional development, needs to face the whole thing and to experience the emotions appropriate to the real situation, and also needs to be carried through by a person professionally re-

lated to him at that time. That is better than having such a discovery always there in a potential future.

Question: At what age should a child be placed? Under the Irish
Adoption Act the mother's consent was not valid until the child
was 6 months old, and there were legal and other difficulties in
early placing.

D.W.W.: I believe the first day is better than the second, the second than the third, and so on. Doubtless there are many snags
and difficulties in practice: but parents feel so differently towards the difficulties they know they are responsible for
(knowing they are responsible for the good things) that I feel all
delays are a nuisance.

Question: Does breast-feeding play a part? It was cut out by very
early placement.

D.W.W.: We shall get into a muddle if we take the words
"breast-feeding" literally. In psychological writings we find the
term "breast-feeding" meaning the kind of care that goes with
personal attention from the mother. Actual breast milk is not
necessary; the mother can bring up her infant perfectly well
without it. Everything depends on her way of doing it. There are
two complicated considerations contained in the question. First,
should one start breast-feeding and then change to the bottle, or
is it better when there is going to be an adoption not to start
breast-feeding at all? Much still has to be learned about this, but
from the infant's point of view I think it is better if breast-feeding
is not started if it is only to be interrupted. But I have found that
even a few days' breast-feeding is something never forgotten. In
normal cases breast-feeding is an enrichment; in the abnormal
case its loss cannot always be helped. The second complication is
that although breast-feeding may be better dispensed with from
the infant's point of view, from that of the mother it may be very
important.

It is possible to have complete breast-feeding followed by
adoption. There may be some sense in that; but a very powerful
relationship between two human beings is developing during
that time, and the baby must be expected to mourn the loss of its

mother, the most important person in the world—in fact, its whole world. However, that situation can be successfully negotiated, provided the infant is well cared for—"well held".

Question: What about the heredity of the child whose mother produced a child for adoption every two years. Might difficulties in adolescence not often reflect the true character of the child's parents?

D.W.W.: There may be genetic factors involved, but I do not want to leave it at that, because the reason why a particular person produces a baby every two years is so complicated that I cannot say if it was inherited at all. For instance, it may be that the mother was herself bandied about as an infant, so that contact with her own mother or a mother substitute was completely lost and never regained. Alternatively, the girl may be one of a low-I.Q. group, who finds life simpler that way. Without knowing the background I should not care to say that this type of behaviour was genetically determined at all; it is more likely to be due to some failure in her emotional development than to heredity.

Part seven

PSYCHOSOMATIC
PROBLEMS

19

Contribution to
a discussion on enuresis

[1936]

The discoveries made through psychoanalysis during the last forty years have rendered possible, among many other things, some understanding of enuresis. Psychoanalysis as a therapeutic method is also able to offer treatment to an individual sufferer; treatment of a child by psychoanalysis would not be considered a success if at the end of it such a symptom as enuresis were still a feature. This does not mean that psychoanalysis has done much, if anything, to help the general practitioner who is asked to treat the symptom. The reason for this is that the emotional development of a child is extremely complex, and involves violently strong forces. Any technique, therefore, which can be used with safety in the treatment of disorders of emotional development is bound to be complex and to require much sacrifice of time from whoever would acquire it. Few general practitioners can afford to make the necessary sacrifice.

Enuresis is one of those myriad symptoms that may mean nothing or a great deal. Bed-wetting may be normal, and at the other extreme, bed-wetting—as we meet it in consultation—is part of a more or less severe difficulty in emotional development, but a great deal of work has to be done in the study of the

151

child's other symptoms, and lack of symptoms, before a guess can be made as to the kind of difficulty that is foremost in his particular case, or as to the prognosis.

Frequently the symptom ceases if left untreated. It is usual in general practice to offer some medicinal treatment, and we need not quarrel as to whether or not the medicine has played a part in the symptomatic cure that may have ensued. On the other hand, enuresis may cease, but the symptom may reappear at puberty in the form of nocturnal emissions, and later may be partly expressed in ejaculatio praecox.

The unconscious fantasy accompanying enuresis may be found on analysis to be chiefly an erotic one, or a hate one; but always the important element for psychological understanding is the *unconscious fantasy*, in fact the different layers of fantasy, of which the dream that may be remembered is an example. The principal emotions expressed by bed-wetting are love, hate, and reparation, and also the urge to be rid of what is felt to be bad. Enuresis may be related to unconscious persecutory fantasies, and may be connected with the attempt to get the bad out. It may also be connected with latent depression, and may be part of an attempt to fill a hole, the hole being the result, in unconscious fantasy, of the emptying of the loved mother, the container of goodness, this emptying being in turn the result of the conversion of love into greed by frustration. Every analyst has abundant evidence, from almost every case, of these things, and would agree that somewhere there always is to be found anxiety of some kind related to the fantasy.

This leads to the next consideration, which is that in enuresis (as in other types of symptom involving "bodily" processes) pleasure is being exploited in the effort to deal with fear. This is fundamentally a normal mechanism. In the human infant it is seldom, if ever, possible to find pure pleasure-seeking; there is always some dealing with fear by sensuous experience, and in the various forms of compulsive sensuality the underlying anxiety, or guilt-feeling, is often fairly obvious to the acute observer. This is no more than saying that a good meal can make you feel better if you are worried, and an extension of the idea to other spheres.

Of course there are some people who cannot accept the fact of sensuality (excitement, pleasure, gratification, satisfaction, anger at frustration, etc.) in connection with the urinary apparatus. In the same way there are some who fail to recognize the intense value to the child of skin excitement, and the gratification infants and children get from contacts, and from rubbing and scratching. Others are incapable of believing in anal, or mouth, or nasal, or genital sensuality, and the part that these play in the infant's and in the child's normal development, as well as (in modified ways) in the adult's attainment to maturity and stability.

It is necessary to point out how much more intense the infant's feelings are than one can tell through empathy. The infant normally sees the pleasure which the body offers in dealing with anxieties, for satisfaction and pleasure mean to him that there is goodness in the world, so that he sets up good people and things inside him; this belief in things enables him to endure pain and frustration, which bring about badness, hate, and make him find bad people and things inside—bad objects which he fears will destroy the good, and which he wants to get out of him if he can feel this may be done safely.

The mother who trains the baby to be clean can be, from the baby's point of view, a creator of evil, since she turns love into anger inside him, and he can only endure this if he has already a firm foundation of belief in the good mother, based on primitive satisfactions. Hence, there is a real danger in the present-day teaching that mothers should train their infants early to "habits". One mother, of a loving nature, may carry through this training without actually doing harm, but the result is frequently a disappointing one. Perhaps, after easily induced cleanliness, the baby begins to refuse to use the pot when about 12 to 18 months old, and a really serious difficulty may be ahead of the mother, who anyway feels humiliated and guilty.

Cleanliness and control of sphincters are only stable when they are the result of the child's unconscious identification, based on love, with clean and self-controlled parents, or ideal figures in fact or fantasy. The best advice to give mothers is the opposite of that usually given. Mothers who ask for advice should be told to avoid conscious efforts at training, and to do no more than to give opportunity for the infant to be clean; moreover, they should be warned that babies often become clean easily at first, but normally become dirty and uncontrolled at times, perhaps for long periods, and that no special training efforts should be made at such times. In other words, they should be told to play for time, and to ignore the unkind remarks of the neighbours.

As for those mothers who do not ask for advice, let them be left alone—they are sometimes the really good mothers, who are not afraid to act on intuition, and who may well know more than the doctor does about how to bring up a child. For the doctor is apt to leave important things out of account; a good mother, for instance, prepares the way for training by a genuine love of her infant's excretions. To her they are love-gifts, good, and not merely physiologically good as they are to the doctor and nurse. Such aspects of mother-love appear in her with the baby, and are often forgotten and even denied by her after all the children have grown up. Yet they are fundamentally important for the healthy emotional development of the individual child. The mother who has recognized her child's gift as such is in a good position to ask of him another gift, the development of control, such as she exerts over her own motions and emotions. It is the lack of these primitive infantile satisfactions that produces the institution child, notoriously liable to enuresis.

There is a psychoanalytic observation that is relevant to this discussion. No analysis could be completed without analysis of the feelings about urinary (and other) incontinence. Continence is part and parcel of the relation of the child to parents, both the actual parents and the inner ones that come to constitute the conscience and the idea. If, in the whole course of the life of an individual, enuresis had never occurred—which is unlikely—still there would have been *fear* of incontinence. Sometimes in the course of analysis of a child who is considered "safe", enuresis appears as a temporary symptom as the child's general sense of guilt becomes less overwhelming. Enuresis is then a sign even of improvement, of emotional development.

The analysis of a little girl of 2½ illustrates this point well, since this child had given no trouble as a bed-wetter, even as an infant, and also enuresis did not appear (as it may do) as a temporary symptom in the course of treatment.

> This child came to hospital on account of severe inhibition of feeding, which began at 1 year and led to some stunting of growth, and recently masturbation, compulsive in type, had occurred. The treatment lasted six months.

> A game which the child introduced, developed, and played with feeling was one in which she acted as strict mother to naughty babies who wetted their beds, the floor, and their mother's lap. The strictness was intense and the punishments even cruel, and the whole setting was in perfect contrast to her own experience; she was the first child in a very happy working-class home, most sensibly brought up, and able to be extremely happy in the family circle as soon as her personal difficulties cleared up.

It would be indeed surprising to find a child who did not play some game with enuresis in it during the whole course of a psychoanalytic treatment.

Frequently there can be demonstrated an anaesthesia of the usually sensitive parts of the urinary apparatus in cases of enuresis. It is found that this anaesthesia is an inhibition of physical sensation, secondary to repression of accompanying fantasy. This anaesthesia disappears as the repression of fantasy becomes less intense, and the part becomes again a source of excitement and pleasure ready to play its part in the child's effort to deal with deep-rooted anxiety.

The most difficult case of enuresis can be the one with no manifest anxiety or depression, so that people say the child would be quite normal but for the bed-wetting habit. In such a case all the emotional difficulties of the child are being dealt with by the one symptom, whereas more normally they are dealt with in a number of different ways, by varying conversion symptoms, by phobias, obsessional behaviour, tempers, moods, and so on.

These findings do not make everyday treatment easier, but it is not the speaker who is complicating the subject; it is the subject that is itself highly complex. The analyst is merely one of those who are trying to understand the forces at work behind enuresis, and behind a hundred kindred symptoms that are common in childhood and sometimes cry out for treatment.

In regard to treatment, there are tricks, of course. There is hypnotism. There is also the treatment of delayed mourning by shock-production of a flow of tears: "You were very fond of your brother, weren't you?" suddenly thrown at the sullen girl of 12 who had become depressed and enuretic after her brother had died from a slow illness, produced violent sobbing and sudden return to normal behaviour at school, at home, and in bed. There may be value in these tricks, but not so much as there is in psychoanalysis and the study of cause, even though this limits therapy to the treatment of a few cases and the giving of better advice that has hitherto been given to the mother who wants to know how best to bring up her child.

20

Papular urticaria
and the dynamics of skin sensation

[1934]

E nough continues to be written, as is shown by the recent papers of Bray[1] and Kinnear[2], on the subject of papular urticaria[3] to justify the assumption that we do not yet fully understand the condition. My object in writing this paper is to examine papular urticaria from a point of view which I think has been neglected, namely, from the point of view of one who is interested not only in the skin condition *per se*, but also, and certainly no less, in the feelings of the child who is the sufferer.

---

[1]G. W. Bray, "Lichen Urticatus or Urticaria Papulosa." *British Journal of Children's Diseases*, 30 (1933), 180.

[2]J. Kinnear, "Urticaria Papulosa." *British Journal of Derm. and Syph.*, 45 (1933), 65.

[3]Papular urticaria is a common skin condition occurring in infants. Winnicott was, of course, aware of the various physical factors associated with the condition, and he is here concerned with a situation in which no demonstrable cause was found. He refers directly to papular urticaria in *Clinical Notes on Disorders of Childhood* in the chapter entitled "Masturbation" (pp. 183–190), specifically on pp. 184 and 188. See also chapter 13 herein (pp. 97–101) for another case study.

In its extreme form my thesis could be expressed in two sentences:

A. Papular urticaria is a normal skin phenomenon, a skin excitement corresponding to the erection of excited erectile tissue (glans penis, clitoris, nipple, mucous membrane of nose, and so on).

This first part of my thesis would be recommended by its simplicity, and I know of no other theory of the condition which accounts for the fact that almost all babies occasionally develop the typical papules, and that these come and go with amazing rapidity, especially in relation to the changing emotional states.

A question immediately arises: what about the distressing characteristics of the fully developed disease, in which the baby or small child is unable to rest or sleep, and which causes such acute distress to parents and doctors? Can this be brought under the adjective "normal"? This leads to the second part of my thesis.

B. When we meet papular urticaria as a distressing disease, we are usually dealing with a complicated psychological disorder, corresponding to obsessive onanism, in which the skin generally has become the battleground of a fight, chiefly unconscious, between an urge demanding gratification, and a sense of guilt which threatens to deprive the child (ego) of an entire pleasure-system. The obsessive quality of the scratching is an indication of the child's fear of loss of a pleasure-system, and the self-mutilating that is so common corresponds exactly to the cruel element that in obsessive onanism is directed on the self, although in the accompanying unconscious fantasies it is fundamentally directed towards an object in the environment.

It is my experience that the statement of this thesis provokes quite strong reactions in the minds of doctors, so that they find it very difficult to discuss the theory on its merits. However, I think that this theory has as much in its favour as others that have been put forward and discussed freely (for instance, the one in which it is held that the disease is caused by bananas), and whereas I am perfectly willing to abandon my theory when it is proved wrong, I am at the moment prepared to sponsor it. Further, one occasionally meets with encouragement from the dermatologists. For instance, in the course of a stimulating lecture to the York Medical Society, John T. Ingram says: "... the skin ... because in man an extension of the mind, an essential part of the individual temperament and personality."[4]

It is common knowledge that in dealing with a child with severe papular urticaria, the problem is to break the vicious circle in which the papules are accompanied by irritation, and the scratching produces papules. Incidentally the scratching also produces abrasions, leading to bleeding, and often to secondary infection and to scarring. It would almost be true to say that we should not mind a child having papules were it not for the distress caused by the conflict "I want to scratch—I must scratch", leading to "I will scratch to show myself I can still 'enjoy' it in spite of feeling guilty, or in spite of mother trying to prevent me". (This is an oversimplification, but will serve.)

We give lotio calaminae, hoping that the business of applying the lotion and letting it dry on will give an interval in which the attention of the child is directed away from that of skin-scratching on to the cooling of the skin, or to the pleasure of seeing a lotion turn to a pink powder. Unfortunately, we are often disappointed by the failure of this and the other prescribed charms. Eventually, exhaustion of the child brings an end to the orgy, distressing alike to parents and child.

It is perhaps because of the part they have to play in the orgies that parents are much more willing to entertain this view of papular urticaria than are doctors; the latter, after all, usually see the skin on the following day, when it may be cold, unexcited, and simply the site of receding papules, scabs, and scars. At this stage, the condition may at times closely simulate chicken-pox, and even smallpox.

In an epidemic, a medical officer of health, experienced in the diagnosis of smallpox, sent to an isolation hospital an afebrile

---

[4] J. T. Ingram, "The Personality of the Skin." *Lancet*, 1 (1933), 889.

child who had been under my care for some weeks, a severe case of papular urticaria. The duration of the rash (if the medical officer of health had felt he could rely on the mother's testimony, which I happened to know was true) might have been taken in disproof of the diagnosis.

Papular urticaria is so common that one hesitates to give cases. The very existence, in print, of a case history is apt to give the impression that the condition is a disease; whereas no amount of recording histories can adequately represent to those who are not in touch with clinical paediatrics the extreme commonness, almost universality, of the condition. However, in my own practice, both hospital and private, experiences are constantly cropping up that seem to confirm my view. I have discussed the condition and given cases elsewhere.

Case 1

A girl, aged 3½ years, has been under my care since 13 months old, when she had acute anterior poliomyelitis, which left her with wasting of a lower limb. Apart from this wasting, she has been in good health, and she gets about quite well in a celluloid splint.

The mother pointed out to me recently that the child was scratching her skin a good deal, and typical papules appeared in varying positions, as is the rule. The mother said she thought the condition was due to the child having eaten a banana. Mothers often say this, and it is often not possible to put down their suggestion to their having heard or read that some doctors share this superstition. In this case, as in some others I have investigated, there was no clear correlation between the taking of bananas and the appearance of the papules. The child had had papular urticaria over a fairly long period, and on one occasion the spots seemed worse after a banana.

Mothers put down all sorts of symptoms to bananas, and it is the job of the medical profession, here, as always, to help parents to understand that certain beliefs are not founded on fact. It is not impossible to see an explanation of the superstition, but this is not the place for such considerations. It is difficult, however, to refer to banana phobia without drawing attention also to fish phobia, since so much stress is laid by dermatologists on the relation between ingestion of fish and urticaria, sometimes on very slender grounds. The following case of mine, although not one of papular urticaria, may be used to illustrate the difficulties to be encountered in this connection in clinical paediatrics.

Case 2

A boy, an only child, was used to being fed by his mother. When he was 14 months old he was one day given some fish by his father. Mother noticed this and had an argument with father in front of the child. She was really jealous of the father who was feeding the child, who had till then been almost exclusively hers. Her rationalization was that fish was not good for a child and would be sure to make him ill. Unconsciously, she was trying to awaken a sense of guilt in the little boy in relation to the taking of food from the father. The diet of fish, therefore, became the subject of a tense emotional situation. That evening the child vomited, and the next day he was limp and good for nothing. From that time, he developed a fish phobia and added an intense dislike of even the sight of eggs and bananas too. This phobia lasted some months, and then spontaneously cleared up.

These were uncultured working-class parents, who only knew how to report faithfully the facts as they had met them. They know nothing of psychology, and certainly had never heard the word "phobia". Anyone might have been inclined to give the vomiting a physical (allergic) relation to the ingestion of fish, but it would take some distortion of facts to account in this way for the associated phobia of eggs and bananas that developed at the same time—a phobia which was probably connected with the symbolic meaning of these foods to the little child.

Case 3

A mother told me: "The child (a girl, aged 6 years) had a perfectly clear skin when I undressed her to be admitted to hospital. She was laid on a stretcher to be carried to the ward, and when the doctor took off the blanket she was covered from head to foot with spots (papules). She was inwardly very anxious at the time, because of being admitted to the ward, and I have often noticed how she gets this rash in a situation of emotional stress."

In this way, mothers constantly impress on me the relation of papular urticaria to the emotions. Indeed, it is common knowledge that a mother, finding papules as she gives the baby the morning bath may, on arrival at hospital, find no lesion to present to the doctor; conversely, a mother may be alarmed to find papules, on undressing her baby for the doctor, when she knew that an hour or so previously she had bathed an infant without blemish. Further, it is well known that papular urticaria is not maintained when the patient is admitted to the ward; like asthma and other diseases with a relation to deep emotions, it tends to appear in the ward only in patients who have become accustomed to the environmental change.

Case 4

A male infant, aged 16 months, was sent me by a welfare centre on account of haematuria. He had a normal urine, and the blood had come from injury to the urinary meatus. The child would want to micturate, but for an hour would scream, and run about with erect penis. At last he would micturate. In the mornings there was a blood clot at the meatus, "as if he had been scratching all night". He also scratched his scrotum in the mid-line, till a sore appeared. Probably the meatal soreness was stimulating genital excitement, and bringing out guilt feelings with threatened repression of genital fantasies and sensation.

Further, the boy had developed severe papular urticaria and "tore himself to pieces".

Case 5

A boy, aged 4 years, is the first and only child of fond parents. He eats well and is happy, but is brought to me because for fourteen days he has been scratching himself unmercifully. He has typical papules, varying in position, coming and going again quickly, except where damage has been done by the scratching. Neither parents nor child have had any peace, and during the fortnight the child has been very bad-tempered, and his hands have been hot.

This is just the sort of picture presented by a child who has started to have a battle over genital masturbation, forming a very common clinical entity at this age. In this case, however, the site of the battle is chiefly the skin.

This boy has further difficulties in regard to the more primitive mouth pleasures. His mother tells me that he has never passed through the normal stage of putting everything to the mouth, and by her attitude to the child during the consultation gave evidence of having herself perhaps transmitted to the child her own sense of guilt over oral interest. The mother was not a bad mother and was loving, but she felt that she ought to stimulate her child's feeling of guilt in relation to both mouth and genital pleasures. I do not know about her attitude towards anal pleasure, but I think that her successful efforts to increase her son's natural guilt over oral and genital pleasure have been a factor in the pathogenesis of his obsessive *skin* onanism. The papules were incidental to this complicated mechanism.

From this it will be clear that I consider that skin excitement and even the occurrence of papules is normal in infancy, and to be expected occasionally in early childhood. In relation to battles over masturbation, it is likely to be emphasized. When, however, the obsessive quality is present I consider that the condition is a symptom of a disease, namely, of a psychological disorder, involving some degree of repression in connection with more advanced (for instance, genital) auto-erotic gratification systems.

My present view is that the disease, *obsessive skin onanism with papular urticaria*, is more closely related to anal than to genital onanism and is, so to speak, a spread-out over the whole skin of a special sensitivity of peri-anal skin and anal mucous membrane; the reason for this spread-out is largely repression in connection with actual anal sensation and the passive fantasies that go with it, though factors may be operative in the direction of encouraging general skin excitement (unsuitable underclothing, infestation, an attack of scabies, a skin experience such as vaccination, chicken-pox, impetigo, and so on).

If the condition under consideration is related to genital masturbation, it is to the obsessive variety, rather than to ordinary normal genital excitability and fantasy accompaniment. The obsessive element indicates unsatisfactoriness, as a form of gratification, and points to an anxiety drive. It is well known that there is a lot of cruelty in (neurotic) obsessive genital masturbation, showing both in the physical treatment of the genitals and in the fantasy accompaniment, and the obsessive quality is related to underlying anxiety.

The relation between the normal skin excitement of the infant, with a tendency to formation of papules, to the "disease" papular urticaria as seen in its worst form in older infants and toddlers would be as the relation of normal genital excitement to obsessive masturbation. The first is simply a stage in normal emotional development, whereas the second is an unsatisfactory attempt to return to an earlier stage as an escape from the dangers inherent in developing object relationships (jealousy, rage, revenge, etc.).

It is hardly necessary to point out that papular urticaria merges into other skin conditions. First, there is no sharp line between papular urticaria and other common urticarias and angio-neurotic oedema. Secondly, by its onanism element, papular urticaria links up with all the other skin conditions that produce or are produced by or kept up by friction.

1. *Sometimes angio-neurotic oedema seems to be an urticaria which has undergone the following change: the itch has been suppressed and the oedema emphasized. In this way the gratification is turned from a physical one (scratching) into a mental one (obtaining sympathy in regard to being ill, etc.).*

Case 6

A boy started at the age of 8 years to suffer from irritating urticaria. He had been a very nervous child from infancy, crying very easily, and was described by mother as "a proper mother's boy" (much to the mother's chagrin). Of the other five children, the eldest was also rather nervous, too, but the others (he came in the middle) were fairly normal. His emotional difficulties became much increased with an illness when he was 2½ years old, in which he had what looked like a "cold" for a week, and after which he was very quiet and only slowly became lively again. He never really regained happiness, and his general nervousness was much increased. However, he was normally intelligent and did well at school.

It appears that his urticaria at first itched a great deal but his mother frightened him off scratching by telling him it would do him harm. As he was nervous about himself, he renounced scratching, but developed oedema of the eyelids, hands, and feet, which came on in attacks. Sometimes he had oedema behind the ears, so that "his ears stood off". The swellings would come and go quickly; for instance, he would go to school with a swollen thumb, and by tea-time the swelling would have disappeared.

He also was liable to a tight feeling on the chest, and he would cry abnormally easily for a boy of his age. I mention this fact because it is not unlikely that this type of urticaria, with a tendency to formation of oedema and so-called "bladders" under the eyes, is, with the crying, related to repressed fantasies connected with micturition, and to suppressed screaming, of which only the tears remain. He was to some extent conscious of difficulties in relation to hostile impulses, and said to me quite spontaneously: "If I sit in school and think about it, it gets worse, and I can hardly breathe, but if I think of something else it goes." I asked: "What sort of things do you have to try not to think of?" He answered "Oh, nasty things—killing anything; that makes it hard to breathe."

He was admitted to the ward in an attack of oedema of eye-lids and hands, and, as is usual with this type of case, the oedema subsided immediately. No evidence of physical disease could be found to account for the symptom.

2.   *That skin is in infancy an erotogenic zone is well recognized by mothers, who wash and dry their infants each day. Normal babies enjoy the warm bath and the friction. It is not rare for a baby to develop an intense bath phobia at an early age, or a hatred of having certain parts (ears, nates, head, etc.) dried.*

We all retain a potential skin erotism, as for instance when the sight of someone scratching himself makes us itch to scratch too. In certain emotional states we are more sympathetic in this respect than we are in others. The social prohibition of scratching illustrates the universal guilt over skin erotism, and presupposes skin pleasure. Any irritating skin lesion is apt to reactivate our skin erotism, and the following instances may be cited:

(i)   Whatever the cause of chilblains, the main problem is the control of the urge to obtain pleasure by friction of the affected parts. This, the patient knows only too well, must lead to worse discomfort, but the urge is so great that he often fails again and again over a long period. If at the outset he can control this urge to gratification, the chilblains tend to disappear. Sometimes the friction is given unconsciously—for instance, in sleep. Unhappy children may find great solace in chilblains and refuse to be cured.

(ii)   Many children and adults have some area of skin which has been developed into an erotogenic zone of a mild kind, friction of which is frankly pleasurable. The cure often prescribed is to suggest friction of another area instead, whereupon the first area will heal. The diagnosis usually made is pruritus.

A special type of this symptom formation is pruritus ani; this is still treated blindly by physical means, as if it had a physical cause, in spite of the work done on the psychological side, which clearly demonstrates its psychological roots in at least certain cases. In childhood the common anus-scratching is usually a passing symptom, corresponding with the passing phase in which the anal zone is more important than the genital. Parents closely link nose-picking with anal erotism, and put down the whole syndrome to worms. Now it is certain that worms can cause quite severe symptoms in certain children, precisely because by causing anal irritation they stimulate the type of fantasy that goes with anal stimulation, and this brings about an unconscious sense of guilt and a corresponding need for strong repression—which leads to increase in neurotic symptoms and wasteful expenditure of mental energy. Further, the *idea* of producing living worms in their bodies is very difficult for some children to face up to.

(iii)   It is common to find horny patches over the malleoli of children who are otherwise in perfect physical health. These horny patches are produced and kept up by constant kicking, and from this is derived pleasure, as well as some degree of relief of tension from the turning in to oneself of aggression, which in the unconscious is directed towards some person in the environment.

(iv)
Case 7

A boy, aged 5 years, has a shiny, hard area of skin on the back of one finger. This is produced and kept up by constant friction with a tooth. If he leaves off biting it, it goes. He is an intelligent boy but has a restless nature.

His symptoms started when he was 5 to 6 months old, when he started an obsessional swaying masturbation; this lasted right on till he was 4 years old. At times the swaying was violent, so that when he was in a ward for observation at 23 months "the cot used to wander". The breast failed when he was 3 weeks old, but he did well on the bottle. He soon was nervous of noise and of travelling. He was subject to sudden and violent jumps, after one of which he had a fit. Micturition was rather precipitate; sleep was restless and disturbed by periods in which he would sit up and sway.

At 4 years, one of his chief symptoms was demonstrated during a consultation, when he *pinched* his mother's arm to hurt. This symptom appeared when he was broken of *biting* his older brother's arm. At that time the mother told me "he bites his own finger instead of biting you", and she showed me the hardened area on the first finger of the right hand. At 5 years he was complaining of "food sticking in his throat" and of "heat bumps". He disliked the idea of being touched anywhere, declaring, "It hurts me".

Now, at 5½ years, the self-biting continues, and the finger still shows the same evidence of this. Otherwise, he is healthy.

(v)   In infantile eczema the clinical problem is the treatment of the baby's desire to scratch. At this early age, he has no guilt about it and will out-Houdini Houdini in escaping from all attempts to keep his hands away from his face. Moreover, if his hands are not free he will certainly rub his face in the pillow till it weeps and even bleeds. The orthodox treatment of infantile eczema reminds one of the primitive and (let us hope) old-fashioned method of preventing masturbation.

The emotional value of skin can only be mentioned here, though much has been written on this subject. Blushing is clearly connected with the emotions. The value of skin texture and of touch is brought out in the perversions and fetishism, but these things also enrich the daily lives of each one of us. The meaning of skin to the child is very varied and complex.

It would be possible to follow up this line of thought almost indefinitely, and to view skin complaints from the point of view of the medical psychologist, who gives full value to the dynamics of infant and child-feelings. For instance, the connection between the recurring boils of adolescent boys and certain types of fantasy might be explored; and it would be interesting to discuss the tendency of skin infections to become chronic in certain children, even when they are not being kept irritated by picking or repeated knocks (lack of desire for health). But perhaps enough points have been made to establish the importance of giving full value to skin sensation and to the associated reactions, and the futility of viewing any childish skin complaint statically.

Summary

1. Skin is normally an excitable organ.

2. Papular urticaria is an expression of this excitement, an "erection".

3. Excitement, showing in the development of papules, can be brought about by:

   (a) External causes—unsuitable clothing, infestation, etc.

   (b) Internal causes, analogous to the erection of erectile tissue; the hands have a function here, as in genital masturbation. In troublesome cases, these internal causes are themselves complicated in various ways and degrees and may indicate difficulties in regard to anal or genital excitement, and the accompanying unconscious fantasies.

4. When papular urticaria is met with as a distressing disease, the skin has become the site of a battle, analogous to the battle over anal or genital masturbation.

5. Apart from the question of pathogenesis, it is advisable not to neglect the dynamics of the child's feelings in the consideration of any skin complaint.

6. Certain common skin conditions are reviewed in their relation to the child's developing emotional state, and lines along which further observation is needed are suggested.

Much interesting work on the skin has been done in the course of psychoanalysis, and some of this is recorded in psychoanalytic literature. I have purposely, however, avoided psychoanalytic material in this paper, and have used only that material which lies at hand and which every clinician, unless he chooses his cases, must meet.

In this way I have hoped to bring about discussion of a theory which, at any rate, has the merit of simplicity.

21

Short communication on enuresis

[1930]

I t is not my object in this communication to go over the whole ground of that common symptom, enuresis. Neither do I claim to be in a position to explain the mechanism of the symptom formation in all cases. Still less is it intended to put forward some drug or trick of management as a cure, experience having taught me to abandon the search for magical effects. My task is to present one point of view of the symptom.

Medical opinion has so changed in the last five years that when I say that enuresis is nearly always a symptom of psychological origin, I may be uttering a platitude, though till lately the literature has dealt with it as a physical disorder almost exclusively.

Here I must make it clear that conditioned reflexes cannot be included in this context under the term "psychology". There is a tendency in some quarters to say: "Yes, enuresis is a psychological phenomenon; it is simply a question of conditioned reflexes." But the symptom cannot be explained along these lines—that is, apart from the emotional life of the child. It is, of course, likely that on Pavlov's solid foundations will be built complicated theories of behaviour which will help to explain what happens when, for instance, a child feels a sense of guilt. But the fact of the feeling of a sense of guilt will remain, and psychology will remain as a separate science; and in the same way enuresis will remain a problem for the psychologist.

The truth is that my point of view is obvious to anyone who makes for himself opportunity for observation of the working of children's feelings, and yet is necessarily obscure and improbable to anyone whose interests lie in other directions.

A physician who is not specially interested in pathology technique can make use of the Wassermann reaction and learn to interpret the results intelligently. In the same way, one who wishes to avoid analysing emotional factors may derive aids to diagnosis from those who wish to investigate the very problems he avoids.

As an example of such an aid to diagnosis, I would submit the following: in the problem of diagnosis of rheumatic chorea, not obvious from the movements and yet possible, the presence of increased frequency or urgency of micturition is an important point against a diagnosis of chorea; it is, on the other hand, in favour of a diagnosis of fidgetiness of psychological—not physical—illness, an indication for treatment very different from that which must be prescribed for chorea on account of the possibly associated carditis.

This non-choreic, anxious fidgetiness leads to the subject of my title, for the increased sensitiveness of the urinary tract in this type of patient frequently leads to enuresis, especially day incontinence. Children so affected are not always brought to the doctor for the enuresis; they are brought for the fidgetiness, the restlessness, because they will not sit still "even at mealtimes", and for other anxiety symptoms, such as abdominal colics, defaecation, dysuria (chiefly in girls), and so on. The enuresis of the patients that fall into this fairly clearly defined group is really one of the by-products of anxiety. The anxiety is the outward show of a sense of guilt accompanying (unconscious) masturbation fantasies.

Just as frequent is enuresis without obvious anxiety. Enuresis is here chiefly nocturnal, perhaps only also diurnal as an expression of the degree of illness. Children with this type of enuresis are usually brought for the incontinence, or for some other clearly psychological symptom such as nervousness, phobias, and stuttering. These children form an enormous heterogeneous group, but in each case the enuresis is the physical accompaniment of a fantasy (usually an unconscious one) of micturating. It may be said that the child has avoided anxiety by expressing himself or herself in a currency that was normal to him or her as a tiny infant, a pre-genital stage where the sense of guilt was comparatively feeble. Enuresis is here part of a regression, and the fantasies belonging to genital sensation have coloured those belonging to micturating. Associated defaecation disorders, when present in patients with this type of enuresis, take the form of incontinence. Sometimes anaesthesia can be proved. The fidgety and restless child must hurry to defaecate, whereas this type of patient defaecates incontinently because he or she is not conscious of any sensation.

Some find it difficult to believe that all children are well equipped with material for fantasies of micturating. And yet to others it is obvious from what children say and play and dream, and from their symptoms, that it is not abnormal for such fantasies to be plentiful. The main affect is a pleasurable one, derived from the infantile experience of micturition in relation to the mother or nurse. The second affect is an aggressive, often cruel one (represented in the toy water-pistol). These points are illustrated in the following cases:

Case 1

Dennis, a very intelligent only child, now just 5 years old, has been under my treatment since he was 2. The picture at 2 was one of extreme apathy, with complete inability to play or to appear interested in anything. After a little, it became clear that this was the reverse side of a picture of very severe anxiety, the symptoms on this side being chiefly screaming attacks of unusual severity and frequency, attacks in which he perspired very freely, fainted or went quite white, attacks in which he even became unconscious, foaming at the mouth with cyanosis. At times he became maniacal, displaying strength quite unexpected in a child of his age. He was the victim of strong auditory and visual hallucinations.

In the course of treatment he has become able to play, and indeed now displays a very rich imagination in the invention of games which represent every facet of his emotional life. Out of the scores of games, I only wish to pick out those which concern fire and water. At first these games represented general burnings and sousings. These have frequently been accompanied by a frank desire to micturate. With the freeing of his personality in the course of treatment, he has become able to play these games on terms which cannot be mistaken by anyone who has opportunity to observe. On the one hand, there is the game of hurting me, maiming me, or destroying something important in my room by pouring hot water over my head, foot, books, and so on. In this game I have to show I am in great pain. On the other hand is a game in which the infant soils and wets in relation to the mother, who acknowledges the gift by means of mild punishment. This, again, in the abnormally free atmosphere of the consulting-room, is played quite openly and without disguise. Having witnessed these games, I am unable to put down his occasional enuresis to physical causes.

Case 2

Edward aet. 11, eldest of three children (brother 9, sister 4), was referred to me by Dr. Helen Mackay because of convulsive attacks which seemed unlikely to have organic basis. His headmaster wrote of him: "General conduct bad; lazy and cunning; evades certain subjects, e.g. arithmetic; plays with boys younger than himself. Unless he is organically affected I have a very shrewd idea of an effective treatment but such treatment is not approved of in these days." Given opportunity to speak freely at regular stated times he produced certain fantasies. We are only concerned with the following groups.

The idea of a big man (Canera) boxing a small man led to the story of a band of robbers ill-treating the King's daughter, who was rescued by her lover. This led to a description of his craving for ill-treatment, which actually led him to see that he deserved punishment.

Superficially this earning punishment had two roots. On the one hand, he expressed a great love for dumb animals, and a fear lest he should be locked up for cruelty to them. (His father was a policeman; the animals were mixed up with the idea of the two younger children.)

On the other hand, there existed a fantasy which illustrates the reason why enuresis is so common. One of his turns was associated with the upsetting of a vase. Recounting this led to a memory of upsetting the chamber-pot in his bedroom just after his mother had cleaned out the room thoroughly. He then made, quite spontaneously, the remark: "A baby sometimes likes to wet what his mother has spent a long time cleaning and drying." He then made it clear that receiving punishment from his mother now gives him feelings representing those originally belonging to this often experienced fantasy of infancy.

Lest anyone should say, "O well, these are only his words; they have no deep roots in the boy's personality", I will add that for a week after this he wet the bed every night, though till then he had not once wet the bed since he was an infant.

It is interesting to note that now, at a later stage, these two wishes are showing as reaction formations; he is undecided, he says, whether to be a policeman like his father and lock people up for ill-treating animals, or to be a fireman and risk his life saving others (and incidentally have opportunity for pouring water over burning houses, though he forgot to mention this).

Two physical conditions may be mentioned in any communication on enuresis. Firstly, nocturnal epilepsy may be unnoticed except by the wet bed found in the morning. Secondly, infected urinary tract may lead to increased frequency and urgency of micturition, and so to incontinence. In practice, the former is comparatively uncommon, but must be remembered, and the second rarely gives rise to real difficulty. The dysuria, the recent onset of increased urgency without increased nervousness, the feverishness, and, most important of all, the microscopical examination of the urinary deposit, lead to a comparatively easy recognition of cystitis. Apart from these exceptions, the common cause of enuresis is in the child's emotional life.

It will be observed that I have spoken of the child and not of the parent. One cannot speak of the parent without logically criticizing the parent's parent, and so on. If a mother is over-keen to get a clean child and so helps to make the normal infantile feelings about wetting over-strong, she helps to lay down a foundation for future troubles should the small child's emotional development suffer strain at a later stage. But the mother is acting in accordance with her own feelings, and who shall say that she is a better mother if she is turned from overcareful into studiously careless? The baby notes chiefly the parent's unchanging unconscious attitude and will not notice the superficial change.

Enuresis represents an abnormal persistence of a normal stage of emotional currency; in psycho-neurosis micturition can become re-invested with feeling which properly belongs to the genital organization, and is in consequence subject to the inhibitions and compulsions and anaesthesias and excitement of that department. No theory of enuresis can be seriously considered that does not take into account the unconscious fantasy material of the patient. Moreover, no "cure" for enuresis can be accepted that is supported by case histories that do not show an appreciation on the part of the observer of the importance of unconscious suggestion on the part of the doctor.

In this paper I have only scratched on the surface, hoping to produce reactions which will make clear the present-day opinion of the profession on the mechanisms that underlie the symptom enuresis.

22

Child psychiatry:
the body as affected by
psychological factors

[ca. 1931]

I wish in this article to classify the bodily changes and symptoms that belong to normal and abnormal emotional states. This is a very big subject, and a complex one, and it needs to be stated and restated by various paediatricians and psychiatrists, in as many ways as possible. My intention is to approach the problem along the lines of developing psychoanalytic knowledge, or my personal understanding of this.

In order to simplify my statement, I propose to make a somewhat artificial and arbitrary division of psychoanalytic scientific progress into three phases:

1. The understanding of personal instinctual life and of interpersonal relationships.

2. The understanding of moods and of the origin of ideas of persecution both within (hypochondria) and without.

3. The understanding of primitive emotional tasks, such as the development of a relationship to external reality, integration of the personality, and the sense of body.

It will be seen at once that the child's body becomes affected in different ways according to the type of task. If two children are quarrelling over a toy gun, the main thing is that each child becomes excited, or angry or frightened: possibly one of them gets a cut or a bang, and then this has to be added.

A child who is depressed has ideas that there are bad things going on inside him, or that he is empty; his fantasy of his body is indirectly affected by this. Lastly, a child who is only just able, at times, to feel he and his body are one, such a child is very much concerned with anything that increases his sense of body, and may even get value out of scabies and skin irritation on this account.

Our first concern in the study of the child along these lines is to understand and describe the psychology of the emotions. A great deal of work could be quoted, but it will perhaps be allowed that there is still room for research on what happens in the body when a child (at various ages) is excited about food, is excited about passing a motion, or passing water, is excited aggressively, is in a state of rage, is afraid of a specific thing, is mildly anxious over a long period of time, and so on.

In each case we want to know about actual instinctual experience, and about the effect of continued excitement without climax, and also the effect on the body of a specific inhibition of an instinctual process. Further, we have to study the effect of a conflict or superimposition of orgies, or of types of excitement, as for instance when a child's excretory process is affected when only half completed by fear of an approaching parent, or perhaps of an idea that has occurred to the child while in the act.

For instance, three children run to school. One runs because he is eager to get there. On arrival he wants to get started quickly, or at any rate to see and greet, and be greeted by the teacher. The second runs because he is late. His mother was late getting his breakfast because the baby had an accident. His aim is to get there in time. The third runs because he feels pursued. His life is dominated by imaginary persecutors. His aim is to get into school, and to some protection from his enemies. He may want to sleep when he gets to school, or if there is no rest for him he must create real persecutors out of the other children or out of the teachers, to gain relief from the unknown.

It will easily be understood that the physiology of these three children on their arrival at school would be found to be of three varieties, had we the delicate instruments to give us exact knowledge. The first would be unlikely to have bodily symptoms; the second would probably be tired and would recover in a half an hour, or perhaps he would faint, or be sick and then recover. The third, the persecuted boy, who would not be robust anyway, and would not be a good feeder, would be liable to complain of internal aches and pains, or of almost anything.

This is only one of the myriad of possible examples to illustrate the way that one activity (in this case a boy running) can have various results according to the emotional state of the child at the time.

One of the most pure emotional states for study is that of the infant in all-out-rage. For a time nothing else counts. In such a state (under 1 year) the heart rate is 220 per minute! At later ages, the memory of rage can be painful and can cause heart disturbance with distress.

23

On cardiac neurosis in children

[1966]

This is a congress of specialists in physical health and in the physical disorders of the heart, notably congenital heart disease. For this the first session you are considering the child in his or her family or other environmental provision, and I am very happy to be taking part just here where there is an integration between the two aspects of paediatrics.

Diseases are things, and there must always be those who like to work with things just as there always will be those who like to be in contact with persons. Some of us are of one kind; some of us are of the other. The children who are our patients do indeed need the two kinds of us to get on well with each other, even though sometimes it is part of their illness to try to make us quarrel.

You will forgive me for the fact that I have not been involved on the physical side in paediatrics for some 25 years. I can claim that from 1920 up to the time of the war I was taking full medical responsibility for cases. Also, as physician at a hospital in the East End of London I was in charge of an L.C.C. Rheumatism Clinic, in which was provided a diagnostic and observation service and which dealt with a large number of cases. This contribution will be based mainly on my experience in this clinic.[1]

---

[1] Annual Report of the London County Council, Senior Medical Officer, Vol. 111, 1928. British Paediatric Association Annual Meeting, Malvern, 1931.

There are various ways in which the student of human growth and development, or the dynamic psychologist, or the child psychiatrist (or whatever you like to call him) may become involved along with the paediatrician who is concerned with children's hearts. The most vital problems, I think, cluster around the prevention, diagnosis, treatment, and aftercare of the rheumatic groups of diseases which carry risk of carditis.

I project myself back into the past, when in London between 1920 and 1940 the rheumatic diseases were rampant and when we were very much concerned with the idea of early diagnosis. Early diagnosis was our only hope in the attempt to prevent what amounted at the time to a scourge: rheumatic heart disease with its immediate threat because of myocarditis and the after-effects (chiefly mitral stenosis and subsequently auricular fibrillation). I am not sure where if anywhere in Europe rheumatic fever is rampant just now. In those two decades, we were still grappling with a common disorder, the one that had confronted Goodhart, Henoch, Cheadle, and Still. Poynton and Robert Hutchison were in process of handing over to Bernard Slesinger and others whom you know in person or by name, and to Bonham-Carter, who is here in this Congress.

As is well known, the rheumatic diseases ceased to be common in the mid-1930s, and no-one has explained this detail of the natural history of a disease which is not (I believe) any better understood now than it was in the days of Hutchison and Poynton in 1920. For this reason, the disease remains a perfect playground for the two kinds of physician, those physically and those psychologically minded. It is necessary to remind oneself how common the disease was, because how else could one explain the extreme measures that were being taken in the early 1920s to diagnose the disease in its earliest stages?[2]

Hutchison had said that we must treat pains in children as evidence of a pre-rheumatic condition, and there followed a phase in clinical practice in which a large number of children were being kept in bed or forbidden to play about, although they were in fact *not* rheumatic.

_____

[2]See Robert Hutchison, *Lectures on Diseases of Children* (London: Arnold, 1904; seventh edition, 1936).

In my L.C.C. Rheumatism Supervisory Clinic, I had opportunity to watch many hundreds of cases, making an initial diagnosis, and making use of an excellent follow-up service. The efficiency of this follow-up service enabled me to take risks. In those days it was terrible to miss an early rheumatic case. There was unusual scope for observation in this clinic, and I can illustrate this by giving the following detail. In one year—perhaps 1932—I was suddenly inundated in the October month by fifty new chorea cases, some new, some recurrences.[3] In this way I was able to recognize a seasonal variation in the incidence of chorea—and this contrasted with the absence of seasonal variation in regard to the other varieties of fidgetiness. In fact, when chorea later became a rare disease, the other types of restlessness remained, as they will always do because they are part of childhood.

The absence then (as now) of clinical tests giving a specific information in regard to rheumatism and chorea threw clinicians back on their clinical sense, and this was good for us. The clinical sense, I would remind you, is not guesswork—it is something that one gradually acquires with experience, and it is based on:

1. very careful history-taking, and
2. the enjoyment of the direct examination of children's bodies.

1. *History-taking*

It is in history-taking that psychoanalysis has a real contribution to make to paediatrics, and indeed to medical practice in general. It is true, I believe, that many acknowledged specialists on the physical side simply do not know how to take a history. In some departments the history is even taken by a junior, who is perhaps required to tick off innumerable items in such a way that the answers can be fed into a computer.

---

[3]Nowadays it would be easy to find a paediatrician who has not yet seen fifty cases of chorea, perhaps not even ten. *D.W.W.*

Whatever is said or felt about psychoanalysis, one thing that it undoubtedly teaches is that no history can be taken by a question-and-answer method. In fact, no picture of the natural history of a disease can be gained except by a time-consuming method whereby the parent or the child or both can gradually display the evolution of the pattern of the organization of the personality in defence against various types of anxiety. This is a vast subject. My meaning can only be made clear on a background of a working theory of the emotional development of the individual in the environment that obtains. I cannot hope to give a satisfactory version of the emotional development of the human being here and now, because this must not be attempted unless time is allowed for proper exposition. For practical purposes, however, it can be said that a history can be taken in an interview or a series of interviews with parents. The parents have always known the child, and they are in their own way specialists in this field. Also, with skill and practice, one may learn from a child patient (2½ years onward) what is needed for an assessment of normality or illness in the personality, and a measure of the child's emotional growth.

Psychoanalysis is in fact a prolonged history-taking, and it is the psychoanalyst who today can best contribute to the study of the natural history of diseases.

It must be conceded that many of the world's famous physicians have been bad at history-taking, and that this is a state of affairs that will continue. Where there are clear diagnostic tests, the absence of a good history matters less, especially when disease is found and a line of treatment is clearly indicated. However, if the tests reveal no disease the laboratory-minded doctor is usually at a loss, because he does not know what to do about the symptoms; he has not been informed as to the symptoms of the healthy.

I would say that many doctors are unable to provide the type of setting in which a clear history of the case can emerge. To get a clear history

a. a doctor must enjoy this part of his work, so that he has the *patience* to listen;

b.   he must be free from preconceived notions, because the parents' irrational *fear* of the doctor makes them (temporarily)
trust him, and makes them want to please him, so that if
possible they give him what they think he is expecting;

c.   he must be free from moralistic attitude: whatever his own
moral code he must be free to meet the moral code of the
clients as he would accept the colour of their hair—in this he
must be like a trained social worker;

d.   he must be able to meet distress without immediate reactions,
like giving money or advice or some drug (this is, in fact, a
matter of self-defence);

e.   he must be able to recognize the ill parent, especially the
mother who is a kind of depressive with a need to have the
child as an object of her own hypochondriacal worry.

Perhaps it is a good thing when busy and preoccupied doctors leave history-taking to the psychiatric social worker. May I
make a suggestion, that the specialist doctor should "sit in" (un-
obtrusively) on the psychiatric social worker interview, without
taking part, and so at least have the experience of the slow evolution of the description of the family pattern and of the
individual child's personality growth and stunting.

The fact is that these cases need unity in the medical service,
because in no other way can the totality of the child or the family
be met and assessed. It is a sad result of the advances in modern
medicine that there is no personal clash between patient and
doctor as whole persons; there is a visit to the doctor, a disease
process is found, treatment is given, and the disease is cured, but
no-one has met anyone, no one person has bumped into another
person.

2. Then, the physical examination

It often happens that the doctor has not even examined the patient's body, and in this way he has deprived himself of one of
the proper incentives to medical care. The physical examination

of all patients provides the doctor with the other root of his clinical sense which must be there if he is to become an experienced clinician.

I wish now to make a brief reference to my work in the clinic that I have mentioned, the L.C.C. Rheumatism Clinic, based on the School Medical Service.

In this clinic that I had in London, I soon learned to put patients into one of five categories, and I put the notes in coloured folders so as to make sure that mistakes in diagnosis would become evident.

Orange. Past or present rheumatic carditis already evident and beyond doubt.

Pink. Probable rheumatic disease but no definite carditis found.

Blue. Other illnesses: congenital heart malformation, etc.

Grey. Chorea witnessed in acute attack, not (on first examination) showing evidence of past or present carditis.

Green. Cases in which diagnosis was definitely
NON-rheumatic
NON-choreic.
In these cases I recommended no restriction of activity, and I made an attempt to give an alternative diagnosis.

It happened that about 50 percent of the cases had green folders (non-rheumatic). Very seldom indeed did the folder need to be changed from green to orange (rheumatic heart disease). This meant that in the case of half the children the parents could be told immediately by me: "Your child is not an ill child and is not liable to heart disease." On this basis it was often possible to offer some help, if it was needed, in the management of the child's difficulties. All these children, therefore, were free to live a full life, and their parents were not under constant strain. It must be remembered that all these children had symptoms, such as pains, that had set some observer (doctor, teacher, parent) wondering. This was the diagnosis in one half of the children referred to the clinic as rheumatic or choreic.

I draw attention to the fact that: "*The diagnosis was made not on the basis of negative tests (there not being any) but on the basis of positive findings in the field of history-taking supplemented by physical examination.*"

Naturally I took a risk in each case, but I was able to take this risk because of the excellent follow-up system that was provided.

At this point it would be good if I could find some way of giving proof of the feasibility of this procedure, but at best I can illustrate what I mean. I must simply state that the folders (shown by their colours) remained accurately descriptive of the cases.

Because of the blitz, and because of the disappearance of the rheumatic scourge in London, the work never got transformed into a statistical statement; but for the purposes of this paper I made a sample study, and I find I can report that the method justified itself.

As a result of this work, it was possible for one to see that in the vast majority of patients with true rheumatic disease, carrying liability to carditis, there was an onset of illness, and at some time or other definite joint involvement, probably flitting from one joint to another, and joint swelling and heat and pain. In other words, in the search for early cases we were *not* well served by using terms like "pre-rheumatic", and we gave them up since this meant putting to bed many children who ought to be up and about.

Also, in chorea there was very seldom a real difficulty. At onset there was a coincidence of weakness and movements in the two limbs of one side, with lability of mood. By the time the examination was made there was usually an obvious generalized choreic state, which it is not necessary for me to redescribe here.

The main conclusion to be drawn from these observations was a general one, affecting the attitude of doctors towards disease. It was found that once a doctor had come to suspect a pre-rheumatic or pre-choreic state, then he would be liable to gather in all manner of other symptoms and signs, especially heart murmurs, overacting heart and frequent heart beat, and premature contractions, and dropped beats, none of which has anything to do with rheumatic carditis.

It is here that it is possible to carry over what I observed to the subject of congenital heart disease.*

Illustration

In an illustration I give one case, that of a girl who had been diagnosed rheumatic on account of pains, and who had been kept in bed by a doctor who found heart disease. I well remember the day I wrote this colleague saying that this diagnosis was wrong and that I had prescribed full activity for the girl.

Briefly, my carefully elicited history had showed that this girl had always had nervousness about herself, and every symptom was exaggerated because of a similar condition in the mother. The father had played but little part, except that he begat her and her little brother.

This girl was highly talented and was clinically a delightful person to meet. She gathered herself together and presented herself in an eager and interesting way, so that everyone liked her, and when she was in the hospital ward she was always Queen of the Ward. She was a true daughter of an actress mother, and at an early age she started herself on a career as a dancer. She was also talented in drawing and painting, and she had a beautiful voice for singing.

When not performing, that is when not engaged in bewitching a friend or a nurse or a doctor, or another child, she was depressed and full of fears about herself, or sleepless because of anxiety dreams. She had pains waiting everywhere for attention, and she undoubtedly suffered greatly from these as well as from persecutory ideas.

She was at her best when performing and when in full activity.

---

* Later speakers referred to the way that once the public has been alerted to the matter of congenital heart disease, there appear in the clinics cases in which the parents are worried about heart disease, and the stage is set for a form of cardiac neurosis. D.W.W.

Naturally, on examination she was found to have an over-acting heart, either thumping away in excitement or else rapidly ticking over in shallow beats, with liability to showers of premature contractions in phases, or else in association with dropped beats.

The fact was that I could account for everything on the basis of a psychiatric disorder, dating from early childhood, and I, *acting on this*, diagnosed her as *non-rheumatic*. This meant that she returned to the ballet class, and that she resumed her preparation for life on the stage. Naturally, I took great trouble making repeated examinations in case I had been in error.

It will be observed that, here, a paediatrician had made positive psychiatric diagnosis the basis for a negative diagnosis on the physical side.

From anxiety, as well as from an affectionate feeling for the girl and her family, I followed her fortunes. I saw her in every kind of dance, and heard her act and sing; in short, I watched her succeed, and also fail as she was doomed to do. By being fixated to her mother who was similarly affected, she missed the climax of every new achievement—indeed, at all critical moments in her career her mother became ill, and the girl would always drop everything and nurse her mother; after a time, no-one would employ her because of her mother's claim on her.

Her own depressive anxieties continued to drive her on and to persecute her. I saw her through unwholesome love affairs with actor-managers and dance leaders, through various abortions and anxieties about venereal disease. There was a suicidal attempt, and eventually she married with theatrical flourish but without love, having found an older man who was well-off and who could afford this mother-in-law. Psychosomatic disorders followed, associated with her sexual inhibitions. When her mother died she became clinically depressed. At length she turned into a grand invalid. She seemed not deeply affected by her husband's death, and the last I saw of her was at a time when she was gripping on to her brother who in turn was becoming a psychosomatic case.

Both were living on the theatrical fringe, always in hope of a job tomorrow, but steadily using up the money mercifully bequeathed by the girl's husband.

In this case the follow-up took three decades, and it fully confirmed the original non-rheumatic diagnosis both in its positive psychiatric aspect and in its negative aspect relative to rheumatism and heart disease. One case proves nothing but can perhaps be used in illustration of an idea.

Summary

The essential element in my communication is that psychiatry gives a definite and positive diagnostic contribution, and when the symptomatology can be accounted for in terms of personality disorder, then the doctor should be able to be definite in saying: "This child is not a rheumatic or choreic subject, and there is no need for special care on account of a liability to heart disease." Careful follow-up can deal with those cases in which there is an overlap simply because personality disorder is ubiquitous and common, and where rheumatic disease is also common then there must be children with both disorders.

Final note

I have not tried to make positive statements about either rheumatic illness or chorea, because I have described all I know in this field in my book, *Clinical Notes on Disorders of Childhood* (1931). See also my paper, "The Psychology of Juvenile Rheumatism", in Ronald G. Gordon (Ed.), *A Survey of Child Psychiatry* (London: Oxford University Press, 1939).

Part eight

AUTISM
AND SCHIZOPHRENIA

24

Three reviews
of books on autism

[1938, 1963, 1966]

Child Psychiatry, by Leo Kanner (London: Bailliere, Tindall and Cox, 1937).

This textbook, which has Prefaces by Dr. Adolf Meyer and Dr. Edwards A. Park, is built on a comprehensive scale and has at present no rival. It is the natural product of the organization at the Johns Hopkins Hospital of the opportunity for cooperation between paediatrics and psychiatry, and colossal indeed must be the clinic of which Dr. Kanner is the head. The amount of work implied in the case material is enough to take away the breath of anyone actively engaged in such work and familiar with its time-eating quality.

Moreover, the type of the case material given is indicative of satisfactory contact between social worker and patient, the latter being always reckoned as a human being with a body, an intellect, and feelings.

An attempt is made to embrace the whole of child psychiatry, and the result is a certain tedium which is perhaps inevitable in so ambitious a work.

In Part I, after a statement of basic principles, a hundred pages is given to examination and diagnosis. Following this is a

191

chapter on therapeutics. This is the least satisfactory part of the book, and gives the reader warning that he must not expect to find in subsequent pages much that is of value to the scientific psychologist.

Part II is in three sections. The first (fifty pages) is headed, "Personality Difficulties Forming Essential Features or Sequels of Physical Illness", and is divided into Anergastic Reaction Forms (brain malformations, mongolism, encephalitis, juvenile paresis, cerebral trauma, etc.), Dysergastic Reaction Forms (delirium, hallucinosis, stupor, coma), Sydenham's Chorea, and the Endocrinopathies.

The second section (seventy pages) is headed, "Personality Difficulties Expressing Themselves in the Form of Involuntary Part-dysfunction", the chapters dealing with the different systems, central nervous, digestive, circulatory, and so on.

The third section (240 pages) is headed, "Personality Difficulties Expressing Themselves Clearly as Whole-dysfunctions of the Individual". Its thirteen chapters deal with all the remaining symptom types, intellectual inadequacy, emotional disorders (jealousy, tempers, fear), thinking difficulties, speech disorders, faulty feeding habits, and so on, including at the end a chapter on children's suicides.

This classification is interesting and is faithfully worked out, but it somehow fails to convince. It necessitates much overlapping, and it is artificial. It pays little tribute to the ordinary psychiatric diagnostic groupings, and fails to point out or to account for the normality of so many of childhood's symptoms.

In fact, it is necessary to make it clear that, in spite of the great amount of work put into it, the book is entirely without originality to the psychologist. And a more serious criticism (since textbooks are seldom original) is that the author is quite out of touch with the psychology of the unconscious, and with psychoanalysis and the results of child analysis as practised and published in England. A good textbook of child psychiatry cannot be compiled today by one who is unfamiliar with the meaning of psychoanalysis. It is unbelievable that a textbook coming from the distinguished Johns Hopkins Hospital should show such lack of knowledge of relevant literature, and it can safely be said that a textbook on physical medicine with a comparable deficiency could not have come from this source.

Actually, if the author believes in the unconscious he does not make this clear. In a rare mention of the word "unconscious" he shows that he thinks that by this word is meant little more than a lodging-house for repressed sexual desires (p. 7). The idea of important unconscious fantasy and of the child's identification of the unconscious with the inside of the body, and such a conception as that of unconscious guilt, these and their like seem to be foreign to him.

In place of an understanding of the psychology of the unconscious, there is to be found throughout the book the usual over-stressing of what might be called "the continuing bad external factor", such as characterizes the publications of all child guidance clinics of American pattern.

Childhood Schizophrenia, by William Goldfarb (Cambridge, MA: Harvard University Press, 1961).

Childhood Schizophrenia is a term that is gradually evolving its own usefulness. The clinical states included under this term are not new, nor are they on the increase, but a recognition of these states is reaching a widening circle of workers in the field of child health. The term autism (Kanner) had value and perhaps disadvantages. The value was that it gave the idea of a nicely defined illness, and this recommended it to paediatricians, who are used to thinking in terms of physical illnesses. But in psychiatry this idea of clear-cut illness is always erroneous, for every condition of psychiatric ill health merges in with deviations that belong to normal development. The details of the illness, childhood schizophrenia, do in fact spread out and around, and can be found in the description of any normal child. In other words, the observer is concerned primarily with the emotional development of the individual, and secondarily with deviations from the normal in such development. Thirdly, the observer is concerned with certain quantitative factors that necessitate a diagnosis of illness. Lastly, the observer is concerned with the physical abnormality that, in certain cases, underlies the disorder of emotional development. These physical abnormalities may be present without producing childhood schizophrenia, and childhood schizophrenia may develop (and usually in fact does) as a purely psychological disorder in children who may be presumed to be physically normal and healthy.

These theoretical complexities are stated in this excellent account of a very well organized investigation. The research is being done at the Henry Ittleson Centre, New York City, and a good feature is that the research team works in with those who are involved therapeutically with the children in the group. The research design is excellent and includes observation of carefully matched controls. Statistically significant results are obtained which confirm much that is known in a more loose way through observations in the course of clinical practice. What emerges from this study is that the diagnosis of childhood schizophrenia, hitherto a clinician's guess, is now becoming amenable to planned observation. Certainly this is already true of the differential diagnosis between organic and non-organic childhood schizophrenia.

Nearly the whole range of childhood schizophrenia as the reviewer knows it is covered in this monograph. What is inadequately stated is the theory of early emotional development of the infant, with the precise manner in which physical disability (for instance, a birth injury to the brain) may interfere with the ways in which the infant and the environment interact and mutually contribute in the establishment of healthy development. However, this subject is approached in an interesting reference to "parental perplexity", a name used in description of the distortions of parental attitudes induced by infancy and childhood abnormalities. This parental perplexity spreads to the staff of the therapeutic group and affects their ability to tolerate the children's illness. Abnormalities in parents can be aetiological factors in a case of childhood schizophrenia, but it is also true that organic or non-organic schizophrenia in a child tends to produce parental perplexity and even gross parental disturbance or family disruption. This book is recommended as a clear guide to this complex subject, although it is written as a report on a research project.

Infantile Autism, by Bernard Rimland (New York: Appleton-Century-Crofts, 1964).

Dr. Rimland offers a comprehensive study of infantile autism, and his book needs to be taken seriously. The approach to the subject is carefully constructed. The various theories are given full attention. Of the literature nothing has been deliberately set aside, and in Part 3 Dr. Rimland attempts to round off the subject by stating his personal opinion and by developing a theory of autism which he claims has implications for a total theory of behaviour. I come to this subject with a certain prejudice, and it is this prejudice that Rimland disagrees with. I came to Kanner's statement of autism with a considerable experience of childhood psychosis, and I have never seen a clear reason why this group should be theoretically cut off from the total subject of schizophrenia of infancy and childhood. Undoubtedly the clear-cut designation "autism" had a value for teaching purposes. Here was something that could be given to the paediatrician comparable to the diseases of the body with which paediatricians are familiar. It was possible to teach students about autism without involving them in a theory of the emotional development of the human being in the same way as it is possible to teach acute nephritis apart from a theory of the evolution in phylogeny and ontogeny of the kidney. There are many workers in the field of child psychiatry who fully support the opinion of Rimland that here too is a disease syndrome, and that, although in more than half the cases no physical dysfunction can be discovered by present methods of investigation, the prediction is that the tools of investigation are not sensitive enough and that in the course of time the whole syndrome will become explained on the basis of a physical dysfunction. All one can do at this point is to put up the claim that a decision on this matter has not been reached. Certainly it is necessary that while methods of examining the physical functions are being refined, other workers in the field should be studying in minutest detail the earliest stages of the establishment of the personality. The arguments for and against are well set out in this book, except that in my opinion Dr. Rimland does not show himself to be fully up to date in regard to the study of the earliest stages of integration of the personality when dependence is near-absolute. It would be possible to stop here and leave the reader to use this book as an important statement of the problem. I feel, however, that it is justifiable to suggest that the last section of the book develops into a system of thought, and that this system of thought has as its basis the area of the author's ignorance of these very matters which have importance in the study of this subject—namely, the theory of early development which leads to the observation that the mental health of the individual (referring to the positive of which schizophrenia is the negative) is being laid down at the beginning by the mother simply through her total care of her child. The author of the book might legitimately throw this back at me and say that my theory in its turn is a system of thought; in other words, this very important matter is still *sub judice*.

I think it is of interest that the extensively planned diagnostic check-list, with seventy-six items, does not contain the question that could produce the significant answer. But such is the way with questionnaires which cannot do more than test the bright ideas of those who are capable of being creative.

25

Autism

[1966]

I t is important for me to be invited to speak to this Society which gives special consideration to autism. Your special-ised interest in this subject must give you certain areas in which you are expert. My own interest in the subject is perhaps more diffuse because as a practising child psychiatrist I have needed to keep my range of interest extended over the whole field of infant and child development and of the distortions of development that are either psychogenic or else secondary to various kinds of physical disorder. My hope is that you will be able to use what I have to contribute in this way to help you with the very real personal problems which belong specifically to your own subject.

I realise that in every case of autism you are concerned not only with a child who is struggling with personal problems of development but also with parents, parents who are disap-pointed because their child is not as rewarding as a normal child would be, and parents who feel guilty, as all parents do quite apart from logic when something goes wrong. I shall have some-thing special to say about this sense of guilt to which parents of autistic children are liable, and I shall want to deal with this because I feel that this phenomenon interferes with our objective examination of the aetiology of the disorder. It need not interfere, but there are reasons why such interference can be a fact. For the time being I will leave this aside, and I will have a look at what is for you the all too familiar picture of the autistic child.

As I have been engaged in the practice of child psychiatry now for nearly half a century, I can look back and compare the present with the past. I would like you to know that the picture which is now called autism was clearly recognizable as early as I can remember doing this kind of work. There is no evidence from my point of view, seeing large numbers of children of all kinds, that there is an increase in the number of autistic children or that there is anything new whatever except in regard to the name and, an important thing, the determination of groups of people to look into the matter and to see how far autism can be prevented and to what extent it can be treated. From my point of view the invention of the term autism was a mixed blessing. The advantages are fairly obvious. The disadvantages are less obvious. I would like to say that once this term had been invented and applied, the stage was set for something which is slightly false, i.e. the discovery of a disease. Paediatricians and physically-minded doctors as a whole like to think in terms of diseases which give a tidy look to the textbooks. It is easy to teach medical students about meningitis of various kinds and about mental defect and appendicitis and rheumatic fever. The student can be taught on the very firm basis of anatomy and physiology. The medical student can make concise notes and can learn about theories of aetiology, symptomatology, and treatment, and the examiner has a nice question always ready with the word autism certainly understood by any students who have done their homework. The unfortunate thing is that in matters psychological things are not like that. To start with, it is not so easy to teach medical students the theory of the emotional development of the individual infant and child as it is to teach anatomy and physiology; and even if it were easy, there is still the matter that there are few teachers with the requisite knowledge that this part of science is far from clear in certain aspects and that the students, each one of them, will have certain resistances to simple learning according to their own experiences. The fact that each student has been an infant and a child is of much more significance when it is psychology that is being taught than when anatomy and physiology are the subjects in the curriculum.

Great advances have been made in this century in the establishment of a body of practical theory of emotional development and of the long and complicated story of dependence on the environment gradually turning into independence of the environment. Without waiting for full agreement amongst dynamic psychologists, which perhaps will never be reached, we can work on the basis of what we agree that we know. When we look at the subject under discussion from this point of view, we see that it is very artificial to talk of an illness called autism. It is this point that I am trying to make in this lecture because I feel that you may be able to get something from me if I concentrate on this aspect of the vast problem. What I wish to say is that for someone who is involved as I have been over the decades with the minute details of the mother's story of herself and her infant, one finds every degree of the organization of a symptomatology which when fully organized and established can be given the label autism. For every case of autism that I have met in my practice, I have met scores or hundreds of cases in which there was a tendency which recovered but which might have produced the autistic picture.

If I am right in this contention then there are certain corollaries, one of which is that the best way to study the aetiology of autism is to study these numerous cases in which one can see the tint and the hue of autism, and where one can account to some extent or perhaps very fully for the onset of the symptomatology as well as for the recovery of the child. It is rather like the subject of anti-social behaviour, which is best studied in respect of the anti-social tendency that manifests in your own rather normal child: it is not very profitable to study this social illness by taking the child who has already become labelled maladjusted or criminal. In any case, in each criminal there was a beginning to the distortion of the individual's socialization process, and it is this that would be rewarding to the investigator.

I now want to make an attempt to look at some of the cases that have come into my practice, in order to illustrate what I am saying. Curiously enough my difficulty is that I am immediately presented in my mind with so many cases that I feel confused. The subject quite quickly becomes one not of autism and not of the early roots of disorder that might have developed into autism, but rather one of the whole story of human emotional development and the relationship of the maturational process in the individual child to the environmental provision which may or may not in any one particular case facilitate the maturational process.

I must interrupt myself at this point in order to make one thing clear. I am perfectly aware that in a proportion of cases where autism is eventually diagnosed, there has been injury or some degenerative process affecting the child's brain. This of course affects the mind and the emotional climate. If the computer is damaged then the use of the computer is unreliable. I suggest that the fact that brain damage can be proved in a certain number of these cases does not affect the issue as I am trying to examine it here. It is extremely likely that in the majority of cases of autism the computer is undamaged and the child is potentially and remains potentially intelligent. The illness is not like that of oligophrenia, where no development can be expected and the symptoms of mental defect depend directly on the poverty of the apparatus. The illness is a disturbance of emotional development and a disturbance that reaches back so far that in some respects at least the child is defective intellectually. In some respects the child may show evidence of brilliance.

I am hoping that what follows may strengthen the argument that the problem in autism is fundamentally one of emotional development and that autism is not a disease. It might be asked, what did I call these cases before the word autism turned up? The answer is that I thought of these cases, and I still think of them, under the heading "infant or childhood schizophrenia". From my point of view this is a better term, if a term has to be used for the purposes of classification. When we are actually examining the problem, we can throw classification to the winds and look at cases and examine details under the microscope as it were.

I will now choose a few cases for presentation. First I will refer to a boy, Ronald.

When I first saw Ronald at the age of 8, he had very exceptional skill in drawing. He was not only an accurate observer but an artist. He drew compulsively all the time that he was awake, and chiefly his drawings were of botanical subjects. His interest covered the whole life history of plant development. Later he turned his attention to animal development, and with help he has become interested in a wide range of phenomena. Apart from drawing he was, however, a typical autistic child. His difficulties dominated the scene at home where two smaller children suffered severely because they were eclipsed, and it was difficult to find a school that could tolerate his need for omnipotent control of every situation all the time.

I will look and see how things developed. The mother herself was an artist, and she found being a mother exasperating from one point of view in that although she was fond of her children and her marriage was a happy one, she could never completely lose herself in her studio in the way that she must do in order to achieve results as an artist. This was what this boy had to compete with when he was born. He competed successfully but at some cost.

The early history of this boy was as follows: The mother thinks of the pregnancy as bad. There was marginal placenta praevia. The birth took place in an underdeveloped country in which an aged doctor with no help had a very big difficulty in bringing the parturition to a satisfactory conclusion. In doing so he broke the mother's coccyx. It is not even certain what kind of presentation the doctor had to cope with, probably a face presentation, and there was a queer shape to the face even at 2 months.

Leading up to the birth the mother had had a lot of sickness. At three weeks after the birth the mother got jaundice, which ended breast-feeding. At two months the mother remembers smacking the baby in exasperation although not conscious of hating him. From the start he was slow in development. He lifted his head up late. There was a nanny at this time who dominated the scene. He sat at 10 months and walked at 22 months. His words were late, and at 2 he had but few words. At 4, he gradually started to talk. There was some weakness of the lower limbs so that he wore special boots, and the mother was told that his muscles were weak. His muscle tone has remained poor. He keeps all his clothes on whatever the weather, and this is part of the whole picture of his abnormal relationship to external reality. The picture here is of a child who was affected physically by the birth process but not necessarily in respect of his brain, though there may have been anoxaemia. His slowness made him fail to awaken the mother's interest in him, which in any case was a difficult task because of her unwillingness to be diverted from her main concern which is painting.

It would be quite easy to expect intellectual limitation in such a child, but the difficulty is that in one respect he always showed a capacity beyond that of his age. This had to do with his adoration of flowers and his drawings of botanical subjects and his early reading of flower books. As can be predicted in such a case, arithmetic meant nothing to him at all, in spite of the fact that his accuracy in regard to the numbers of petals and other details was absolute. There are interesting details here: his interest in flowers started with a preoccupation with balloons dating from 18 months. There was a history to this in that he spent his infancy lying watching his favourite rattle, which was made of three or four tiny coloured balls. At a very early age he had a preoccupation with colour, and as soon as he started to paint he knew about colour mixtures. At a very early age he knew that yellow and black make khaki and that blue and green make peacock. It is easy to see that his mother can have given him opportunity for making these discoveries, but the management of her other children makes her feel that it was this boy himself who because of some inner drive and some innate capacity specialized in this direction. An example would be that he was taken to the circus. At the circus he did not see the elephants but he said: "Look"—and pointed out that something was rust red and not scarlet. He did have concern in the lion act because he disliked watching a man controlling an animal.

Very early he had an intolerance of being in the wrong, and indeed his illness controlled the whole home to the detriment eventually of the younger children. When he got cross he was so upset that everyone quite naturally avoided producing this degree of distress. The parents had to be firm quickly to forestall frustrating him and to avoid the inevitable scene in which the boy was obviously in a state of intense mental suffering.

This boy was affectionate with his mother but not with his father. The parents, who are quite able to cope with the ordinary problems of child management, have been perplexed by this special problem of the management of their child, who in fact is rather typically autistic. This could be taken as a good example of the difficulty that faces anyone who studies the aetiology in a case of autism. No-one can sort out with certainty the various factors which do show in this case:

1. The mother had a very special interest of her own and her first child needed to compete with her painting. When the pregnancy and the birth and then the child disappointed her and failed to arouse her maternal concern, she was not only puzzled but she also could not avoid resenting the fact that he was this challenge to her career as an artist. Soon the father joined in being puzzled and disappointed.

2. The disturbance around the birth may or may not have affected the child and perhaps did affect the brain. Nevertheless the result was not mental defect but patchy intelligence, and specialized emotional preoccupation.

3. The failure of the early infant–mother relationship resulted in a state of affairs in which it can be said that the parents had to

be all the time thinking out what to do instead of knowing it in their bones.

It happens that these parents have thought it out a great deal. They have had two normal children who have made them realize that they could have been normal parents to the first child if he had awakened the proper responses in them. This makes them feel less guilty and less ashamed. They have also been able to arrange for a specialized education of this boy who will either be a genius in his own line or else simply a person who is boring because of having a one-track mind. The trouble is that he always strikes people as much more interesting than a normal child, but you can well understand that these parents would give anything to have a less interesting child who could be lost in the crowd. He is now 15, and it looks as if he might come through to being someone who can earn a living. But the parents will be lucky if he does actually achieve emotional independence.

The words "one-track mind" will ring a bell for anyone who has had care of these children. As I think back over the cases that I have come across, I think of a specialist in old tin-cans, a boy who filled the back-yard with precious tins which he accurately classified, and he put everything into this specialization which someone else might put into stamp collecting.

I think of a boy whose full intelligence only showed in regard to his knowledge of what used to be called Bradshaw.[1] In other respects he was somewhat restricted intellectually. He was a borderline case in that eventually he became able to make a living out of knowing all that was to be known about the running of every train in the United Kingdom. His skill was such that his colleagues put up with his awkward temperament in order to have amongst themselves a living and always up-to-date railway timetable. There is no need for me to continue in this vein because the fact of these specialities is well-known and there seems to me to be no sharp line between the speciality that cannot be socialized and the one which makes a man or woman famous. There can be no essential difference in quality between the normal and the abnormal here; all one can say is that in the autistic

---

[1] A comprehensive train timetable guide.

child the specialization is boring in that it is like rocking and head-banging, a compulsive activity that at its worst seems to be devoid of fantasy.

Another example is a man of restricted personality whom I first saw when he was 8. This boy eventually became a specialist in traffic signals in the London streets, and he made a classification of these with such accuracy that everyone was astounded. The only trouble was that this was a useless ploy.

The story of this boy was something like this. His birth was considered to be a perfectly normal one although he was a big baby, nine and a half pounds, and the first child. There was no reason to think that there had been any head injury. The mother according to her own account was, however, a very ill person for reasons unconnected with the birth of the child. For the first eighteen months of this boy's life, because of a physical disability, she was sleeping badly and was very irritable and she was quite unable to devote herself to the baby in the way that she would have liked to have done. The baby yelled almost continuously though steadily growing in a physical way. He was breast-fed for four months. Because of the mother's illness there were frequent changes of nurse, and these changes were due quite largely to the fact that the baby did nothing but yell and this wore them out one after another. Though large and fat, he was walking well by 13 months, and speech was late except for the fact that he said "no" and "or not" at a very early age. He could sing simple tunes like "Three Blind Mice" correctly at [the number is missing] months, and it seemed to the mother that the yelling gradually subsided as he became able to hum and use notes. She noticed him deliberately turning the notes of the yelling into musical notes. Also music made him cry. Gradually the mother noticed what she called a very negative tendency in every way along with the development of an extremely strong will. She never felt that there was a void, but that from very early there was definite and deliberate opposition, exasperating to anyone trying to care for him. By the age of 2, his backwardness in speech was noted, and this again was the result of deliberate opposition, accompanied by the shutting of his lips when expected to repeat a word. By the time he was 4, he was very liable to physical disorders.

The mother summed up her feelings about him at this stage by expressing the difficulty that she had in making him take notice of his surroundings. She said there was an almost unbelievable indolence. This was combined with a certain amount of ambition. For instance, although he would not try to read or write it was found suddenly that he could do both. Every achievement was an under-the-counter phenomenon in spite of refusal to try or to learn. Gradually an expression of pig-like stupidity developed as a part of a set attitude against any kind of learning. He had what the mother called a trick memory, as if by innate intelligence he could arrive without travelling. The expert in autistic behaviour can recognize in this material the beginnings of autism. Gradually the boy began to escape into repetitive activities. By the time I saw him when he was 8, he could pray for two hours without repeating himself, keeping up a reverent tone. His parents were not particularly religious. It was not long before he developed the usual characteristics of autism including transposition of pronouns so that he would suddenly go up to his grandmother and say: "You have dirtied your knickers." In this way he was taking hold of the words that he expected her to use because it was he who had dirtied his knickers. The grandmother said, "I remember when his father was like that as a little boy", and this gave the parents some hope; but unfortunately in this case the boy, while remaining potentially brilliant, in actuality did not recover sufficiently to be able to have a life of his own or a profession. This detail of the reversal of pronouns indicates what is called projective identification of a degree which leaves the child without an identification with the self.

I now wish to give clinical material in illustration of the more delicate aspects of this subject. It has always seemed to me that the smaller degrees of disturbance of the mind that I am trying to describe are common and that even smaller degrees of the disturbance are very common indeed. Some degree of this same disturbance is in fact universal. In other words, what I am trying to convey is that there is no such disease as autism, but that this is a clinical term that describes the less common extremes of a universal phenomenon. Difficulty has arisen out of the fact that many clinical studies have been written either by those who deal with normal children and who are not familiar with autism or childhood schizophrenia, or else they are written by those who because of their speciality see only ill children and who by the nature of their work do not get caught up in the ordinary problems of the infant–mother relationship.

As I choose illustrative material, inevitably I come up against the very big difficulty: what case shall I choose? At this the more normal end of the problem, not only are the cases extremely numerous but also they are protean. Until one has described a hundred or so cases, one has not done justice to the subject, whereas of course one can describe autism in terms of a half dozen cases because of the set pattern of the extreme case. I choose a case simply because of recent contact.

It concerns a little girl whom I will call Sally, aged 17 months. The mother consulted me because I had played a part in the management of her own childhood when she was in distress on account of the death of her father when she was 5. In fact, this mother was not well cared for as an infant, because of her own mother's difficulties which again went back to troubles in the relationship of Sally's grandmother to the great-grandmother. Sally's grandmother had lost her mother when she was an infant. Sally's mother was terrified that she was going to continue this process of handing on difficulties by failure in the initial stages of infant care. What I found in this case was that Sally's mother was indeed inadequate as a mother in spite of her very strong wish to do well. The reason why Sally was in a fairly good state was that Sally's father was a very maternal type of person, and he had given the baby much of what the mother was unable to give. This was evident during the consultation when Sally at 17 months went all the time to her father who treated her with the utmost understanding. One could say that he is so maternal

that one wonders how he will manage when he becomes
needed as a male man and as a true father.

There were two sets of troubles. The first was that Sally employed compulsive rhythmical movements more than babies
usually do. In spite of being quite a delightful child and up to
standard in most respects, she had resorted to head-rolling
and rocking and other repetitive compulsions whenever at a
loose end. The mother had had a great deal of this compulsive rocking and swaying, and in her case the movements
lasted on into childhood and she can remember them, and
she also knows how in her case they were connected with a
feeling of intense loneliness and lack of contact with her
mother. She was very worried to find these same symptoms
appearing in her own infant. Sally employs these techniques—which could be called boring because of their freedom from fantasy—when tired or unable to find distractions
or just waiting for food in her high-chair.

In the history of this case, Sally had been breast-fed and this
was very satisfactory. Suddenly, when Sally was 11 months
old, the mother conceived, and in spite of every effort to control herself she altered in her relationship to the baby. She
suddenly stopped breast-feeding, and at the same time her
routine was altered by the fact that she was told by the doctor
to stay in bed. There was a succession of good people coming
in to look after Sally, but there was seldom one person there
for more than a week. In reaction to this, Sally started her
compulsions, which had persisted. When Sally is 18 months
old, the new baby will be born. Naturally the parents are very
worried as to the further effect of this on her. This is the
second thing that they wished to discuss.

They had had the baby early because the mother felt that in
this way she could avoid all the troubles that come from the
birth of a sibling. She now, of course, realized that at 17
months one cannot tell a baby to expect a brother or sister,
and this mother, because of her own difficulties, had particular trouble in communicating anything so subtle to a small

child. She could not conceive of the fact that a 17-month-old baby would be affected by the physical changes of her pregnancy or that a child of that age could have the idea of something coming from the inside that might in fact turn out to be a baby. The father, by contrast, could easily see these things and get to the feeling that belongs to them.

There was one further detail of importance. As the pregnancy advanced, Sally was more and more liable to go into a little trance, a withdrawal state during which she had no contact with the world around her.

Through the sensitivity of the father, arrangements of the best possible kind were being made for the care of Sally during the mother's confinement. She was to be looked after by an aunt in a house where there were other children and where everything was familiar. Moreover, the father was planning to visit Sally at least every other day. Nevertheless, he could feel that Sally was in danger of increasing all her symptoms and becoming therefore an ill child. The mother also saw this danger but her reaction was more one of fear and bewilderment and helplessness.

In my opinion there is a very real danger here which we may not be able to avert, and if the worst comes to the worst Sally may become autistic. If the danger can be averted, this must be largely due to the fact that the mother got help from me when she was a child and therefore came to me for help about her own child in spite of feeling paralysed in her bewilderment at being in the position of handing down to her daughter what had been handed down to her.

A further symptom did in fact develop. In the consulting-room, I saw it when Sally lay on her front and almost withdrew, though she just managed to clutch on to a soft toy of which she was fond. This was a recent development, and it gradually developed into another compulsive activity, a kind of masturbation accompanied by withdrawal. The case is still under observation.

Now let me give briefly a very different type of case. I refer to a boy who is now in his late teens. He probably does come into the category of genius, and in his chosen profession in the arts he shows exceptional talent, and he is creative in a way that is generally thought of as being highly original (I have written this case up in some detail).[2]

When I first saw this boy at age 12, he was a rather typical psychotic, tolerated at his prep school in spite of his bizarre behaviour. He was like the proverbial professor who walks along with one foot in the gutter and the other on the pavement and does not know. He combined superior intelligence with being unable to do up his shoelaces and being quite unsafe in the road. His relationships with other children were disturbed by the fact that he lived in a subjective world, and any impingement was liable to be a persecution to which he reacted violently. With a certain amount of help, this boy did adjust himself to external reality and, in fact, he made very good use of his public school, and when puberty came he quickly developed into a man. He might now be taken for normal. At 12, however, the whole future of this boy was problematical, and it was not considered that he would become an independent person. In the early history of this boy, there were certain interesting details. Both parents have exceptional intelligence. When the mother became pregnant she was at the height of her profession, and she waited for six months after conception before transferring her preoccupation from her job, which was a very exacting one, to the baby that she was expecting. This was her third child. She enjoyed having babies, and she fed this boy for three months. After this time, however, the mother began to think about her job again and allowed a very possessive nanny to take him over. When the boy was 2, the nanny went. It is likely from the parent's story that the main trauma to this boy was the loss of the nanny, from whom the mother rescued him because she was so possessive. He found it very difficult to make use of his mother.

---

[2]See Case 9, "Ashton", in *Therapeutic Consultations in Child Psychiatry* (1971).

Hereditary factors played a part from the start and in his development he was very like his father had been. Developmentally he seemed to be copying many of the things that we call autistic. For one thing he had a very severe learning difficulty from the beginning. By means of his exceptional intellectual equipment he got round this by cheating in the sense that he was able to teach himself while refusing to be taught. He taught himself to read at 3½ and to multiply before he was 4. He took it for granted that all women were stupid, in particular his mother. His mother had been a piano teacher of repute, but he refused to allow her to teach him anything and taught himself to play at a very early age, picking up from her, in spite of the learning difficulty, all the things that she in fact considered important in teaching a pupil to play. Apart from Meccano, this boy's play had almost entirely to do with sums and the manipulation of figures. In spite of his disparagement of his mother, he was entirely dependent on her presence in the background. When he went to school at 6, he was always at the top of the class, and this disturbed his relationship to his peer group. The only thing he was good at was cross-country running, of which it was said "he runs like a lunatic", the idea behind this being that he was running away from persecutors, rather than to get somewhere or to win.

And so he eventually arrived at the prep school, where fortunately his eccentricities were accepted. He became rather religious. For bedtime employment he specialized in the Latin translation of *Winnie the Pooh*. It could be said that the main difficulty with this boy was related to his complete lack of confidence in external reality, which from his point of view could never be trusted to behave itself.

My point of view can be illustrated therefore by this case, which I consider to be a recovered childhood schizophrenia. There were periods when the word autism could be used correctly in description of his clinical state. He might easily have been mentally defective in spite of having a good brain, but it just happened that in his case, by use of his exceptional intellectual capacity, he got round the difficulties that have to do with a severe block in learning, and this has now made it possible that he will be able to make a valuable and original contribution to the world through one of the arts. The future is not yet clear, however, and indeed it can be said that the future of any artist who may be outstanding must be unsure. It can be said that this boy could not take his place in the world as an ordinary person, and I am sure that he will not earn his living as a bus conductor. He would indeed find it difficult even in late puberty to survive without the continuation of the stable and understanding environment provided by his parents.

Perhaps my main argument has now become clear. There are certain difficulties that arise when primitive things are being experienced by the baby that depend not only on inherited personal tendencies but also on what happens to be provided by the mother. Here failure spells disaster of a particular kind for the baby. At the beginning the baby needs the mother's full attention, and usually gets precisely this; and in this period the basis for metal health is laid down. This in all its details becomes established by constant reinforcement through the continuation of a pattern of care that has in it the essential elements.

Naturally, some individual infants have a greater capacity to go ahead in spite of imperfect care, because of inherited tendencies or because of the variations that exist in the amount of damage actually done to the brain either in the critical stages of pregnancy or during the birth process. On the whole, however, it is the quality of early care that counts. It is this aspect of the environmental provision that rates highest in a general review of the disorders of the development of the child, of which autism is one.

This is a matter of aetiology. As far as possible we are studying the facts in order to arrive at an accurate and valuable theoretical statement, without which we are stuck.

What we are not talking about here is responsibility. I may say of a particular case of a series, the autistic picture in the child results from this or that that was, or was not, a feature in the child's early management, but this is very different from saying to a mother or a father: "This was your fault."

Now, I find that, if a mother is worried about these matters, if I can meet her I can explain what I mean quite easily. She understands that we have to look for all the causes of any disorder and also of health, and we cannot hold back our statements for fear of hurting someone. In the case of thalidomide children, it was obvious that paediatricians had to say out loud, "this is due to thalidomide medication of the mother in the second month of pregnancy", whatever the effect this may have had on doctors and mothers who in fact unwittingly did cause the disaster of 250 babies born with defective limbs.

Mothers do, of course, tend to feel guilty; they tend to feel responsible, quite apart from logic, for every defect that manifests itself in their children. They feel guilty before the baby is born, and they so strongly expect to give birth to a monster that they must always be shown the baby the very moment he or she is born, however exhausted they may be. And the father too.

Nevertheless, most people are rational beings in their best moments, and they can then discuss the relationship between autism developing in a child and (in some cases) a relative failure in infant care. What is much more difficult is to deal with this problem in social terms, in terms of the public and the public's attitude to the parents. Collectively people are less rational than individually. No doubt parents of any ill child have a serious social problem.

It is easier, however, if society can get the idea that the illness is due to fate, or an act of God. Even the sins of the fathers will do quite well. The moment society gets the idea that a child's abnormality is due to the parents, then ruthlessness takes over.

For this reason, I would love to be able to say to the world that I find that the attitude of parents does not really have anything to do with autism, or with delinquency, or with adolescent insurgence. But I cannot. In fact, if I could, this would be tantamount to saying that parents play no part when things go well. In terms of autism, it would be claiming that it does not matter what goes on in infant care until a certain age—say, 3 or 4, when the baby tends to become an autonomous child and starts to reach towards independence. If follows that parents of children with abnormalities have to put up with a certain amount of discomfort socially. It is sad but it can't be helped. This is why there are all these specialist groupings, for instance:[3]

The Spastic Society

The Society for Blind Children

The Society for Deaf Children

The Society for Thalidomide Children

The Society for the Educationally Sub-Normal Child

The Society for Children with Fibrocystic Disease

The Society for Children with Haemophilia

The Society for Children with Hole in the Heart, and other congenital heart malformations.

I am sure that parents of children with tuberculosis, cancer, disseminated sclerosis, rheumatic heart disease, hydrocephalus, dwarfism, giantism, obesity, etc. would all need a localized group for support because of the loneliness that the illness of the child produces. Also, parents need to feel that all that is possible is being done, and that their particular problem is not being neglected in the Ministry of Health plans.

This Society for Autistic Children has a very real function, as I see it, to deal with society's tendency to wash its hands of any problem that is not a vote-catcher in the political scene. The parents of autistic children are puzzled, and lonely, and potentially loaded up with guilt feelings, and yet they do have to go on caring for these children whatever the cause.

The Society does not concern itself with the cause (except that it has a scientific interest in aetiology). It is concerned with the special plight of parents who have one child, who instead of giving the usual rewards that belong to emotional growth towards independence, continues to need special adaptive care, soon to the detriment of the other children in the family, certainly to the detriment of the parents themselves in their individual lives and in their lives together. Moreover, who can tell how long?

---

[3]These were their titles in 1966.

How much easier it was when these children just got lost in the educationally sub-normal pool, and no-one bothered. But parents who know in their hearts, because of definite indications, that their boy or girl has a good brain, which, however, has not reached satisfactory functioning, do feel unable to let the child become classified mentally defective without a struggle to establish what is the truth.

Sometimes I have diagnosed autism and I have wished I had said primary defect. Also, sometimes I have diagnosed mental defect and I wish I had been clever enough to see that, in fact, the child had a potential perhaps for a normal mind or even an intellect of special quality.

My trouble, as I have said, is that in the description of these intimate details, there is so much clinical material at my disposal that I am bewildered and do not know how to choose. As I write this paper, a colleague tells me of a boy who is under treatment.

The boy is 6 years old, and the mother is also under treatment by the same doctor. The boy is typically autistic and his one preoccupation is with jugs. His relationship to human beings is minimal. My friend tells me that it was two years before the mother became able to tell him how the illness in her son started. It was at the time before the baby was a year old when she had a long phase of depression, moderately severe. During this phase she was completely unable to stand the sound of a baby crying; and to deal with this she kept a bottle always ready, and the moment the baby started to cry she simply put the bottle into his mouth, and in this way she managed to stop the crying without having to do anything personal to the baby, without having to make contact with him, and certainly without taking him up and handling him. From this time the baby fitted into her scheme of things and substituted a relationship with the bottle for a relationship of interpersonal type. There was a direct line from this to the boy's preoccupation with jugs and the whole of the negative aspect of the autistic picture.

I give this to illustrate the way in which one cannot come by the details in the past history of a child by questionnaires and by brusque enquiry. A mother has to gain confidence in the enquirer, and then perhaps she may be able to report the details of her relationship with the baby in so far as these can be relevant in the aetiology of the disorder in the child.

This oversimplified description of a case leads on to the question: what is it that happens automatically when things go well in the early infant–mother relationship, but which when disturbed leads to faulty development of the autistic type? The subject is complex, and I have tried to deal with it in its complexity. Here I would like to follow up the clue that my friend got from the mother, who pointed out that she gave the baby satisfactions but dealt with her own anxiety and failed either to let the baby enjoy crying or being angry, or else failed more basically to make contact in a human way with the baby. In other words, to cure this child someone has to be able to give him the rudiments of human contact, and it may be that in such a case physical care including actual handling has more importance than anything that can be done by verbal interpretation. If in the treatment of an autistic child, something can be done to make up for what the mother failed to do at the critical moment, then the child can reach to a place from which it makes sense for him or her to be angry about the failure. From this position he can go on to rediscover his capacity to love. When parents are doing all the minute things of infant care, and this often includes doing nothing at all except being alongside, then in terms of the infant's personal development a great deal is happening. The foundation is being laid for many things, some of which can be enumerated. I choose to enumerate, firstly, the whole process of integration which leads eventually to the baby's becoming autonomous; secondly, the baby's ability to come to terms with his own body, leading eventually to psychosomatic coexistence which includes firm muscle tone; and, thirdly, the baby's initial steps in object-relating, which lead to the ability to adopt symbolic objects and to the existence of an area in between the baby and persons in which play is meaningful.

All these things belong to the maturational process which the baby inherits, but nothing in the development of a baby can take place without something from a human being which meets the baby almost exactly in the way that is needed. One of the most difficult of all these, unless it happens naturally, is simply coexistence: two people breathing together and doing nothing simply because doing is not a state of rest. I am aware that to some this idea comes easily, but to others it appears mystical and disturbingly complex. It is this sort of thing that we do find, however, when we examine these intimate matters with the microscope, so to speak, and we have to state them in so far as we are able to find words to describe what we mean.

My hope is that this Society will flourish and will perform its dual role of counteracting the loneliness of the parents and of fostering scientific or objective enquiry into this form of schizophrenia, which starts in infancy or early childhood. In the end, it is the aetiology of the illness that gives the clue for prevention.

26

The aetiology
of infantile schizophrenia
in terms of adaptive failure

[1967]

Part 1

I much regret having needed to reverse my original intention of being present at the Conference. All I can do is to offer a brief account setting out my personal point of view.

Much of what I give here is to be found in the writings of others (notably Bettelheim, *The Empty Fortress*[1]), but my own view developed in the course of my work as a paediatrician in the 1920s and 1930s, and became reformulated in the 1940s when I began to have my own way of stating the essential stages of the intertwined physical and emotional development of the human infant.[2]

Naturally, I was strongly influenced by Kanner's formulation of autism,[3] but in the years prior to this important contribution I

---

[1] Bruno Bettelheim, *The Empty Fortress: Infantile Autism and the Birth of the Self* (New York: Free Press; London: Collier-Macmillan, 1967).

[2] See *The Child and the Family* (1957) and the lectures gathered together in *Collected Papers: Through Paediatrics to Psycho-Analysis* (1958).

[3] Leo Kanner, *Child Psychiatry* (London: Balliere, Tindall & Cox, 1937).

had simply dealt with these cases under the heading Infantile Psychosis. It was always clear, at one extreme, that in a proportion of these cases there had been brain damage and, at the other extreme, that the condition could appear as an illness in a child who had the equipment to be of average or above-average intelligence. Among mental defectives, we knew we could always find the odd case in which mental defect was secondary to what we then called "infantile psychosis" or "childhood schizophrenia".

A further point is that in the early 1920s we had temporarily the epidemic of encephalitis lethargica to complicate the problem of diagnosis and aetiology.

It is not certain to me whether all was gain in Kanner's labelling of the cases "autistic". The loss, it seemed to me, was that this label gave paediatricians, used as they are to syndromes and disease entities, a false trail which they followed only too willingly. They could now look for autistic cases and place them conveniently in a group with an artificially clear boundary. It could then be held that there was a disease, aetiology not yet known, and the picture of the disease could easily be given to students.

But there is not a clear-cut boundary to the condition, which I think should not be thought of as a disease. Any one of the many descriptive elements can be looked at separately and can be found in children who are not autistic, and even in children who are called normal and healthy.

However, this is not to decry the positive value of Kanner's contribution.

It has to be remembered that whether autism is called infantile schizophrenia or not, we need to expect resistance to the idea of an aetiology that points to the innate processes of the emotional development of the individual in the given environment. In other words, there will be those who prefer to find a physical, genetic, biochemical, or endocrine cause, both for autism and for schizophrenia. It is to be hoped that at this conference the full range of possibilities will be allowed, and that those who hold the view that the cause of autism is a physical cause that has not yet been discovered will allow those who claim to have clues to follow these up, even if they seem to be leading away from the physical and towards the idea of a disturbance in the delicate interplay of individual and environmental factors as they operate in the earliest stages of human growth and development.

It is necessary to refer to one detail which should not give trouble in a scientific meeting, except that those who participate are nearly all in practice. It is not good to distort the truth in order to avoid hurting the feelings of clients. No doubt the doctor who believes that the ultimate explanation of autism is physical will be more at ease with parents than the doctor who feels that evidence leads towards the idea that the parents, or one parent, actually caused the disorder by some distortion of the "average expectable environment".[4] It is bad enough to have an autistic child, and if, added to this, the parents are to feel that they caused the condition, then their burden may be intolerable. But it is not always so. Parents feel guilt-laden in any case when their child is abnormal (e.g. if there is a primary defect or even a deformity such as syndactyly). I have known parents who preferred to be told about all the possibilities, including the possibility that the aetiology of the child's condition involves one or both of them to some extent.

In any case, scientific enquiry must go behind this kind of human consideration.

Part II

I do not feel that this conference needs direction. Nevertheless, I wish to offer the following ideas:

(A) There is only obscurity to be got from thinking of the autistic picture in terms of regression.

(B) Autism is a highly sophisticated defence organization. What we see is *invulnerability*. There has been a gradual build-up

---

[4] H. Hartmann, *Ego Psychology and the Problem of Adaptation* (London: Imago, 1958; first published 1939).

towards invulnerability, and in the case of a stabilized autistic child it is the environment and not the child who suffers. People in the environment may suffer greatly.

(C) The child carries round *the (lost) memory of unthinkable anxiety*,[5] and the illness is a complex mental structure insuring against recurrence of the conditions of the unthinkable anxiety.

(D) This very primitive kind of anxiety can only happen in states of extreme dependence and trust, that is, before there has been established a clear distinction between the *I AM* central "me" and the repudiated world that is separate or external.

This is the reason why Bettelheim's title "The Empty Fortress" has value. It is not necessarily true, however, that the fortress is always empty. When the disorder develops very early, there may indeed be almost nothing there to be defended except just something of a self that carried the body memory of anxiety that is completely beyond the infant's capacity to cope with. The mental mechanisms for coping have not yet become established. In many cases, however, the condition starts late, as when a child has to deal with the presence of a new baby when he or she is 12 or 13 months old. In such cases, it is to be presumed that there is a very great deal that is being defended in the fortress.

(E) If environmental provision is made which tends to restore the status quo ante, and a long period of reliability seems to the child to give confidence, then the startling result is a *return of vulnerability*. Clinically, this means increased trouble, and it is now distressing to see the child suffering in a way that did not obtain when the autism was firmly established. For this reason, therapeutic work with autistic children is maximally exacting, and constantly makes the worker feel: is this worthwhile? There is but slight possibility of a "cure"— only amelioration of the condition and a great increase in the child's personal experience of suffering.

---

[5]Winnicott, *The Maturational Processes and the Facilitating Environment* (1965).

(F)   In search for the aetiological factor, it is necessary to have a
theory of the emotional development of the human child that
is as free as possible from what Bettelheim calls myth,
derived from wish and fear. It is necessary to see through
the "psychoanalytic myth" (now happily disappearing) that
early infancy is a matter of satisfactions relative to oral eroto-
genicity.

(G)   From my point of view, the essential feature (from amongst
the vast sum of features) is *the mother's* (or substitute mother's) *capacity to adapt to the infant's needs through her healthy
ability to identify with the baby* (without, of course, losing her
own identity). With such a capacity she can, for instance, hold
her baby, and without it she cannot hold her baby except in
a way that disturbs the baby's personal living process.[6]

(H)   It seems necessary to add to this the concept of the mother's
unconscious (repressed) hate of the child.[7,8] Parents naturally
love and hate their babies, in varying degrees. This does not
do damage. At all ages, and in earliest infancy especially, the
effect of the repressed death wish towards the baby is harmful, and it is beyond the baby's capacity to deal with this. At
a later stage than this one that concerns us here, one can see
a child all the time making effort *in order to arrive at the starting
post*—that is, to counteract the parents' unconscious wish
(covered by reaction formations) that the child should be
dead. At the earlier stages that relate to the subject of autism,
the baby can only show the *distortion* that results from his or
her having been cared for by someone whose positive actions
are all reaction formations; direct or spontaneous free and
adaptive movements would all reveal the (repressed) death
wish.

Such ideas call for courage on the part of those who discuss
them, and yet without these ideas there is no hope, in my
opinion, that any body of scientists will move towards an
understanding of the aetiology of autism.

---

[6]See Winnicott, *The Maturational Processes and the Facilitating Environment*
(1965), and throughout his writings.

[7]See Bettelheim, *The Empty Fortress.*

[8]See p. xxx and footnote 1, pp. xxx–xxxi.

(I)   Many writers have expressed the view that an understanding of autism would widen our understanding of human nature. I also feel that this is true, once a true statement has been made of the aetiology. Also, I feel that this statement will be a helpful aetiological contribution not only to the subject of autism, but also to that of schizophrenia in general.

Part nine

PROFESSIONAL CARE
OF THE GROWING CHILD

27

Training for child psychiatry: the paediatric department of psychology

[1961]

The psychological aspect of paediatrics has especial importance at this time because of the interest that doctors have
developed in the human beings whose diseases at one
time claimed almost exclusive attention. Medical students now
expect to be introduced to dynamic psychology along with
medicine and surgery and the specialities, and just as they are
taught organic medicine on the basis of physiology and
anatomy, so they begin to need to be taught about dynamic psychology on the basis   ychoanalysis.

Teachers in organic medicine must not be expected to be able
to teach dynamic psychology, and the same applies the other
way round. In other words, there must be paediatric specialists
in psychology. It has become customary to call these specialists
child psychiatrists, but this is a pity because there is a much
closer relationship between child psychiatry and physical paediatrics than there is between child psychiatry and general
psychiatry. Psychiatrists are, in fact, concerned chiefly with end
results and breakdowns, if not actually with disorders based on
brain or vascular degeneration, and on the whole they do not
know very much about the emotional development of the infant
and the small child, and of the functioning of the mother and
father and of the family and the school. Paediatricians them-

selves also have been slow to recognize that child psychiatry is essentially a sibling of physical paediatrics, and that much is lost when a child psychiatry department is set up, either under the aegis of psychiatry or of educational or academic psychology. There is, of course, room for all kinds of clinics, and there are areas of overlap between psychiatry and child psychiatry, and between child psychiatry and academic psychology. But a paediatric department of the future must have a psychology department as one half of itself. The paediatrician and the child psychiatrist in this way work together, on equal terms, and each is pleased to find that a territory exists which belongs to either or to each.

This state of affairs has existed at Paddington Green since that hospital came under St Mary's; and before that time the psychology department was a theoretical concept within the general medical out-patient department which existed in virtue of my appointment as assistant physician (later physician) on the staff of Paddington Green in 1923. My retirement now because of my having reached the age of 65 brings this matter to a head, and perhaps justifies the editor in inviting me to write this comment in which I give my personal view.

It should be stated clearly that it is the view of psychiatrists in general that child psychiatry ought to be a part of psychiatry. In many clinics this state of affairs obtains, and the overall control is from psychiatry, and I know of no instance in which the yoke is rubbing the ox's neck. Nevertheless, if this were to be the universal rule, a great deal would be lost which is not known to the psychiatrist of adults, and which can only be known to those who work at one and the same time in physical and psychological paediatrics. To take one example, there is a vast amount of psychology in the field of infant feeding. This is, indeed, a far cry from general psychiatric practice.

In the matter of training in child psychiatry, the essentials are physical paediatrics and psychoanalysis. It is not necessary for all child psychiatrists to be qualified in adult psychiatry. Moreover, adult psychiatry today tends to get further and further from the problems of human nature and veers towards the exploration of drug treatments, biochemistry, and the various shock therapies. Nothing could be further from paediatric psychology, or from the advice you would give a mother who finds it difficult to wean her baby, or from what you must know in order to advise a father who must decide whether to let his little boy exploit his wife at bed-time to the extent that he never sees her, and so on. No, child psychiatry is a thing in itself, and it belongs naturally to physical paediatrics, not to psychiatry.

In fact, on the theoretical side, the psychoanalysis of children and the practice of child psychiatry have together contributed a great deal to the study of adult psychiatric disorder, whereas adult psychiatry has given practically nothing to child psychiatry, not even a classification that has practical value.

Child psychiatry obviously overlaps with psychiatry, and on this common ground there is no reason why two disciplines should not meet in a friendly way. In some clinics there will be the one kind of set-up, with psychiatry dominant, and in other clinics paediatrics will claim child psychiatry as essentially part of itself. This is as it should be.

The factor that has brought about the change is the tremendous advance that has been made in the last three decades in the treatment of physical disease, with penicillin as the most important one discovery. It is now possible to see that the psychological aspect of paediatrics is the greater half of paediatrics, although it will be very many years before half the paediatricians will be child psychiatrists, because of the long extra training that is needed.

It follows that the University Chair in Paediatrics will need to be a tandem, to accommodate two professors, the one in physical and the other in psychological paediatrics. This is a measure that is already overdue. The main thing for the purpose of my argument here is that there is no place for a tandem chair for adult psychiatry and child psychiatry, there being relatively little affinity between these two activities. The one activity concerns adults, and the other concerns infants and children and parents and child care generally.

It is my one hope on my retirement that the Paddington Green psychology department will not be lost to paediatrics. Having been engaged in this work since 1923, I am in a good position to hold a personal opinion, and my personal opinion is that a great deal will be lost if the principle I have enunciated is violated, so that paediatric psychology is claimed by psychiatry, and lost to paediatrics.

Summary

Child psychiatry is a speciality on its own account, whereas general psychiatry is concerned with degenerative processes and with neurological phenomena that are not important in the average child psychiatry department. Child psychiatry is concerned with the emotional development of the individual child and with the interferences with maturational processes that come from the environment and from conflict within the child. This makes child psychiatry akin to paediatrics.

The general psychiatrist or the paediatrician needs additional training of the kind provided by psychoanalysis and analytical psychology. These institutes also provide machinery for selection.

There will always be those who come to child psychiatry from general psychiatry, but it is important to keep open the route through paediatric practice.

28

Notes on
the time factor in treatment

[1961]

When asked for a title for this lecture I gave "The Time Factor in Treatment" (including social work). I had several reasons for wishing to take up this theme; the theme of time, the great physician, a phrase which I find comes from Disraeli. There are innumerable references to time which could be quoted here: "Time, not our time, rings the bell" is T. S. Eliot's way of drawing attention to the power of the unconscious. I could make another quotation, this time from myself, which refers to maternal adaptation enabling the baby to catch hold of time.

Since I thought of this title, nearly all my patients have contributed-in, and last Sunday I was talking to a friend, a psychoanalyst, who was asked by a patient why there could not be a cure in a few minutes by hypnotism or shock treatment or something, and my friend had said:

"But you have been able to waste me for four years—this has been the important thing in your treatment; how could you have condensed this into a moment of time?"

We are so often asked why we do not favour short cuts, and I think that in order to answer the question we need to study the time factor and its place in our work.

Again, when I was asked whether I would speak here, I had just seen a man about one of his children.

> He has a happy home, and he came to me because his second child had been diagnosed defective and he felt that she was really intelligent; in fact, he was right and the child was deaf. This man and his wife have moved house in order to get to London so that this child may get the education that is necessary for a deaf child, and this means a long journey every day for the breadwinner, who has a good job in a country district where there are no facilities. I felt that I was dealing with a healthy man and woman properly concerned about their healthy children. The interesting thing from my point of view is that I have had to wait for this since 1928 when I gave this man child analysis as far as I was able at that time, before I had met Mrs. Klein. The treatment was a very interesting one as you can imagine, this little boy being only 3 years old. He had a very possessive mother, and what I was not able to show immediately was that a small child cannot kill his mother or run away from her; he has to endure her, and my treatment of this boy did no more than enable him to defend himself against his mother's pathological grip on his personality. I got no result until the war broke out and the question of the boy's military service came up for consideration. By this time, the boy had developed fits, and the mother gave me a very clear account of a very ill child, asking me to let the military authorities know that the boy was unfit for service. What I did in fact was to write to the Medical Officer and suggest to him that the boy's abnormalities were quite largely due to the mother's grip on his personality and that they would be taking a good risk in accepting this boy for the army. He had actually told me in personal interview that he hoped that he would be accepted. It was interesting that he quickly became normal in the army, and after the war, which he enjoyed in spite of all its dangers, he maintained a distance between himself and his mother, of whom he continued to be very fond. Soon he married well and obtained a good job.

This case has nothing very unusual about it, but I was interested in the case just when I chose to speak to you about the time factor.

I would suggest that in your work, and in mine, we have to distinguish clearly between what the patient gets out of the treatment and what we get out of it. For the patient, the treatment is not life. If the treatment is successful, it enables the patient to start, perhaps at a late date, or to make a better start, or to start with better equipment. For ourselves, the work must be interesting in itself, i.e. we must have an interest in our work which is not dependent on getting results. It is very tempting for us to try to copy our colleagues in other professions; the surgeon, for instance, who often saves a life. Much of our work produces a result, but after an interval which is beyond our capacity to hold; by the time the result can be recorded, we have really lost touch with the beginnings of the treatment and even with the crises of the mid-way stages. In this way, we report diagnostic interviews and we report phases in early treatment and phases in late treatment, and then we survey results. These are all separate endeavours; how can we possibly report total treatments? When we attempt to report total treatments, we are either bogged down with an unmanageable mass of material or else—and this is the point I am making—we get lost between the beginning and the end, between the problem that presented itself and the result which may easily not be ready for description for many years after our initial contact with the case.

What I am talking about, therefore, is the fourth dimension in integration. In the emotional development of the human individual, the tendency to integration is innate. Conditions have to be bad if integration does not become a fact. Integration can be pictured in terms of the three dimensions of space, but in this case we must add the fourth dimension of time. We all know that when a patient begins to talk about the past, he is at the same time beginning to think of the future. We meet restless individuals, especially among potential delinquents, who are integrated at any one moment in a way which easily deceives us unless we remember that they are not at all integrated in time, and in fact they are incapable of relating now with then. This could be said to be a fault of existentialism, that some of those who find a sort of religion in existentialism are escaping into the present moment from their inability to relate to the past and the future.

A little child who stands on the sand castle and says, "I'm the King of the castle; and you're the dirty rascal", is only concerned with the fact of his or her existence at that one moment. Already we see in the "you're the dirty rascal" the perception that if time is taken into account, someone is soon coming to appear to claim the kingship of the castle.

In the integration of the healthy child and adult, integration in time is just as important as any other kind of wholeness. In our work, we have to stand the strain which our cases put on us when results are not by any means immediate, and when we have learned to distrust immediate results. We develop other interests in our work, interests in our technique and in the money we get for it, because we cannot, and indeed we must not, ignore the time factor in the process of the patient's delayed development or cure.

29

The Association for
Child Psychology and Psychiatry
observed as a group phenomenon

[1967]

This would seem to be the sort of occasion that could call for an assessment of our Association in its relation to itself. Has it an identity? What makes it be and keeps its existence going? Such an assessment is certainly relevant, it may possibly prove encouraging, and it runs the risk of being painful.

We must be prepared, if we look into the matter of our own group-self, to find that no integrating factor can be found. Our history would allow for this, since we came into being in a rather haphazard way, the immediate purpose being that there should be a body in Great Britain corresponding to the I.A.C.P.P.,[1] able to invite the I.A.C.P.P. to hold occasional conferences within our shores. In order to be on a footing with the representatives of other nations, we more or less had to set up our own Association, although it was somewhat artificial for us to do so. (The recent successful Edinburgh Conference could not have taken place if the A.C.P.P. had not been set up, although we are very

---

[1] This set of initials refers to the IACAPAP, as they are now called, the International Association for Child and Adolescent Psychiatry and Allied Professions, a body speaking on behalf of children, adolescents, and the professions that serve them.

236 PROFESSIONAL CARE OF THE GROWING CHILD

much aware that we of the 1966 Council had but little to do with the planning and the work involved, this having been the responsibility of the International President and of his Committee.)

In this country, because of our history and because of the great battle over the centuries for freedom of thought, we are able to think of social service simply because that is what we want, and not as something arising out of indoctrination by a church or a religion or a philosophy. So we have the freedom to look and see what we find in human nature, as it has evolved and as we find it. We count among our number many who are in some way or other affiliated. In practice, affiliated and unaffiliated people need to be able to meet together, as we are doing now, for certain purposes of discussion and action; and while we may stand on any of the many platforms that our complex culture provides, we may all shout out about the same thing. The theme is that of the individual child growing in his or her own way in the environment which exists, or which we are challenged by the nature of any one case to provide.

We look at human growth and development, and take what comes. A corollary must be (and I can't help it) that anyone who, because of an affiliation, must bring a preconceived plan, and who cannot look freely at what is found when a child is observed, must feel out of place in this Association. Science means just this, that when one observes and builds theories to coordinate observations one is free from affiliations, and anyone who knows the answers in advance, who has seen the light, so to speak, is not a scientist, and must be out of place among scientists.

Science, in other words, is not a matter of proving this or that by statistics; it is a matter of being free from knowing in advance. (Knowing in advance belongs to poetry.) You or I may need or enjoy an affiliation for the purpose of living our own lives, but this has nothing to do with what we observe, with science. Many people have been burnt alive in defence of this principle.

I assume that we are all scientists, though we may differ from each other in the degree of our involvement in scientific enquiry.

In our title we only mention psychiatry and psychology. This is just a matter of verbal economy. We include in our group:

education   paediatrics   psychiatry   psychology
psychoanalysis   psychotherapy   social work

Absent are:

religion   philosophy   poetry
and alchemy, which tries to ride the two horses at once.

From the point of view of the planning of our programme each year, it is important that the problems of the inter-relationship of these disciplines be constantly kept in mind, because in a practical way it could easily happen that we could have a series of meetings with little or no overlap of participants. This can happen and it has happened.

Obviously, any discussion can be of interest to everyone, but we have limited time to live, and often there is a clash in the matter of dates because of the number of societies with regular meetings in London, if not in other big cities, and it is only by careful planning that your committee manages to keep the interest of all the groups for each meeting. Here, the main theme of my lecture turns up practical planning on the part of your committee, whose work I have watched for a couple of years. From this it can easily be appreciated how vital is this matter of a periodical assessment of the reason for our existence as a group.

A first step is for us to look at the potential antagonisms that the A.C.P.P. contains within its own skin. As there are but few opportunities for looking at the divergencies of the various elements in the Association, I want to try to say everything now that I can think of saying about the reasons why this group is *not* a group. We have three words to play with: unintegration (which is used for a primary state prior in time to integration); disintegration (which I think we all use for describing the violent result of an attack from within on integration); and Michael Fordham's word de-integration, which has value in description of the idea of the undoing of integration, as in splitting as a defence. We can employ all three if their employment gives us help.

I am concerned with everything that makes *against* cohesion. I would like to make it seem to be a miracle that the group claims to be a group. If there is mutual suspicion, then I want to examine mutual suspicion. The risk has to be taken that, if we look at ourselves, we actually disintegrate. But if we fail to take this risk, then we are bound together by a fear of disunity, which is a negation factor.

Self-selection

In order to get a stage further in my investigation, I want to look at the various groups in terms of *self-selection*. This idea of self-selection seems to me to be a key that opens the way to the problem, and I think that it has more importance for our purpose than training.

If looked at this way, we fall naturally into groups. I know that no-one is entirely committed to one line of life, and yet for purposes of discussion I shall be talking in terms of extremes. I am calling a teacher a teacher, and a spade a spade. It is unlikely that anyone here knows of a man or woman who could, with equal drive from within himself or herself, be a teacher or a paediatrician or a psychiatrist or a psychotherapist or a psychologist of the so-called academic variety, or a social worker. There are, of course, sub-groups in each of these sections about which a similar statement could be made.

Now I shall go over the various groups thinking in terms of self-selection.

Teaching

Teaching is based (is it not?) on a fundamental acceptance of something. The teacher *knows* something. The job of teaching is to impart this knowledge to someone else. It may be a skill, a body of knowledge, or a code of behaviour. It is true that there can be good and bad teaching and that there are ways of imparting knowledge which do not violate the pupil's natural revulsion against indoctrination or propaganda. Nevertheless, in comparing the teacher's job with that of the other members of groups in this Association, one must be crude and (as I said before) one must look at the extremes. The result of teaching is that something the teacher knows reaches a place in the pupil. Teaching is like feeding in one respect, since feeding a child has as its basis the axiom: there is one thing more important than eating—that is, *not* eating. The teacher needs to assume that the child has emerged from the land of paradox, having been sponsored there by his paradoxical parents. Now the teacher hopes for the exploitation of whatever degree of compliance the child has attained.

A further thing to be said about teaching, especially if one ignores nursery-school age and the beginning of primary education, is that the teacher is "at one remove" from the pupil. In teaching there is an avoidance of a total human interrelationship. The teacher and pupil may have an intense interrelationship of a localized kind, but already teaching is being interfered with when the teacher develops a powerful *emotional* involvement; and if a teacher enters too much into the life of the child, teaching becomes impossible. I am referring to the difficulties that show in practice when a teacher does, in fact, need to have his or her own child in among the other pupils. Also, I could refer to the fact that some woman teachers experience a great shock when they marry and have children of their own and they find themselves not so well equipped to be mothers and fathers as they expected to be. In fact, the adjustment from being a teacher to being the mother of a baby is maybe so great that teachers must not be expected to make the change easily. Nor do they easily make the change the other way, when they have been mothers and wish to become teachers again. No doubt there are many factors at work here but it is important to recognize the reality. Self-selection determines the preponderance of women among teachers of the younger children.

Is it not true to say that the man or woman teacher self-selected joins the teaching profession and gets support from being a member of that profession and expects to move up gradually towards the position of head? There is a general acceptance of a hierarchy. Society has a very definite place for the teacher. These things have been worked out well by teachers in the course of their long experience.

In practice, it is not every teacher who is suitable to change over into becoming a school counsellor, that is to say abandoning the task of teaching and moving towards the role of social worker. Here, however, is a link between two of our groups. In order to get on with his or her job, the teacher must take for granted the development of the child in terms of personality and character and therefore must assume that the parents have done their job fairly well. Some of the parental functions are carried on by the teacher, and there is permanent discussion as to how far the teacher is responsible for moulding character.

In practice, one thinks of teaching in terms of the imparting of knowledge, and a separate category is needed for the schooling of children who are difficult, that is to say, whose families or parents have not succeeded in producing teachable material. The school for difficult children is by definition *not simply a teaching proposition*, because here teaching takes second place to management, and the subject has now moved over away from education towards social work and psychotherapy—though, curiously enough, the Ministry of Education is principally involved. In the war it was the Ministry of Health. It could be the Home Office because of the link with Approved Schools.

Roughly speaking, it can be claimed that teaching is based on the imparting of knowledge to teachable children. Teachable children do on the whole want to know, hence the universal service of the teaching profession.

Children who are "bold and unbiddable" interfere with the teacher's job. Teachers know they are in danger of overvaluing the biddable child because of his or her teachability. Some of the successes of teaching turn out to be psychiatric casualties, perhaps false personalities—that is to say, young men and women who do not know what to do with success when they have academically succeeded.

Teachers need not to have to deal with psychiatric illness. Imagine a referendum: "Shall teaching be abolished or psychotherapy?" There is no doubt that the teachers would come out of this well, since most children are normal and want to learn.

Their parents nearly all want them to have been taught. Some even want their children to be and to feel educated, that is, in touch with the cultural matrix of social living.

Psychology

Psychologists could gain from being aware of the difficulty that psychotherapists and those who work in the dynamic area do have in regard to the borderline between their two areas of operation. Psychologists come into their own in the organization of research, and it is they who most nearly fulfil the conditions which research workers in other fields (like physics) require.

There is, therefore, plenty of ground for difficulty in the relationship between the academic psychologist and all those who get involved with individuals. In psychotherapy and social work, nothing is achieved if there is no involvement. I could also say, I believe, that it is the psychologists who are most critical of the sort of thing that psychotherapists and social workers do.

There is another point that should be mentioned: self-selection in academic psychology is based on academic prowess and may not be based very much on personality structure or on such a thing as the capacity to make contact with a child. As compared with this, the teacher cannot proceed without some capacity for making contact, and the psychotherapist absolutely needs to be both able to get deeply *en rapport* and also to get uninvolved, not according to his or her need but according to the need of the child-patient.

I would claim rather provocatively that psychologists constantly show that they are aware that they are operating in the intellectual field and that this is not the psyche of psychosomatic living. If there is a split-off intellectual field of the intellect, then there is much opportunity for mutual misunderstanding; I tried to show this in a paper on psychosomatics in the *International Journal of Psycho-Analysis*.[2] because it *is* easy to discuss the subject

---

[2] "Psycho-Somatic Illness in Its Positive and Negative Aspects", *International Journal of Psycho-Analysis*, 47 (1966): 510. Also in *Psycho-Analytic Explorations* (1989).

from a split-off intellectual position. The difficulty comes when it is the clinician who is hopelessly involved in the patient's illogical dissociations. On the positive side, if the psychologists can help dynamic psychologists and social workers with their very difficult task of evaluating the results of the treatment of the individual, then they have an important task to perform, but they must not expect to receive material that can be put into a computer.

I suggest that psychologists and social workers find it difficult to discuss together, either theoretically or in terms of any one child's problems. Even if a common language is employed, the psychologist and the dynamic psychologist talk in two distinct layers of word-usage. The psychologist is usually unconcerned with unconscious motivation, for instance, while the social worker is looking for troubles just there. The teacher, too, is dealing with teaching, not with troubles. (But why not, since from the teacher's point of view most children are normal.)

Paediatrics

The paediatrician is in one respect in a similar position to the psychologist. He may be at the top of his profession and yet be unsuitable for intimate dealings with the mind of a child, or for that matter with the personalities of parents. (What is there to prevent this?)

Doctors who specialize in paediatrics have a very special place in the medical profession. They are the only doctors who deal with the whole individual, although of course they may specialize. But even when the paediatrician is a specialist, he has a whole individual in his care; and he has the opportunity, moreover, to think of the child in the family and social setting, and to be at one and the same time the doctor of the patient's body and of the patient's mind. He could be the most privileged of all of us. Does he use or fail to use this privilege?

In practice, it works out that paediatricians as a whole concern themselves by self-selection mostly with the body and its function. They tend to be "good with children", but they need not be, and no-one stops a doctor from being a paediatrician because of his personality or character. We have to take paediatrics as we find them and to recognize that there is such a tremendous amount for the paediatrician to concern himself with on the physical side that it is understandable when he or she has not the time or the emotional reserve for the study of the half of paediatrics which concerns the child's person rather then his physiology and anatomy.

There is a borderline, however, which has great importance for us; this is where a physical malformation or defect or illness affects the mind or the personality or the character. I refer to mental defect, encephalitis, coarctation of the aorta, chronic rheumatic heart disease involving a long period of hospitalization, etc. etc. Cooperation between paediatrician, teacher, social worker, and psychotherapist becomes an essential in this work.

The difficulty about paediatrics for us is that the doctor tends to be in a position of importance simply because he is a doctor. He takes responsibility for life. He is qualified to make mistakes that kill. The trouble starts when the doctor begins to throw his weight about, or begins to use this artificial position he finds himself in to exert authority outside his speciality.

He has saved a child's life, and then perhaps he calmly gives advice on a matter of management. "You should send your child away to school." The parents tend to think that the doctor who saved the child's life knows about these other matters, and they may take his advice. But this way of dealing with the parents' problem is a wrong one. What is needed in response to the question the parent asks which leads the doctor to give advice is an investigation, perhaps by a team, and the institution of case-work. The doctor ought to know how to keep out of these areas in which he has no jurisdiction; indeed, he has no more authority than the questioner. There is no way of altering the doctors, but presumably it may be possible to educate the public in the use of doctors so that the special skills that doctors have may be used in the areas in which these skills have relevance.

We forgive the paediatrician only because of the immense importance he acquires when he is our own doctor when our children are ill. But this is a local and temporary matter and must not be allowed to colour the way we work together outside the area of our own doctor's ministry.

Psychiatry

We need the psychiatrist, along with the paediatrician and the G.P. for taking medical responsibility, most especially to provide cover in case of suicide.

In the case of the psychiatrist, it is necessary to think in terms of the amount that he or she has been able to unlearn from the experience of work with adults, since many adult patients will have had diseases that children do not have or have been affected by old age, or by degenerative processes such as arteriosclerosis affecting the blood supply to the brain.

The domination of adult psychiatry over child psychiatry is a phenomenon that distresses me, and I believe that child psychiatry has much more to offer adult psychiatry than can ever be true the other way round. It is among the child psychiatrists in particular that mental disorder is thought of in terms of the emotional development of the individual in the family and the social setting.

In a way, there is a problem here only in so far as the training in child psychiatry must needs be implanted on the training in adult psychiatry. We must leave it to the individual psychiatrists for them to see how to fit everything into a short life—but we do need them to know about the practice of medicine and the practice of paediatrics, and to have had experience of psychotherapy of a dynamic kind.

What we know we need is psychiatry in terms of special knowledge of the fields bordering on that of neurology—that is, mental defect, epilepsy, brain damage, after-effects of encephalitis, concussion, and the rare brain diseases, including tumour.

Social work

Next I come to social workers. Social workers bear the clinical burden in child psychiatry. They are self-selected in respect of a drive to be directly involved in the dynamics of individual and group life. They want to be of use in the direction of undoing the tangles that belong to human growth and inter-relating. Perhaps more than (those of) other groups, social workers represent the voluntary workers of the days prior to the welfare state. They are also more or less rigorously *selected* according to personality, character, and relative freedom from certain interfering trends (such as the need to manage, to cure, or to pass on a personal affiliation by propaganda). "Client acceptance" is a phrase used in social work but not obviously applicable to the essential attitudes of the other groups. "Meeting the challenge of the Case" is a description of social work and of child psychiatry.

It is the social worker who refuses to offer a solution except that which may emerge on the basis of casework. In the course of time, casework having been instituted, because of the frame that the social worker puts round the persons essentially involved, a new confidence begins to be felt by one or more of the child, and family, and the teachers. In a good proportion of cases that are held well, a solution arises *by internal resolution of personal and interpersonal conflicts, and reorganization of defences.*

The social worker, then, on the basis of the new equilibrium, uses any of the rest of us who are needed in order to implement some tendency that unfolds, and so what we do has a chance to be effective. After a while, the case ceases to be in need of casework, and the various persons involved gradually forget the social worker and the clinic.

In teaching, the end is the school-leaving age, or the moment at which the boy or girl passes the exam that qualifies. In social work the case may end in ten minutes or in ten years, according to the continuance of need. In this and many other ways we may compare the jobs.

Because social workers are carrying the clinical burdens, they do not usually play an active part on committees and in discussions. In discussion, they cannot always get detached quickly enough from the actual case to the theoretical principles that lie behind all our work. Here they are like the psychotherapists. (We have to accept this, and yet somehow entice them to the work of the Association.)

Groups within social work

The Social Work group is a very big one which can properly be looked at in all its complexity, at the movement towards what is called generic (as opposed to specific) training. Each sub-group of the social work group needs to be looked at in respect of the concept of self-selection. The point is to see how different we are from each other.

The generic concept of training avoids the question of self-selection. Even if a training could produce social workers trained to do any kind of social work, the question arises: would they want to? But it is more complex, because in each training scheme an important part of the training is an insistence on placements during the training period. It is not always clear to me that a child care officer wishes to do geriatric social work even for three months, or that an almoner student wishes to do child care. And, all the time, one needs to remember that the various social work agencies have to carry the student, with as little damage to the work of the agency as possible. These placements in the various agencies ought to break down barriers, but there has to be accepted, also, the fact that self-selection can make sense of these very barriers, and can make a man and woman keen to be one type of social worker and none other.

In this Association, we need to find all the various types of social work represented, and to examine their inherent unrelatedness where this exists—that is, in the temperament and unconscious instincts of the social worker.

Probation officers

Probation officers (men or women) tend to be identified with a "masculine" attitude towards children. The majority are men, which points again to self-selection. They work in easily with the authoritative courts. Their clients have met the reality principle in terms of the court, and so the probation officers' social work is based on the chance their work gives them to be more nearly identified with the child than the magistrate or the court official can afford to be. They humanize the mechanical operation of legal decision. The majority of the children who are on the active list of the probation officer are forced by law to attend. If the child's wish to be helped is present, this has to be found—it is not because of a wish to be helped that the child at first attends.

The vast majority of these clients are basically "deprived children", although secondary gains may have put a curtain between the present delinquency and the past moment when deprivation was a fact. Probation officers, concerned as they are with the management of delinquency, may hardly know that the anti-social child occupies a small part of the total work of child psychiatry.

Hospital social workers

The medical social worker likes to work with a doctor. This partnership often proves a fruitful one, as is well known. But doctors vary tremendously in the way they use social workers. Those who work in hospital run the risk of finding themselves caught up with a medical man or woman who learns nothing from the case, but who simply wants someone to implant the medical edict. Find this boy a holiday home! See this girl gets a splint, or that one attends more regularly at the orthoptist's clinic! Get that mother to stop talking so much, and tell her the child will only be "in" three days for tonsillectomy and will be benefiting from not seeing her over that time!

With better luck, the hospital social worker can do casework in a subtle way on the doctors and nurses and can exert lasting influence as well as enjoying herself.

Family Welfare Association social work

A social worker working in the Family Welfare Association is part of a voluntary organization. People apply to the Family Welfare Association for help, so the clients are self-selected, and so I suppose are most of the social workers, men and women, who choose this agency. Their work is based on casework and is just like that of other social workers; but there is this important thing, that the organization is a voluntary one. Many workers in voluntary agencies must have got there by chance, but in the scheme of things there seems to be a place for being a paid worker in one of these voluntary agencies.

Child care³

The basis of child care is *casework*, as with all social workers, but the child care officer has *statutory obligations*, and these have to be fitted in with client-need. It is not possible for a Children's Department to say: "We are too busy to take this case on." The case is "on" by its very existence, and work on the case is assumed to have been done. It has been said as a sort of joke that self-selection in child care is based on ignorance of what the job is like; in other words, child care officers can be heard saying that the burden of responsibility is so great in this work that they would not have taken it up had they known what it would involve in terms of responsibility. But it continues to draw workers.

There are important features in child care that affect self-selection, and it should be remembered that there is no medical

---

³Now included in general social work.

man on the case, unless the child, like any other child, should happen to get measles or something. The worker has total responsibility, that is, relative to the Children's Officer who is responsible to the Committee, the chairman of this committee being responsible to the local authority. This undoubtedly makes the work more rewarding to the worker. In so far as it is successful, it is the worker's success. Undoubtedly, this brings out the best in many men and women, even if it kills them.

What about sub-groups? Now let us look into a Children's Department. Do we find unity there? I would say not. The specialist worker in adoption has an orientation that is different from that of the specialist worker in foster care. The workers chiefly associated with residential work have different loyalties again, and so have those who deal chiefly with the physically handicapped. Another worker is completely caught up in court work. Open other doors and you will find yet others who are collected together under the Children's Officer, and who meet at the 11 a.m. waterhole for coffee. I am only making these observations in order to draw our attention to the fact that we are essentially various and there is more reason why we should avoid each other than meet, unless we include something that I am calling sophistication.

Residential child care

It is convenient here to refer to residential care. The workers in this field carry the can. They have 24-hour responsibility. There must be personal involvement or else nothing happens, and what does happen when the work is good is often nasty and is periodically hellish.

It is natural that residential staff tend to be suspicious of all those who pay flying visits and think they are in charge of the case. It is like the problem of white-collared workers and the workmen who used to wear a red handkerchief with white spots.

The trouble is that heavily involved persons need intermediaries between them and the social provision, intermediaries who are less involved and who have time to think.

To cater for self-selection, and at the same time to attract people into residential work, presents a real problem. No doubt the answer is to offer better and universal training for residential workers, who are social workers indeed. Some, after training, will want to self-select themselves into another category, one that does not involve washing, cooking, and feeling guilty when a child absconds.

The important thing here and now about all this is that the child whose home life is disrupted needs the residential worker and *also* needs the child care or other worker who is relatively detached, but who is more closely identified with social provision. The child does not need these two to understand each other or even to like each other. Sophisticated cooperation could be enough.

At the deep level of psychosomatic living, there are natural divisions between people, and cooperation becomes effective when sophisticated thinking processes are brought to play and an artificial state of affairs is created in which coffee-breaks enable people to meet each other and to communicate about other things for which they have a common language.

The nearer a worker is to the child, the more difficult it will be for him or her to discuss theory without being overwhelmed by a sense of the unreal. Theory seems futile to someone who wants to know what to do *now* with a problem of management. I get this in private practice, where a mother comes for consultation and I find that what she needs is for me to *see* the child or children, the results of her work; discussion of the theory of infant and child-care leaves her cold, and I am glad.

Psychiatric social workers

Psychiatric social workers, like all social workers, are selected by careful procedure. They have always been distinguished by the fact that their qualification includes being educated in terms of the theory of the emotional development of the child—the child individually and relative to the family and to society. Psychiatric social workers have always been dynamically involved people.

Since the mid-1930s in this country (earlier in the United States), the psychiatric social worker has been bearing the clinical burden of psychiatry, both in the psychiatrist's work with adults and in child psychiatry, as for instance in Child Guidance Clinics. The psychiatric social workers may indeed have played a major part in the slow change that has undoubtedly taken place in this country in regard to the recognition of the mentally ill as of the same stuff as those who are supposed to be mentally healthy.

The psychiatric social worker is self-selected, one would think, by looking at mental illness, just as the doctor wishes to look at physical illness as a distortion of growth or an example of environmental deficiency or persecution. One could postulate a capacity in the psychiatric social worker to identify with the mentally ill person, to stand in mad shoes, and to walk under a mad hat—that is, without loss of personal sanity. A degree of personal maturity has been indeed needed for this work, and an absence of trends, tendencies, and affiliations.

There are many others in the wider grouping of social work—those drawn to geriatric social work, people who operate meals on wheels, who help deaf patients to use hearing aids, who are officials administering old-age pensions or national assistance. One could add: school counsellors, marriage guidance workers, those who operate play groups, operate the open door for agoraphobics, alcoholics, and suicides anonymous—a full list would constitute a history of our times.

Psychotherapy

I have left to last my sub-group—psychotherapy. I am an analyst, trained in the Freud school, but whatever I say must do for all psychotherapists. For this work, self-selection is found to be only a first step. Selection is excessively difficult, since each student is having an analysis during training. Self-selection continues during the years of training, and, in this way, many students change their minds and go back to psychiatry or teaching or take up gardening.

Psychotherapists must have a theory on which to work, and this theory, it will be found, derives from Freud's immense contribution, and from the work of those who followed this up or who reacted against certain elements in it. Jung needs to be mentioned by name, as much of Jung is just Jung, and not a development from or a reaction to Freud.

It is part of the analyst's job to understand unconscious motivation, and so (one would think) to tolerate unresolved conflicts in interpersonal relationship.

Someone said: "The Vietnam War will go on for 100 years." This seems to me to be good psychology. Whoever said it could be a caseworker or a psychotherapist.

People get tired, and war shifts from one to another area of the globe. Someone else said: "Only victory will satisfy us." This is bad psychology because it means intolerance of conflict that does actually exist, and the inevitable result of victory (in terms of the unconscious) is defeat.

A psychotherapist cannot do without this backbone to psychotherapy that has been built up in the past seventy years. The analyst has a great responsibility for the teaching of theory and for the development of theory according to what the patients are all the time trying to teach us, thereby giving strength to the whole wide area of work with children, of whatever kind.

The A.C.P.P. function

The A.C.P.P. is essentially a heterogeneous group or (in another language) a motley crew.

"Que faites-vous dans cette galère?", a probation officer whispers to a colleague while a teacher describes the staffing arrangements in a comprehensive school.

I am not asking for a rush towards unification. This ecumenical tendency can be looked at and dissected, and perhaps it reveals a fear of confusion, disharmony, disunity, disintegration. Nothing based on fear can satisfy us.

The unit that depends for its existence on flight from disunity contains within itself the seeds of its own dissolution. I do not believe we can start to talk about the A.C.P.P. as a unit except on a basis of full acknowledgement of the mutual antagonisms and suspicions of its sub-groups. As I have taken the trouble to look for these and to point the way to many others that are not immediately to the fore, I feel I have qualified for the task of looking for something to justify our existence.

When I try to state this I come back to the fact that the collective child—well and ill, mentally defective and clever, well-cared for and neglected, infantile or nearly mature—the collective child may need us to exist. To meet this need we have to allow ourselves to leave the area of our own speciality, where each one of us feels real, and to operate in sophistication, tolerating the sense of artificiality that this generates in us.

It would be valuable if one could link each service with some place in the scheme of the individual developing in the environmental provision.

The teacher (as I have suggested already) acts as substitute for parents, who have done the foundation-laying in the years before school starts.

The social worker's interest in the child comes from the point where environmental provision is not good enough, so that the process of individual emotional development is held up or defences are being organized that distort the personality or character. Social workers are organized to bring social provision to the rescue of the child.

The probation officer comes to the work in relation to the part the father plays as he comes or fails to come into the infant–mother relationship in his male role. Here there must usually be a punitive element, at any rate in the form of a background of legal machinery.

The psychotherapist finds drive from an identification with the individual who is being in some way distorted, or who just finds his or her own human nature too difficult anyway. There is a link with the child's distress.

The residential worker's work links with the early and later stages of family provision that failed in its functioning.

The psychologist cannot be described in these terms, because a child does not naturally call out for a psychologist. The need for psychology comes from the psychologist, who is not, by definition, a helpful person.

A normal child wants and gets his or her own parents, and family, and the extensions of the family, this in wider and wider circles till the Welfare State is reached.

Am I alone in feeling this artificiality? I think it is in assessing the use that we can be to each other, since we are made of such variable stuff, that we can call on the psychologists to help, because they seem to be able to operate in a world of the split-off intellect, where feelings are shed, where psychosomatic living is temporarily ignored. Your new president is a psychologist and your secretary too, so you are well-served.

Let us say that there is a zoo, and it has in it animals that have reached the top of the profession. Lions, giraffes, hippopotamuses, bats, ospreys, mice, and red admiral butterflies. They scarcely know each other, and they have nothing in them that would make them form a zoo. But children need to be able to go with their fathers and mothers on Saturday afternoons, and to see these fine specimens and then go home and read about them. Our justification may be simply in the fact that the collective child needs just this zoo. That could be enough, because we are made up individually, and self-selection or unconscious motivation leads us to special work to which we develop loyalty.

We all have been children, and perhaps that is all that joins us. This could be sufficient to enable us in committee to work out a year's programme that caters for all the aspects of life that the collective child would employ. Such a child would, I hope, invent and employ the A.C.P.P. committee, and would perhaps enjoy watching the groups misunderstand each other. And, I assure you, we do. We have constantly misunderstood each other. And we shall . . .[4]

---

[4]The text ends here and was Winnicott's second (incomplete) lecture on psychologists as a group.

30

A link between paediatrics and child psychology: clinical observations

[1968]

My purpose is to use this special occasion as an opportunity to direct your attention to the exciting prospect that lies before any young doctor or other worker coming into the field of clinical medicine at the present time.

I wonder what you will be thinking about as I utter these words. You will have all manner of special skills already at your disposal, and you will be thinking in terms of the clinical application of physics, nuclear physics, biochemistry, physiology, biology. You may have already gone so far as to consider the possibility of the transplantation of a dead man's whole body on to a live man's soul. I cannot tell.

For me, I simply mean the opportunity everyone has for original clinical observation.

Such big things happen all around us that we may feel small and insignificant. As I write, someone is playing Beethoven's Emperor piano concerto, and I know, as I listen, that my tinklings on my piano will not go down to history. Political events overtake us, and the facts of economics shape our ends whether we like it or not. Let us not forget, however, the example set us by the great masters of clinical medicine who loved to observe and to record, and who live in our minds and in our

255

affections because of their belief in the value of small details, carefully noted and collated.

Beside me, alongside the radio and Beethoven, I have Henoch's two volumes, *Lectures on Children's Diseases*.[1] May I ask you to go and read these if you have not already done so? These lectures do not make us feel hopeless, because, after all, we are in Henoch's position, involved with people, people who come to us because of illness or distress; and we can use Henoch and Gee and Sydenham and Osler and Tommy Horder as a basis for our own attitude. Each one of us can enjoy writing a sonata or two, even if we do not achieve the immortal concerto.

I will start from Henoch. But first I must acknowledge the undoubted fact that clinical medicine is a bit overcrowded on the *physical* side—Henoch was lucky in that he had the whole field for his wanderings. Henoch did not even need to distinguish between physical and emotional determinants when ordering the material garnered during his day of clinical involvement.

For you, if you are heavily loaded on the physical side, there has been a century of close observation since Henoch's day. Can there be anything left? I believe there can be. But it is not my job to explore the physical side of the clinical scene.

What I wish to do is to draw attention to the vast uncharted areas awaiting your attention in the area of the psyche half of the psychosomatic partnership. I hope that dedicated somatics who may be present will bear with me as I try to give you a glimpse of the psyche.

We are short of words here. I do not mean to refer specifically to disorders of the split-off intellect. That would take me to academic psychology. The opposite partner of the soma in life's waltz is not the mind. What I refer to is individual emotional development—a subject that has its size equivalent to the size of physiology. I refer to the development of the individual person in the environment, the establishment of the personality, the attainment of a sense of I AM, and of ME and YOU, the building up of a personal inner reality; and I include the unconscious as well as the conscious roots of behaviour. I am considering the long,

---

[1]E. Henoch, *Lectures on Children's Diseases* (London: The New Sydenham Society, 1889).

often painful, often joyful journey towards maturity, and the living of the life of a mature person, an adult in the community, the achievement of socialization without loss of individual integrity.

We take so much for granted, if we are healthy, and why should we not! But as clinicians we may use our health to look at the meaning of health, and at the cost in terms of child care, and we may scrutinize the points of failure of development and examine the organization within the personality of defences against intolerable anxiety.

Now let me return to Henoch, leaving you to read his description of purpura and all that, and choosing a case that I can follow up with an observation of my own. Here is an extract from Volume 1:

> Thus on 5th January, 1878, a child of one year whom I have already mentioned, who had been perfectly well and in whose family epilepsy was unknown, was brought to me at the poly-clinic. Five months before, the child while sucking had bitten its mother's breast with its two incisors (which were prematurely developed), and, when she screamed violently, at once fell into severe convulsions, its whole body being affected in the fit. These convulsions had since then been repeated four times without any cause and without any tendency to rickets being observable. Such cases cannot but rouse anxiety lest the disease should become habitual and develop into epilepsy.

You note the baby's bitings and the mother's unpreparedness for this, and her intolerance and violent reaction. This is not only a matter of prematurely developed incisors.

At risk of presumption I give a case out of my 1931 book, *Clinical Notes on Disorders of Childhood* (p. 165).

Case

> A girl (2463) first attended hospital (in the 1920s) when 6 months old, with moderately severe infective gastro-enteritis. She was the first baby, breast-fed.
>
> At 7 months, she was brought again because she began to lie awake, crying. She was sick after food and did not enjoy the

breast-feeds. Supplementary feeds had to be given, and weaning from the breast was completed in a few weeks.

At 9 months she had a fit, and continued to have occasional fits, usually at 5 a.m., about a quarter of an hour after waking. The fits affected both sides and lasted five minutes.

At 11 months, the fits were frequent. The mother found she could prevent individual fits by distracting the child's attention. In one day, she had to do this four times. The child had become nervy, jumping at the least sound. She had one fit in her sleep. In some of the fits she bit her tongue, and in some she was incontinent of urine.

At 1 year she was having four to five fits a day. It was noticed she would sometimes sit down after a feed, double up, and go off. She was given orange juice, then went off. She was put to sit on the floor, and a fit started. One morning she woke and immediately had a fit, then slept; soon she woke again and had another fit. At this time the fits began to be followed by a desire to sleep, but even at this severe stage the mother could often stop a fit in the early stage by distracting the child's attention. I made at the time this note: "Taken on my knees she cries incessantly, but does not show hostility. She pulls my tie about in a careless way as she cries. Given back to her mother she shows no interest in the change and continues to cry, crying more and more pitifully right on through being dressed, and so till carried out of the building." At this time I witnessed a fit, which was marked by tonic and clonic stages and followed by sleep. The child was having four to five a day, and was crying all day, though sleeping at night.

Careful examinations revealed no sign of physical disease. Bromide was given, 3 to 15 gr. in the day, according to need.

At one consultation I had the child on my knee observing her. She made a furtive attempt to bite my knuckle.[2] Three days later I had her again on my knee, and waited to see what she would do. She bit my knuckle three times so severely that the

[2]This is the link with Henoch's case, where biting is involved. *D.W.W.*

skin was nearly torn. She then played at throwing spatulas on the floor incessantly for fifteen minutes. All the time she cried as if really unhappy. Two days later I had her on my knee for half an hour. She had had four convulsions in the intervening two days. At first she cried as usual. She again bit my knuckle very severely, this time without showing guilt feelings, and then played the game of biting and throwing away spatulas; *while on my knee she became able to enjoy play.* After a while she began to finger her toes, and so I had her shoes and socks removed. The result of this was a period of experimentation which absorbed her whole interest. It looked as if she was discovering and proving over and over again, to her great satisfaction, that whereas spatulas (and socks, I might have said) can be put to the mouth, thrown away, and lost, toes cannot be pulled off.

Four days later the mother came and said that since the last consultation the baby had been "a different child". She had not only had no fits, but had been sleeping well at night— happy all day, taking no bromide. Eleven days later the improvement had been maintained, without medicine; there had been no fits for fourteen days, and the mother asked to be discharged.

(I visited this child one year later [1931] and found that since the last consultation she had had no symptom whatever. I found an entirely healthy, happy, intelligent, and friendly child, fond of play and free from the common anxieties.)

Imagine my happiness when I discovered that Henoch had already been over this territory, which by the way is still awaiting exploration by yourselves. I must impress on you the fact that this was before 1930, and that if you go here now in 1968 you must not only know how to interpret the EEG, but also you must be familiar with the theory of the emotional development of the infant, and especially of that part that concerns the arrival of oral sadism on top of what is sometimes called a pre-ambivalent phase in which the destructive potential has not yet become evident. I can tell you that extremely complex theoretical problems present here, but to encourage you I say that the great need is for *your clinical observations*. The psychoanalyst may gain insight into these matters in his therapeutic work, and even an adult patient may tell us what to look for in infancy, but it is you who observe infants who can let us know what makes sense and what makes nonsense. Please Help! The dichotomy between paediatrics (physical) and child psychiatry is the saddest thing we have to bear in our professional lives. I can say this here because of the positive and pioneer attitude of your professor.

Now let me go back to the stage of a baby's development, that is, to *absolute dependence*. The baby is newborn, full of genes and genetic potential, but not able to realize anything except through the agency of the adaptive environment. At first the environment is the mother who (in health) is identified with her baby to a remarkable degree, that is, for a few weeks before the baby's birth and for some weeks or months afterwards, till she begins to separate off according to the baby's growing need to have her as a separate thing.

Here is an account of a mother's reaction to having her first child. You see her *slow* awakening from a state of career girl to one of what I call maternal preoccupation. Later, having had three other babies, she easily achieved the state that the baby needs, in which all the career aspect has been set aside at least pro tem. (This is one of the difficulties of being a woman.)

Mark's mother

"I have always wanted to have children, though the reason seems rather obscure. To say that I love children would be good enough except that my experience of young children was absolutely nil. I had the kind of feeling, though, that unless one had a child one wasn't really 'doing one's bit', and I thought that a baby would be like an animal who I could feed, pet, and do with exactly as I wished. I had no conception that having a baby meant really hard work, nor that a baby was very much an individual who screamed when things weren't going well and who demanded, or seemed to demand, things endlessly.

"Then there was all this business about 'born mothers'. I presumed that I would be able to care for it without any trouble since I presumed that all the knowledge I hadn't got would pop out of a little drawer in my brain as soon as I had given birth. It's rather like the fantasy of being able to sit down at a piano and play a Chopin étude immediately, and perfectly.

"Well, I had a fairly miserable labour, although I was reasonably well looked after and, of course, I was terribly excited about the 'end product'. When the boy was born, it was about nine o'clock at night, and from nine to ten they left him with me and I just lay there, holding him in my arms, ravenously hungry (I'd not eaten lunch) and deeply moved and excited by him. But from the moment he lay there, alive with wide-open, unblinking eyes, I began to feel frightfully nervous, too. He was so solid, somehow, and so much a presence and a person already. When he looked at me he seemed to expect so much of me, and it was then I realized that I knew absolutely nothing about babies.

"I would have liked to have given him the breast because I felt it might give me courage and him comfort, but no one suggested it and I wasn't sure whether he might not be sick, or have a fit, or something if I did. Well, then they took him away and at midnight gave me a bowl of stale corn flakes with milk but no sugar. I still feel resentful about that! And then, for two days, or maybe it was only one day, I can't remember now, he was cot-fed, which meant I couldn't hold him and I didn't see him either. They did this with babies who have had a fairly difficult arrival so that they can sleep a lot and not be disturbed by being lifted out of their cots. So, when he was finally wheeled to my bedside, I felt that I had, in some way, failed him already. I longed to hold him and establish a relationship with him, and I felt that this gap had damaged something.

"When I finally breast-fed him, I couldn't have enough of him and I loved holding and feeding him and being 'at one' with him. This is the best time really, because one is not tired by household chores and the conditions that prevail with a newborn baby at home. Otherwise, as you know, it was utterly horrible in hospital, but those times with the baby were a little oasis in the day. That part of it could have gone on for ever!

"Getting home meant that I had lots of other things to do, and I resented doing them and began to feel guilty again. I felt that the baby expected me to be there for him and that I had 'fallen down' as a mother if I didn't rush to him at the slightest peep. Since I had left hospital after only five days, I had to stay in bed anyway, and Mum came to cook so that I could concentrate on the baby. It was a very hot summer, and I was getting in and out of bed all the time to attend to him and so developed a frightful cold which made everything uncomfortable since I had to wear a face mask when I fed him! Once again, the only bearable time was when I was feeding him, but since it became more and more obvious that he wasn't getting enough from me, I felt inadequate yet again.

"To make it more specific, I felt inadequate:

(1) Because the milk supply wasn't lasting.
(2) He screamed at me and turned away from the empty breast.
(3) I never seemed able to make him comfortable and 'at peace'.
(4) I was resentful because he was cross with me and this made me feel more inadequate still.

"Well, the tension that was built up became absolutely unbearable. I was always tired and always resentful. We had a daily at that time who used to take him for walks for me, and she would take him to Boots chemist shop and weigh him. She'd always come back from there and say that the people in the shop said how pale he was, even though he appeared to be gaining weight. God knows how. And she, the daily, thought he should be having more to eat. We used to argue about this, and I insisted that as he was gaining weight, he *must* be getting enough to eat. I therefore came to the conclusion that the reason he screamed at me was because he hated me. I cannot be specific about why I thought he hated me except that I felt I was making a mess of things generally. I didn't put him on to a bottle because this, again, would have made me feel totally useless. Also, I wanted to build up his immunity and willy-nilly, screaming or not, give him the much-talked-about contact with the breast.

"The relief when he went on to the bottle—at 3 months—was immense. He slept better and became much more contented. But I felt that the damage was done and that he was on the road to ruin. I, therefore, felt that since I was so inadequate as mother, the less I had to do with him the better. I, in the meantime, was fat, resentful, and felt a complete and utter failure. Whenever I took him for a walk, usually over the weekends, my thighs were so fat that they used to rub together and get terribly sore, and I loathed these walks for that reason. Everything ached and was uncomfortable and there was no pleasure in anything. From being a smart, elegant career girl, I had deteriorated into a fat housewife, and, on top of this, part of me had opted-out as a mother. At home, I did a lot with him: I played with him when he was awake; I showed him picture books from a very early age; we listened to music together. He had a great deal of his father, too."

You will only get true statements like this one if you believe in what you hear. If you believe what mothers and fathers say, you can glean these descriptions of *feelings*. It is feelings that matter. Factual errors can be corrected at leisure.

Now I want you to jump with me to the observation of a little girl who played while I was having a consultation with the mother. From the girl's point of view, she dominated the scene and it was her interview. This was something that the mother and I allowed in order that we could have an hour together, which we needed in order to discuss the fate of her little boy who was a mongol with a congenital heart defect. As this was not a therapeutic consultation, I was able to keep the play going by being playful myself; a picture is given, therefore, which includes ideas that come from me. It is possible to detect in this material the way in which this girl of 5 identifies with her parents in respect of their very great problem while at the same time she retains her own childhood irresponsibility and spontaneity.

Diana

I had to conduct two consultations in parallel, one with the mother, who was in distress, and a play relationship with the daughter, Diana.

My contact with the mother lasted an hour. The child was with us all the time, and my task was a threefold one: to give the mother full attention because of her own needs, to play with the child, and (for the purpose of writing this paper) to record the nature of Diana's play.

As a matter of fact, it was Diana herself who took charge from the beginning, for as I opened the front door to let in the mother an eager little girl presented herself, putting forward a small teddy. I did not look at her mother or at her, but I went straight for the teddy and said: "What's his name?" She said: "Just Teddy!" So a strong relationship between Diana and myself had quickly developed, and I needed to keep this going in order to do my main job, which was to meet the needs of the mother. In the consulting-room, Diana needed all the time, naturally, to feel that she had my attention, but it was possible for me to give the mother the attention she needed and to play with Diana too.

In describing this case I shall give what happened between me and Diana, leaving out the material of the consultation with the mother.

When we all three got into the consulting-room, we settled down, the mother sitting on the couch, Diana having a small chair to herself near the child table. Diana took her small teddy bear and stuffed it into my breast pocket. She tried to see how far it would go down, and examined the lining of my jacket, and from this she became interested in the various pockets and the way that they did not communicate with each other. This was happening while the mother and I were talking seriously about the backward child of 2½, and Diana gave the additional information: "He has a hole in his heart." One could say that while playing she was listening with one ear. It seemed to me that she was able to accept her brother's physical disability due to the hole in his heart while not finding his backwardness within her range.

In the playing which Diana and I did together, playing without therapeutics in it, *I felt free to be playful*. Children play more easily when the other person is able to be playful. I suddenly put my ear to the teddy bear in my pocket and I said: "I heard him say something." She was very interested in this. I said: "I think he wants someone to play with." And I told her about the woolly lamb that she would find if she looked at the other end of the room in the mess of toys under the shelf. Perhaps I had an ulterior motive, which was to get the bear out of my pocket. Diana went and fetched the lamb, which was considerably bigger than the bear, and she took up my idea of friendship between the teddy bear and the lamb. For some time she put the teddy and the lamb together on the couch near where the mother was sitting. I, of course, was continuing my interview with the mother, and it could be noted that Diana retained an interest in what we were saying with some part of herself, a part that identifies with grownups and grownup attitudes.

In the play, Diana decided that these two creatures were her children. She put them up under her clothes, making herself pregnant with them. After a period of pregnancy, she announced that they were going to be born, but they were "not going to be twins". She made it very evident that the lamb was to be born first and then the teddy bear. After the birth was complete, she put her two newly born children together on a bed which she improvised on the floor, and she covered them up. At first she put one at one end and the other at the other end, saying that if they were together they would fight. They might "meet in the middle of the bed under the clothes and fight". Then she put them sleeping together peacefully, at the top of the improvised bed. She now went and fetched a lot of toys in a bucket and in some boxes. On the floor around the top end of the bed she arranged the toys and played with them; the playing was orderly, and there were several different themes that developed, each kept separate from the other. I came in again with an idea of my own. I said: "Oh look! you are putting on the floor around these babies' heads the dreams that they are having while they are asleep." This idea intrigued her, and she took it up and went on developing the various themes as if dreaming their dreams for the babies. All this was giving the mother and me time which we badly needed because of the work we were doing together. Somewhere just here the mother was crying and was very disturbed, and Diana looked up for a moment, prepared to be anxious. I said to her: "Mother is crying because she is thinking of your brother who is ill." This reassured Diana because it was direct and factual, and she said, "Hole in the heart", and then continued dreaming the babies' dreams for them.

So here was Diana not coming for a consultation about herself and not being in any special need for help, playing with me and on her own, and at the same time caught up in her mother's state. I could see that the mother had needed to bring Diana, she being herself too anxious for a direct confrontation with myself because of the very deep disturbance which she felt on account of having an ill boy. Later, the mother came to me by herself, no longer needing the distraction of the child.

When at a later date I saw the mother alone we were able to go over what happened when I saw her with Diana, and the mother was then able to add this important detail, that Diana's father exploits Diana's forwardness and likes her best when she is just like a little grownup. There can be seen in the material a pull towards premature ego development, an identification with the mother, and a participation in the mother's problems that arise out of the fact that the brother is actually ill and abnormal.

Looking back on what happened, I find it possible to say that Diana had prepared herself before she set out to come, although the interview was not arranged for her benefit.

From what the mother told me, I could see that Diana was organized for the contact with me just as if she knew she was coming to a psychotherapist. Before starting out, she had collected together the first of her teddy bears and also her discarded transitional object. She did not bring the latter but came prepared to organize a somewhat regressive experience in her play activities. At the same time, the mother and I were witnessing Diana's ability to be identified with her mother not only in respect of the pregnancy, but also in respect of taking responsibility for the management of the brother.

The play was of a self-healing kind. The result was comparable with a psychotherapeutic session.

Now perhaps you would look at something rather different. Here is a tiny detail from the story given me by the mother of a girl of 7.

Linda

I hope you will understand that these tiny details do not arrive unless one gives the parents the opportunity to take their own time discovering what they feel can be reported in the situation of special trust and confidence which belongs to the professional set-up.

The tiny detail which I choose to report is as follows:
Linda is the middle child of five children. The mother noticed something when Linda was 10 months old. She felt uncertain of herself when she started to tell me what was in her mind. She and her husband have a very satisfactory marriage, and the home is a going concern. When this child was 10 months old the mother went away with her husband because of something important in his job which needed not only that he should visit another country, but also that he should if possible be accompanied by his wife. The child was left with the excellent nanny, in whom everyone had great confidence, so that the parents had no anxiety about what they were doing, and in fact they felt there might be no difference from the

child's point of view since the ordinary routine would be kept and the only thing would be that the child would not see her mother for three days. The child was quite used to not seeing her mother for one day.

You can see how carefully this mother was thinking of her children by the fact that, when she was away for three days, she became very much concerned with what might be happening to the child of 10 months, and she became more and more worried. When she came home, she could not wait to see that all was well, so she rushed up to the nursery without taking her hat off. Perhaps all would have been well if she had not been in such a hurry and if she had not been so anxious. As it was, the child froze up. There is nothing more distressing to a mother than this condition in a child who completely loses for the time being all capacity for response. The mother was terribly upset and immediately gave herself over to mending what she knew might be a disaster. She took the child and kept her with her, making no demands but simply waiting, and eventually the child began to relax and then the child and the mother were in contact with each other again. This took many hours or perhaps a day or two to become an established fact, after which it could be said that the mother had mended the harm she had done. From this point onwards, the child resumed her development normally except for one thing. *She developed a phobia of women with hats on.* Wherever she was, if a woman appeared in a *hat*, she would scream to such an extent that the mother took great trouble to avoid this kind of situation. Evidently a woman with a hat brought to the child this terrible feeling that she had experienced of having no feelings and of being frozen, as the saying is, and of being unable to respond.

Eventually, this phobia of women in hats disappeared as a symptom. Nevertheless, I can say that in my consultation with the child about other matters, when she was 7½, there were many drawings and there were, as if by chance, many women's hats. In this way it can be seen that even at 7½ years there was the residue built into the child's personality struc-

ture of the trauma   e mother's disappearance and sudden
return, at 10 months, and of the exceedingly painful phase of
being frozen or unable to feel feelings.

Now finally one more clinical detail, which illustrates a practical use of theoretical understanding.

Rosamund

The father of a little girl of 20 months wrote and asked me to
discuss with him and his wife the illness that they had
watched developing in the child. They are thoughtful and
thinking people, academics. They told me that they had been
able to watch the process by which the symptomatology had
developed, so that an illness pattern had gradually become
manifest. They said that the child had developed irrational
fears connected with pot training, and that these were getting
worse progressively.

I saw the parents once and I did not see the child. I found the
parents to be able to discuss their home affairs intimately and
freely. The consultation was in January 1967. At the time
when Rosamund was 12 months old, in March 1966, an *au
pair* girl was employed in the household and she certainly
played a part in the determination of the symptom formation. In fact this *au pair* girl, of whom the child was very
fond, gradually developed into an acute obsessional psychiatric case. She was obsessed with the idea that there was something wrong about the baby's motions, and as she felt that
these were filthy she changed the napkins as infrequently as
possible. Soon she began to be worried about dirt on her
hands, and the baby began to take over some of the fears. At
13 months the child was having a bath and passed a motion
into the water. This caused a very severe disturbance in the
au pair girl. It was worse still when, at 14 months, the child,
sitting at table, took a lump of motion out of her clothes with
her hand and put it on the table where there was food. The
au pair girl had a violent hysterical outbreak, and it was not

long before she was asked to leave as she had become a se-vere psychiatric casualty.

At 16 months the child again did a large motion in the bath. The mother was in charge and she deliberately paid no atten-tion, hoping to neutralize the bad effects of the previous epi-sodes. In spite of the mother's attitude, the process had started up and the symptomatology of a diffused kind devel-oped.

The next day the child refused to get into her bath. I may say that the parents are not in the least obsessional in type; per-haps they are even opposite to obsessional, and one has to consider the possibility that, without knowing it, they em-ployed a rather obsessional *au pair* girl to counterbalance their own ideas of letting nature take its own course and not training a child to cleanliness. In two words, these parents give the impression of being normal parents, but in psychiat-ric work one has to look out for tendencies of one kind and another even in normal people.

It was now easier to see the illness pattern. The next develop-ment was that the child became worried about a whole lot of phenomena that could be said to be symbolical of faeces in the bath. An example was seaweed floating on water. This is often moving, and after a holiday at the seaside she had a well-developed phobia of everything moving on its own account. This included trees moving in the wind, which terri-fied her, although she could already be helped by an explana-tion about the existence of wind.

Between September and December (at 18 to 20 months of age), the family went on a journey because of the father's work. There was now a new baby. It interested me that I was told about this new baby in this off-hand way, and I believe that the parents were taking some time to gather up courage to deal with this fact of the birth of a new baby after so short an interval. They returned to details later in a consultation.

During this journey, the child had repeated panics of a severe kind, and always she had to be picked up and reassured.

These panics belonged to displaced versions of incontinence as, for instance, when she was playing with a ball and the ball moved *behind* her. The parents accepted at this stage that pot training instituted at the time of the *au pair* girl was a total failure and should be abandoned. Only once did the child manage to do a deliberate motion. All the other times she just made a mess on the floor without acknowledging the existence of the mess.

May I remind you that this was a happy marriage with the two young parents well settled in academic life and very much wanting this child and the next one. The pregnancy and the birth had been easy, and the child had been breastfed at first. It now emerged in consultation how it was that the *au pair* girl came on the scene. She was brought in to help three months before a new baby was expected. In other words, the mother had conceived again when the child was 3 to 4 months old. In this way I learned that she had a brother. Her brother was born when she was 14 months old, and the symptomatology that I described had developed around about this time. She was never jealous of the boy and accepted him easily, except at the very beginning. Rather, she was in need of a constant reassurance about the baby, and one of her most frequent remarks would be : "Where's the baby?" It should be added that micturition had very seldom been deliberate, and, like the motions, it was still something that just happened in the napkins. At the time of the birth, when Rosamund was 14 months old, the mother was two days in hospital, but the father was constantly looking after her and she seemed to need him to be in sight the whole time that she was awake. It could be said that she had rather a gay personality with a good ear for music and plenty of play in her. She was obviously highly intelligent. Life at the time of the consultation was a happy one in the family, except that it was spoiled all the time by the child's fear of anything moving, which produced panics of a severe kind that needed immediate attention.

The question now was, what could be done? Would it be possible to give advice to these parents who were obviously doing everything as well as could possibly be done? It will be understood that when I come to a practical problem like this, I bring to the problem not only the summation of a long experience of the psychotherapy of children, but also a theoretical structure. This is exactly comparable to the way in which, if you were vaccinating a child or arranging for the management of a suspected intussusception, you would bring to the case all that you know and take for granted about anatomy and physiology and physics and biochemistry. It was fairly clear to me that, taking everything into consideration, this child had probably been given as much information as she could take in regard to the question of where babies come from, but that she had been denied some of the infantile and early childhood play or fantasy about babies.

Before children are able to use exact information about the origin of babies, they have their own theories, although, of course, these theories may not have been formulated in the mind or in an intellectual way on the basis of verbalization. I had to speculate in the way that I am describing and make a test. I therefore asked the question: "Is she interested in tummies?" The idea in my mind, based on a very considerable experience, was that this child was at a stage in which what comes out of the body is related to what goes in. In other words, babies that come out of mothers started with the mothers' appetite and with their eating and the fantasies that go with eating. From observation of a direct kind, as well as by theoretical reformulations, we know that little children from 9 to 10 months onwards appreciate the relationship between intake and output, and on the basis of this they become interested in the unknown or mystical experiences that join ingestion and excretion.

This child might have lost the ability to make the connection between eating and defaecation and I felt I must know, and for this reason I gave the mother a chance to contribute. As it turned out, the parents were astonished that I should ask this question because, as they went on to tell me, the child was "preoccupied with bellies". They described the way in which she was constantly showing her own tummy with pride and she had an oft-repeated game in which she would do a kind of striptease, saying "Jacket"; and then lifting that up—"Skirt"; and then "tummy", going in from layer to layer. In the same way, she had a compulsive interest in her mother's tummy, and the mother allowed this. The mother was able to say that she expected Rosamund to be interested in her breasts, but her interest in breasts was not in any way comparable to her interest in tummies. As a further detail, the mother was able to tell me that Rosamund would always become very upset if the baby vomited. Even if the baby seemed to be liable to be sick, she would be alarmed and warn the parents.

I now had confirmation of the theory that I had formed in my mind about this child, although, as the father described when he was explaining why he was worried about her state, the symptomatology had seemed to be spreading out. This illness would have as its centre the threat of a loss of connection between eating and defaecation, and the obsession with tummies would therefore be an important link remaining, one which could possibly be used in therapy. The child had become worried about all kinds of displacements of the idea of faeces, such as mud on shoes and dirt on fingers, and she was beginning to be frightened of anything that looked at all like what she called "pluff" on the floor. In other words, she was beginning an illness in which faeces had no meaning except the getting rid of bad things or else perhaps had no meaning at all, as was evidenced by her incontinence, which she seemed to be no longer able to own up to, so that she was completely unconcerned about her own faeces on the floor of the nursery.

The environmental situation, and especially the illness of the *au pair* girl, had played into her own tendency to lose the essential connection between intake and output. My job would therefore be to reinforce what remained of her ability to retain this connection. You will see that what she had lost was the ability to think that something good could be formed in the inside in this time interval between ingestion and excretion. These are matters which concern small children deeply, so that they become specialists in this little area of life and living.

I have had to introduce a certain amount of theory here in order to explain what I did to help these parents in the management of the child. I would like to add that, playing with her doll, she was doing a great deal of strict toilet training and was satisfied when she was able to use the word dry after examining the doll's bottom. In this way, she was imitating the *au pair* girl. There was also a certain amount of identification with the baby brother, so that she wanted to be like him in the feeding situation.

I must leave out the various ways in which this child's development was going well, although these were important details because they encouraged me to think that here was some simple procedure which would alter the pattern which was rapidly becoming a pathological one.

Having summed up the parents as rather normal people who would probably not have had this ill child if it had not been for the *au pair* girl, who was badly chosen, I decided to give them an idea. I now want to tell you what I said to the parents, but I want to make it clear first that I only give advice very reluctantly. I said: "Next time the child gives you the opportunity, showing an interest in her own and her mummy's tummy, give her in words that she would understand describing what she knows already in a non-verbal way. Say to her: *'The inside where babies are made out of what you eat.'"* You will perhaps be able to see that I wanted the parents to say this thing which, as it seemed to me, they had missed out, which had to do with a very early childhood form of knowledge, something which gives a positive value to inside things and happenings and which even makes sense of constipation, which at this stage is a pregnancy.

I made notes of all these things, and the parents went away, thinking perhaps that they had consulted someone with funny ideas; but they had certainly listened, and I knew that they would try to find a natural way of taking my advice even if only as an experiment. I suggested that they should not rush at this thing but should wait until they might either come to accept my idea or reject it.

There is a sequel to this story, because the parents quite soon found an opportunity and did what I had suggested. In a letter, the father wrote that Rosamund "received the explanation with great interest, and returned to the subject on her own several times in the following two days. She also seemed to become rather *bashful* about her own tummy (instead of exhibitionistic) as if she now understood that it had two differing important functions."

In the letter, the father went on to say: "Whatever went on in her mind, her behaviour changed with dramatic suddenness. All her symptoms disappeared instantly, and they have not returned." He wrote this after ten days, and he has been good enough to keep me informed so that I know that the change was a lasting one.

Following on this, Rosamund's development went ahead in a straightforward way, and the parents have almost forgotten that there was ever any trouble. It is rather interesting that Rosamund's attitude to her little brother changed at the same time. The main thing was that she became for the first time *jealous* of him in the rather normal way that was absent before. "Jealousy" had been "unnaturally absent", as the father observed. In other words, she had been traumatized by the confusion around the idea of the pregnancy which she had not been able to understand in her own terms, and the lack of jealousy of her brother had been a symptom of her inability to think of him as truly her brother.

Later the mother was able to write me outside the astonishment which she shared with her husband at the dramatic change in the child, and she was able to report residual symptomatology, all of which really made Rosamund into a child more like other children. As can be imagined, the parents were very willing to postpone all efforts at Rosamund's toilet training, because these matters seemed to be unimportant as compared with the phobias and compulsions which had so dramatically disappeared.

I have a year's follow-up in this case, and I have permission from the parents to refer to the case in this lecture. This has been rather a long lecture, and I only hope that Catherine Chisholm would have liked it. I could have given you a potted version of the psychoanalytic theory of the emotional development of the human child, and perhaps you would have found it tiresome. I chose instead to give you some examples of the simplest possible variety, of the kind that you can collect yourselves in your clinical work, day by day, in the hope that you will not think that these matters are for psychoanalysts only. Indeed, they belong specifically to your position in the medical field. I hope that I have also indicated that there is a great deal that can be learned in the field of theory, and if you wish to write concertos, then you must collect information, become proficient in specialized techniques, and acquire some wisdom; and all these things take time. So start soon.

31

Child psychiatry, social work, and alternative care

[1970]

I wish to use this opportunity for a moment of personal re-thinking on the subject of our work with children. This, of course, includes work with parents, families, guardians of all kinds, schools of various types, social groupings and other environmental facts and factors, and indeed the state of society here today and tomorrow.

I shall not hesitate to use the indisputable given—that I am 74 years old, and that I look at life from that age-platform. This age seems unbelievable to many children. A boy asked me last week, after accusing me of having rings around my eyes and of being old, "Do you remember steam trains made to go by coal?" "Did you actually travel in the Flying Scotsman?" More seriously, since I passed the 60 mark I have found that adolescents find me agreeable in the consultation situation, since I have passed out of the parent category into that of grandparent, and the murder theme is in consequence somewhat obliquely seen, instead of directly threatening in the transference.

I want to be positive and not to waste time knocking down enemies, much as this exercise can give satisfaction. I want to say how it is that I'm glad I have for my work a background of psychoanalysis, that is, basic theory that belongs to what we have come to call dynamic psychology. Our work is always a meeting point between us and persons, not between us and an experiment, or a thesis or a planning committee that is arranging for *others* to meet the child, the parent, the nurse, the school teacher, the social worker, the university tutor.

The name of this Association gives evidence that there is room in the world for all kinds of people and work; for me, however, the subject for study is intercommunication between me and the patient as individual persons, meeting on equal terms, each teaching the other and getting enriched by the experience of involvement.

What we do together is always quite a natural thing; something limited is taken from the natural procedures of child care and home life, or of being a child growing or failing to grow in the setting that obtains. If we find we are doing something or behaving in a way that has no counterpart in ordinary life and living, then we pull ourselves up and think again.

What we do in our work is to arrange a professional setting made up of time and space and behaviour, which frames a limited area of child or child-care experience, and we see what happens. This is the same as form in art. Religious people of Christian persuasion use the phrase, *whose service is perfect freedom*, which is the same as the sonnet form accepted by Shakespeare or Keats which allows of spontaneous impulse, and the unexpected creative gesture. This is what we wait for and value highly in our work, and we even hold back our own bright ideas when they come, for fear of blocking the bright ideas that might come from the child or adult patient.

I now want to have a go at classification. Without classification, we cannot plan our work in this huge area that covers child psychiatry, social work, and alternative care.

For my own part, I start with the assumption that every human being is all the time growing and developing, according to the hereditary growth factors, and according to the stage the individual is at in the progression from absolute dependence through relative dependence towards independence. Dependence remains, but the individual has ways and means, as development proceeds, for seeming independent and for feeling independent; these ways and means include the development of a capacity to identify with the environment and, indeed, to internalize an environment.

It is further assumed that, in the early stages, absolute dependence is a fact, and this means that environmental failure ("not good enough" is the phrase that I use) spells personal disaster. As dependence becomes relative, so environmental failure ceases to be necessarily, and immediately, disastrous, and indeed graduated failures of adaptation take their place as positive features of the environmental function.

In other words, there is an evolution of the environmental provision tailored to the changing needs of the individual undergoing emotional development. All this is extremely complex, and is beyond computer skill, and it can only be done "well enough" by a human being who has this particular relationship to the one baby, child, adolescent that we usually call love; love that implies concern and a continuing sense of responsibility, and an easy acceptance of being needed changing into being wanted or not wanted.

I have used the term "primary maternal preoccupation"[1] to describe the thing that has happened to mothers (and fathers) for millions of years, and that can be found to some extent in lions and cats and penguins.

Now I am ready to give my working classification. Individual emotional development is precarious, and when all goes well it involves great pain as well as joy, and the element of luck enters in. We can see that in some cases the environmental provision is good enough. Difficulties arise from minute to minute, but a special effort at adaptation to need made soon enough mends the hurt. The child begins to collect evidence that when things are awful they can be put right, that someone is (as we would say, and the child learns to say) concerned. This is life, and if this is the way a child's life can be described, then we can think in terms of health. We can cut right across symptom details and ignore the categories that belong to adult psychiatry, practised in

---

[1] "Primary Maternal Preoccupation" (1956), in *Collected Papers: Through Paediatrics to Psychoanalysis* (1958).

mental hospitals. Here, we say, is health. Health may have flown out of the window tomorrow, but today the diagnosis is HEALTH. We need to be able to use this word, and not as a reassurance to the parents and to ourselves, but simply as a descriptive term that is appropriate.

On the other side of a line we see ill-health; that is to say, we see environmental provision that is not able to maintain itself, either because of defects in the field of reliability, or because the strains and provocations of the growing individual child (and then of the children) ask too much of the human beings who collectively form the emotional environment, so that the innumerable hurts and moments of agony in the child's life are not being all the time mended—instead, they are building up into an accumulation of insults, against which the child must build up defences. Here is ill-health in the psychiatric sense, a disaster brewing, even when the body is healthy and functioning well.

Alas, even the best paediatricians can be deceived into thinking all is well with a child when the body is lovely, and per contra they can fail to see psychiatric health that may be a fact when physical disability is crippling and when there is an acute or a chronic need for the doctor's and nurse's skills on the physical side.

Now we have two categories, the lucky ones with good-enough environmental provision in terms of adaptation to need, and the unlucky ones who are the true "have-nots", whose environmental provision does not in practice cope, for one reason or another. As these latter children grow, they show by their rigidly organized defences that they carry round with them the unthinkable agonies that belonged to one or repeated or oft-repeated environmental maladjustment.

To add insult to injury, society labels certain of these children "maladjusted". This is wrong indeed.

In between, we find, if we look at our cases, a vast collection of children whose environmental provision somehow failed to maintain a standard that could be called good enough, in terms of adaptation to need and reliability of all kinds. In each case, we must decide how to use the crude classification that I give.

This is a useful classification. It has practical value in that it allows us to use the word health in the face of behavioural abnormalities and psychosomatic malfunctioning and mood disorders and where schizoid tendencies present. We can, of course, try to give personal help to these children who are in distress, and we may sometimes bring about a change which enables a wobbly environment to function adequately and even to grow to acquire the stability that the child needs of it.

Psychotherapy operates in this area.

It is important to recognize the not-good-enough environment as quickly as possible so that time is not wasted on giving psychotherapy when what is needed is specialized child care. This often means temporary or permanent alternative management—residential care, fostering, adoption, and social workers of one kind and another are specialists in this aspect of the practice of child psychiatry. In each case "casework" is needed, and long-term planning is a regular feature.

I have to say that I think that, on the whole, doctors are not good at this job. There is no need to be worried, because paediatricians have an immense amount to their credit on the physical side. I have watched physical paediatrics from 1920 till the present time, and I really do know something of the genius that has gone into the theory and practice of paediatrics in this half-century. But, on the whole, paediatricians are exactly where they were in the other half of paediatrics which has to do with the emotional development of the individual, the maturational process in its relation to the facilitating environment. Social workers have been carrying the burden of the practice of child psychiatry all these years, and it is to social work that we must look for an extension of psychiatric practice to cover all types of case and to engage in preventive work.

So, it is from social work that we must expect the feedback into politics, local and general, into paediatrics, into legal practice, into adult psychiatry. Strangely enough, adult psychiatry has added very little, as I see it, to child psychiatry in the 50 years, at any rate, that I can see with my own eyes.

It may be asked, where does psychology come in? I think that we must use the psychologist where we find that a psychological test gives valuable pointers. It is probably in only a small proportion of the cases in our case-load that such tests give us guidelines.

GLOSSARY
OF MEDICAL TERMS

Anergastic reaction forms: (from *anergasia*) used to describe a psychosis caused by organic lesions of the nervous system—for example, disease or physical damage to the brain. An archaic term.

Angio-neurotic oedema: comparable to urticaria (*q.v.*), but localized and usually short-lived. Severe swelling may occur and, if the larynx is involved, may endanger life.

Anoxaemia : a lack of circulating oxygen, which if prolonged leads to brain damage and, subsequently, death.

Auricular fibrillation: (nowadays *atrial fibrillation*) irregular heartbeat due to damage to the atria of the heart. Commonly associated with rheumatic heart disease (*q.v.*).

Carditis: inflammation of the heart. Commonly associated with rheumatic heart disease (*q.v.*).

Chorea: involuntary irregular movements of the extremities and face—frequently part of a syndrome following an infection. It may follow rheumatic fever (*q.v.*); see also Sydenham's chorea.

Clonic stage, of fit: a stage characterized by uncontrolled spasms of the body.

Coarctation of the aorta: a congenital narrowing of the main artery leading to the heart. Frequently found with other congenital car-

284 GLOSSARY OF MEDICAL TERMS

diac abnormalities. In modern times surgical correction is possible, but when Winnicott was practising medicine patients with this condition died in early adulthood.

Disseminated sclerosis: (now known as *multiple sclerosis*) many lesions occur in the white matter of the brain and spinal cord, resulting in failure of the nerves involved and progressive disability. The disease is variable in its course, often with many relapses and remissions, and may result in gradual deterioration or else be rapidly fatal. Symptoms are also variable: visual failure, weakness and loss of limb control, slurring of speech, and incontinence are common.

Dysuria: painful urination.

Dysergastic reaction form: a mental disturbance due to toxic factors, such as metabolic disturbance or poisoning. An archaic term.

Encephalitis lethargica: an acute viral infection of the nervous system, with fever and severe lethargy, sometimes coma. Sequelae include mental change, paralysis, and Parkinsonism. The illness occurs in epidemics and was last rife in Europe from 1917 to 1920.

Endocrinopathies: diseases of the endocrine glands—for example, thyroid disease.

Haematuria: blood in the urine.

Hydrocephalus: an abnormal increase of fluid surrounding the brain. May be congenital, due to malformations of the brain and surrounding tissues, or acquired, due to infection or trauma. Brain damage and consequent mental and physical deficit was at one time inevitable; today, surgical intervention may be helpful..

Intussusception: a condition in which a section of the intestine becomes invaginated into the adjacent portion, leading to bouts of acute pain, clinical shock, and intestinal obstruction. A serious condition requiring emergency surgery.

Malleoli: protuberances such as those on either side of the ankle.

Marginal placenta praevia: a condition in which the afterbirth is situated low in the womb, leading to a high risk of haemorrhage before or during labour, and a consequent threat to the lives of both the mother and her baby. An indication for Caesarian section.

Mitral stenosis: a narrowing of the mitral valve of the left side of the heart, commonly due to rheumatic heart disease (*q.v.*).

Oligophrenia: constitutional intellectual deficit.

Papular urticaria: a common skin condition occurring in infants, consisting of red blotches and white wheals with intense irritation. Small blisters may imitate chicken pox. Usually due to insect bites or allergy, but in some cases no cause can be demonstrated.

Pruritus: intense itching.

Pruritus ani: itching in the anal area.

Purpura: haemorrhages in the skin or mucous membrane, often giving a purple appearance. May be due to abnormalities in the blood or blood vessels, or due to severe infection.

Rheumatic chorea: *see* chorea; rheumatic fever.

Rheumatic fever: a potentially serious illness following a streptococcal infection and consisting of inflammation of the joints. Frequently there is carditis (*q.v.*), leading to permanent damage to the heart—for instance, mitral stenosis (*q.v.*). The illness is now less common than before.

Rheumatic heart disease: heart disease following rheumatic fever (*q.v.*).

Sydenham's chorea: (St Vitus' Dance) a form of chorea (*q.v.*).

Syndactyly: congenital webbing of the fingers or toes.

Thalidomide: a sedative drug prescribed briefly in the 1960s for insomnia. It was discovered to cause malformations in the developing foetus, particularly of the limbs.

Tonic stage, of fit: a stage during which the body becomes rigid.

Urinary meatus: the opening through which urine is voided (i.e. in boys) at the tip of the penis.

Urticaria: a rash resembling that caused by nettle-stings.

Vascular degeneration: degeneration of the blood vessels.

ORIGINAL SOURCE
OF EACH CHAPTER

1. "Towards an objective study of human nature." A lecture given, by invitation of the High Master, to the Eighth Form of St. Pauls's School, London, in 1945. Also in *The Child and the Outside World* (1957).

2. "Yes, but how do we know it's true?" A talk given to students of psychology and social work at the London School of Economics, in 1950.

3. "Primary introduction to external reality: the early stages." Part of a series of talks given to students of The Institute of Education, University of London, in 1948.

4. "Environmental needs; the early stages; total dependence and essential independence." Part of a series of talks given to students of The Institute of Education, University of London, in 1948.

5. "The bearing of emotional development on feeding problems." A Symposium on Environmental Health in Infancy at the Royal Society of Medicine, organized by the Gerber Baby Council, 17 March 1967.

6. "Sleep refusal in children." Published in *Medical News Magazine* (July 1968).

7. "The effect of loss on the young." A talk written for the directors of the Cruse Club at their A.G.M. in 1968. The Cruse Club was

founded in 1959 and organized self-help groups for widows and their children; it has now been replaced by Cruse Bereavement Care, a nationwide counselling service with 195 branches.

8. "Out of the mouths of adolescents." A book review published in *New Society* (September 1966) of E. M. Eppel & M. Eppel, *Adolescents and Morality* (London: Routledge & Kegan Paul).

9. "The delinquent and habitual offender." Probably written in the early 1940s before the Evacuation.

10. "A clinical approach to family problems: the family." Introductory lecture and course on Human Growth and Development given to postgraduate social work students at the London School of Economics, in 1959.

11. "Mental hygiene of the pre-school child." A talk given on 25 September 1936 to nursery school teachers at the Conference of the Nursery School Association at Hull.

12. "The teacher, the parent, and the doctor." Paper read before the Ideals in Education Conference, Oxford, Easter 1936.

13. "A clinical example of symptomatology following the birth of a sibling." No known source [ca. 1931].

14. "Notes on a little boy." Published in *The New Era in Home and School*, *19* (1938).

15. "The niffle." No known source [undated].

16. "Two adopted children." This article is based on a talk given to the Association of Child Care Officers, 5 December 1953. Also in *The Child and the Outside World* (1957).

17. "Pitfalls in adoption." Written for the *Medical Press* (December 1954). Also in *The Child and the Outside World* (1957).

18. "Adopted children in adolescence." A 1955 report to the Standing Conference of Societies Registered for Adoption.

19. "Contribution to a discussion on enuresis." *Proceedings of the Royal Society of Medicine*, *29* (1936), 1522–1524.

20. "Papular urticaria and the dynamics of skin sensation." *British Journal of Children's Diseases*, *31* (1934), 5–16.

21. "Short communication on enuresis." Printed in *St. Bartholomew's Hospital Journal*, *37* (April 1930), 125–127. Based on a paper read before The Section for the Study of Disease in Children, Royal Society of Medicine.

22. "Child psychiatry: the body as affected by psychological factors." Fragment of a paper, dated 1931. No known source.

23. "On cardiac neurosis in children." A paper given at The Association of European Paediatric Cardiologists Annual General Meeting at Helsinki, 29 June to 2 July 1966.

24. "Three reviews of books on autism." *Child Psychiatry*, by Leo Kanner (London: Bailliere, Tindall & Cox, 1937); from the *International Journal of Psycho-Analysis, 19* (1938). *Childhood Schizophrenia*, by William Goldfarb (Cambridge, MA: Harvard University Press, 1961); from the *British Journal of Psychiatric Social Work, 7* (1963). *Infantile Autism*, by Bernard Rimland (New York: Appleton-Century-Crofts, 1964); from the *British Medical Journal* (10 September 1966).

25. "Autism." A paper prepared for the Society for Autistic Children, Leicester, 26 March 1966.

26. "The aetiology of infantile schizophrenia in terms of adaptive failure." A paper prepared for a study day on Psychosis in Infancy, held in France at Maison de la Chimie, 28 Rue Saint-Dominique, Paris, 21–22 October 1967.

27. "Training for child psychiatry: the paediatric department of psychology." Published in *St. Mary's Hospital Gazette* (September 1961), under the title "The Paediatric Department of Psychology".

28. "Notes on the time factor in treatment." Preparation for a Lecture given to the West Sussex County Council Children's Department, 4 June 1961.

29. "The Association for Child Psychology and Psychiatry observed as a group phenomenon." President's Address, Association for Child Psychology and Psychiatry, 17 February 1967.

30. "A link between paediatrics and child psychology: clinical observations." The Catherine Chisholm Memorial Lecture, Institute of Child Health, Manchester, 24 May 1968. Catherine Chisholm [1878–1952], a Fellow of the Royal College of Physicians, was active in the field of children's health, particularly in the Manchester area.

31. "Child psychiatry, social work, and alternative care." A talk given to the Association of Child Psychology and Psychiatry, Newcastle, in 1970.

BIBLIOGRAPHY

Compiled by Harry Karnac

List of volumes

W1 *Clinical Notes on Disorders of Childhood.* London: Heinemann, 1931.

W2 *Getting to Know Your Baby.* London: Heinemann, 1945.

W3 *The Ordinary Devoted Mother and Her Baby.* Privately published, 1949.

W4 *The Child and the Family.* London: Tavistock, 1957.

W5 *The Child and the Outside World.* London: Tavistock, 1957.

W6 *Collected Papers: Through Paediatrics to Psycho-Analysis.* London: Tavistock, 1958. New York: Basic Books, 1958. [Reprinted as *Through Paediatrics to Psycho-Analysis.* London: Hogarth Press & the Institute of Psycho-Analysis, 1975; reprinted London: Karnac Books, 1992].

W7 *The Child, the Family and the Outside World.* London: Penguin, 1964. Reading, MA: Addison-Wesley, 1987.

W8 *The Family and Individual Development.* London: Tavistock, 1965.

W9 *The Maturational Processes and the Facilitating Environment: Studies in the Theory of Emotional Development.* London: Hogarth Press & The Institute of Psycho-Analysis, 1965. New York: International Universities Press, 1965. [Reprinted London: Karnac Books, 1990.]

W10 *Playing and Reality.* London: Tavistock, 1971. New York: Methuen, 1982.

W11   *Therapeutic Consultations in Child Psychiatry.* London: Hogarth Press &
      The Institute of Psycho-Analysis, 1971. New York: Basic Books,
      1971.

W12   *The Piggle: An Account of the Psychoanalytic Treatment of a Little Girl* (ed.
      Ishak Ramzy).   London: Hogarth Press & The Institute of Psycho-
      Analysis, 1977. New York: International Universities Press, 1977.

W13   *Deprivation and Delinquency* (ed. C. Winnicott, R. Shepherd, & M.
      Davis). London: Tavistock, 1984. New York: Methuen, 1984.

W14   *Home Is Where We Start From* (ed. C. Winnicott, R. Shepherd, & M.
      Davis). London: Penguin, 1986. New York: W. W. Norton, 1986.

W15   *Holding and Interpretation: Fragment of an Analysis.* London: Hogarth
      Press & The Institute of Psycho-Analysis, 1986. New York: Grove
      Press, 1986. [Reprinted London: Karnac Books, 1989.]

W16   *Babies & Their Mothers* (ed. C. Winnicott, R. Shepherd, & M. Davis).
      London: Free Association Books, 1987. Reading, MA: Addison-
      Wesley, 1987.

W17   *The Spontaneous Gesture* (selected letters, ed. F. R. Rodman).
      Cambridge, MA: Harvard University Press, 1987.

W18   *Human Nature.* London: Free Association Books, 1988. New York:
      Schocken Books, 1988.

W19   *Psycho-Analytic Explorations* (ed. C. Winnicott, R. Shepherd, & M.
      Davis). London: Karnac Books, 1989. Cambridge, MA: Harvard
      University Press, 1989.

W20   *Talking to Parents* (ed. C. Winnicott, C. Bollas, M. Davis, & R.
      Shepherd). Reading, MA: Addison-Wesley, 1993.

W21   *Thinking about Children* (ed. R. Shepherd, J. Johns, & H. Taylor
      Robinson). London: Karnac Books, 1996. Reading, MA: Addison-
      Wesley, 1996.

Alphabetical list

*** Indicates that the entry does not appear in volumes W1 to W21.

Aggression in Relation to Emotional Development   1950   W6:204–210
Aitken, Mrs. P.: Letter to [Jan. 13th]   1967   W17:163–164
Aims of Psycho-Analytical Treatment (The)   1962   W9:166–170
American Correspondent (An): Letter to [Jan. 14th]   1969   W17:183–185
Antisocial Tendency (The)   1956   W6:306–315
Antisocial Tendency (The)   1956   W13:120–131
Anti-Social Tendency Illustrated by a Case (The)   1962
  A Criança Portuguesa Vol. 21
  Also appears as Case VII in: W11:110–126
Anxiety   1931   W1:122–128
Anxiety Associated with Insecurity   1952   W6:97–100
Appetite and Emotional Disorder [read before the Medical
    Section, British Psychological Society]   1936   W6:33–51
Art versus Illness by A. Hill [review]   1949   W19:555–557
  Brit. J. Med. Psychol. 22
Arthritis Associated with Emotional Disturbance   1931   W1:81–86
Association for Child Psychology and Psychiatry Observed as
    a Group Phenomenon (The) [President's address,
    A.C.P.P.]   1967   W21:235–254
Asthma: Attitude & Milieu by Aaron Lask [review]   1966   ***
  New Society 17/11
Autism [paper prepared for the Society for Autistic Children] 1966   W21:197–217
Babies as Persons (Further Thoughts on)   1947   W5:134–140
  New Era in Home & School 28/10:199 under title "Babies are
    Persons"
Baby as a Going Concern (The) [B.B.C. radio broadcast]   1949   W3:7–11
Baby as a Going Concern (The)   1949   W4:13–17
Baby as a Person (The) [B.B.C. radio broadcast]   1949   W3:22–26
Baby as a Person (The)   1949   W4:33–37
Balint, Enid: Letter to [March 22nd]   1956   W17:97–98
Balint, Michael: Letter to [Feb. 5th]   1960   W17:127–129
Basis for Self in Body (On the)   1970   W19:261–283
  Nouvelle Revue de Psychanalyse [1971]
  International Journal of Child Psychotherapy [1972]
Bearing of Emotional Development on Feeding Problems (The)
    [Symposium on Environmental Health in Infancy at the
    Royal Society of Medicine]   1967   W21:39–41
Becoming Deprived as a Fact: A Psychotherapeutic
    Consultation   1966
  J. Child Psychother. 1
  Appears as Case XVII in: W11:315–331
Beginning of the Individual (The)   1966   W16:51–58
Beginnings of a Formulation of an Appreciation and Criticism
    of Klein's Envy Statement (The)   1962   W19:447–457
Behaviour Therapy [letter]   1969   W19:558–560
  Child Care News [June 1969]
Berlin Walls   1969   W14:221–227
Beveridge, Lord: Letter to [Oct. 15th]   1946   W17:8
Bick, Esther: Letter to [June 11th]   1953   W17:50–52
Bion, Wilfred R.: Letter to [Oct. 7th]   1955   W17:89–93
Bion, Wilfred R.: Letter to [Nov. 17th]   1960   W17:131

Child Therapy: A Case of Anti-Social Behaviour   1965
  In *Perspectives on Child Psychiatry* ed. J. Howells
  Appears also as Case XV in: W11:270–295
Childhood and Society by E. H. Erikson, 1965 (Review of)   1965   W19:493–494
  New Society [Sept.]
Childhood Schizophrenia by William Goldfarb, 1961 [review]   1963   W21:193–194
  Brit. J. Psychiatric Social Work 7
Children and Their Mothers   1940   W13:14–21
  New Era in Home & School 21
Children in Distress by Alec Clegg & Barbara Megson [review]   1968   ***
  New Society 7/11
Children in the War   1940   W5:69–74
  New Era in Home & School 21/9:229
Children in the War   1940   W13:25–30
Children Learning   1968   W14:142–149
  In *The Family & God,* Christian Teamwork Inst. of Education
Children's Hostels in War and Peace   1948   W5:117–121
  Brit. J. Med. Psychol. 21/3:175
Children's Hostels in War and Peace   1948   W13:73–77
Child's Needs and the Rôle of the Mother in the Early Stages
  (The)   1953   W5:13–23
  [An excerpt] published in series *Problems in Education*
Classification: Is There a Psycho-Analytic Contribution to
  Psychiatric Classification? [postscript dated 1964]   1959   W9:124–139
Clinical Approach to Family Problems (A): The Family [lecture
  at London School of Economics]   1959   W21:54–56
Clinical Example of Symptomatology Following the Birth of a
  Sibling (A)   1931ca W21:97–101
Clinical Illustration of "The Use of an Object"   1968   W19:235–238
Clinical Regression Compared with That of Defence
  Organisation (The Concept of)   1967   W19:193–199
  In *Psychotherapy in the Designed Therapeutic Milieu* ed.
    Eldred & Vanderpol [1968]
Clinical Study of the Effect of a Failure of the Average
  Expectable Environment on a Child's Mental
  Functioning (A)   1965
  IJP 46:81
  Appears also as Case IV in: W11:64–88
Clinical Varieties of Transference   1955   W6:295–299
  IJP 37 [1956]:386
Close-Up of Mother Feeding Baby [B.B.C. radio broadcast]   1949   W3:27–31
Close-Up of Mother Feeding Baby   1949   W4:38–42
Colleague (A): Letter to [Sept. 4th]   1967   W17:165
Collection of children's books reviewed under the title "Small
  Things for Small People" (A)   1967   ***
  New Society 7/12
Collinson, J. D.: Letter to [March 10th]   1969   W17:186–188
Comments on My Paper "The Use of an Object"   1968   W19:238–240
Communicating and Not Communicating Leading to a Study
  of Certain Opposites   1963   W9:179–192

Development of the Capacity for Concern (The)   1963   W13:100–105
Dibs: In Search of Self by Virginia Axline [review]   1966   ***
  New Society 28/4
Discussion of War Aims   1940   W14:210–220
Discussions on Ian Alger's paper "The Clinical Handling of the
    Analyst's Responses"   1966   ***
  Psychoan. Forum 1:3
Disease of the Nervous System   1931   W1:129–142
Dissociation Revealed in a Therapeutic Consultation   1965   W13:256–282
  In *Crime, Law and Corrections* ed. R. Slovenko [1966]
  Also published as Case XIII in: W11:220–238
Disturbed Children ed. Robert J. N. Tod (Foreword to)   1968   ***
  Longmans' Papers on Residential Work Vol. 2
Do Progressive Schools Give Too Much Freedom to the Child?   1965   W13:209–219
  In *Who Are the Progressives Now?* ed. M. Ash [1969]
Doctor (The), His Patient and the Illness by M. Balint, 1957
    (Review of)   1958   W19:438–442
  IJP 39
Dowling, R. S. W.: Letter to [Dec. 8th]   1967   W17:174–175
Dreaming, Fantasying, and Living: A Case-History Describing
    a Primary Dissociation   1971   W10:26–37
D.W.W. on D.W.W.   1967   W19:569–582
D.W.W.'s Dream Related to Reviewing Jung   1963   W19:228–230
Early Disillusion   1939   W19:21–23
Educational Diagnosis   1946   W5:29–34
  National Froebel Foundation Bulletin 41:3
Effect of Loss on the Young (The) [talk written for the Cruse
    Club]   1968   W21:46–47
Effect of Psychosis on Family Life (The)   1960   W8:61–68
Effect of Psychotic Parents on the Emotional Development of
    the Child (The)   1959   W8:69–78
  Brit. J. Psychiatric Social Work 6/1 [1961]
Ego Distortion in Terms of True and False Self   1960   W9:140–152
Ego Integration in Child Development   1962   W9:56–63
End of the Digestive Process (The) [B.B.C. radio broadcast]   1949   W3:17–21
End of the Digestive Process (The)   1949   W4:28–32
Environmental Health in Infancy   1967   W16:59–68
  Portions published in *Maternal & Child Care*
Environmental Needs; The Early Stages; Total Dependence
    and Essential Independence [talk given at The Institute
    of Education, Univ. of London]   1948   W21:29–36
Envy and Gratitude by M. Klein, 1957 (Review of)   1959   W19:443–446
  Case Conference [Jan.]
Envy and Jealousy (Contribution to a Symposium on)   1969   W19:462–464
Ernest Jones: Obituary & Funeral Address   1958   W19:393–407
  IJP 39
Evacuated Child (The) [B.B.C. radio broadcast]   1945   W5:83–87
Evacuated Child (The)   1945   W13:39–43
Evacuation of Small Children [letter: with J. Bowlby & E.
    Miller]   1939   W13:13–14
  Brit. Med. J.

Grief and Mourning in Infancy by J. Bowlby (Discussion on)	1953	W19:426–432
PSC 15 [1960]		
Group Influences and the Maladjusted Child: The School		
Aspect	1955	W8:146–154
Group Influences and the Maladjusted Child: The School		
Aspect	1955	W13:189–199
Growing Pains	1931	W1:76–80
Growth and Development in Immaturity	1950	W8:21–29
Guntrip, Harry: Letter to [July 20th]	1954	W17:75–76
Guntrip, Harry: Letter to [Aug. 13th]	1954	W17:77–79
Hallucination and Dehallucination	1957	W19:39–42
Hate in the Countertransference	1947	W6:194–203
IJP 30 [1949]:69		
Hazlehurst, R. S.: Letter to [Sept. 1st]	1949	W17:17
Haemoptysis: Case for Diagnosis	1931	***
Proceedings of the Royal Society of Medicine 24:855–856		
Health Education through Broadcasting	1957	W20:1–6
Mother and Child 28		
Healthy Individual (The Concept of a)	1967	W14:22–38
In *Towards Community Health* ed. J. D. Sutherland [1971]		
Heart (The), with Special Reference to Rheumatic Carditis	1931	W1:42–57
Henderson, Sir David K.: Letter to [May 10th]	1954	W17:63–65
Henderson, Sir David K.: Letter to [May 20th]	1954	W17:68–71
History-Taking	1931	W1:7–21
Hobgoblins and Good Habits	1967	***
Parents 22:9		
Hodge, S. H.: Letter to [Sept. 1st]	1949	W17:17–19
Hoffer, Willi: Letter to [April 4th]	1952	W17:29–30
Holding and Interpretation: Fragment of an Analysis	1986	W15:1–202
An earlier version published in *Tactics and Techniques in*		
Psychoanalytic Therapy ed. P. L. Giovacchini [1972]		
Home Again [B.B.C. radio broadcast]	1945	W5:93–97
Home Again	1945	W13:49–53
Hospital Care Supplementing Intensive Psychotherapy in		
Adolescence	1963	W9:242–248
How a Baby Begins to Feel Sorry and to Make Amends	1967	***
Parents 22:7		
How to Survive Parenthood by Edna J. LeShan [review]	1967	***
New Society 26/10		
Human Aggression by Anthony Storr [review]	1968	***
New Statesman 5/7		
Human Nature	1988	W18:1–189
Ideas and Definitions [probably early 1950s]	n.d.	W19:43–44
Human Relations	1969	***
Physiotherapy 55		
Importance of the Setting in Meeting Regression in Psycho-		
Analysis (The)	1964	W19:96–102
Impulse to Steal (The)	1949	W5:176–180
Indications for Child Analysis & Other Papers by A. Freud		
(Review of)	1969	W19:511–512
New Society [Aug. 1969]		

Location of Cultural Experience (The)   1971   W10:95–103
    IJP 48 [1967]:368
"Location of Cultural Experience (The)" (Addendum to)   1967   W19:200–202
    IJP 487:368
Lowry, Oliver H.: Letter to [July 5th]   1956   W17:100–103
Luria, A. R.: Letter to [July 7th]   1960   W17:130
Main, Thomas: Letter to [Feb. 25th]   1957   W17:112–114
Man Looks at Motherhood (A) [B.B.C. radio broadcast]   1949   W4:3–6
Manic Defence (The)   1935   W6:129–144
Masturbation   1931   W1:183–190
Maternal Care and Mental Health by John Bowlby, 1951
    (Review of)   1953   W19:423–426
    Brit. J. Med. Psychol. 26
McKeith, Ronald: Letter to [Jan. 31st]   1963   W17:138–139
Meaning of Mother Love (The)   1967   ***
    Parents 22:6
Meltzer, Donald: Letter to [May 21st]   1959   W17:124–125
Meltzer, Donald: Letter to [Oct. 25th]   1966   W17:157–161
Memories, Dreams, Reflections by C. G. Jung, 1963 (Review of)   1964   W19:482–492
    IJP 45
Mental Defect   1931   W1:152–156
Mental Hygiene of the Pre-school Child [talk given to the
    Nursery School Association]   1936   W21:59–76
Mentally Ill in Your Caseload (The)   1963   W9:217–229
    In *New Thinking for Changing Needs*, Association of Social
    Workers
Metapsychological and Clinical Aspects of Regression within
    the Psycho-Analytical Set-Up   1954   W6:278–294
    IJP 36:16
Micturition Disturbances   1931   W1:172–182
Mind and Its Relation to the Psyche-Soma   1949   W6:243–254
    Brit. J. Med. Psychol. 27 [1954]
Mirror-rôle of Mother and Family in Child Development   1971   W10:111–118
    In *The Predicament of the Family* ed. P. Lomas [1967]
Money-Kyrle, Roger: Letter to [Nov. 27th]   1952   W17:38–43
Money-Kyrle, Roger: Letter to [Sept. 23rd]   1954   W17:79–80
Money-Kyrle, Roger: Letter to [Feb. 10th]   1955   W17:84–85
Money-Kyrle, Roger: Letter to [March 17th]   1955   W17:85
Moral Paradox of Peace and War (The) by J. C. Flugel [review]   1941   ***
    New Era in Home and School 22:183
Morals and Education   1963   W9:93–105
    In *Moral Education in a Changing Society* ed. W. R. Niblett,
    under the title "The Young Child at Home and at
    School"
Mother, Teacher and the Child's Needs   1964   W7:189–198
Mother's Contribution to Society (The) [published as
    Postscript]   1957   W4:141–144
Mother's Contribution to Society (The)   1957   W14:123–127
Mother's Madness Appearing in the Clinical Material as an
    Ego-Alien Factor   1969   W19:375–382

In *Tactics & Techniques in Psychoanalytic Therapy* ed. P.
   Giovacchini [1972]

Mother-Foetus Relationship (A Note on the) [probably mid-1960s]	n.d.	W19:161–162
Mother-Infant Experience of Mutuality (The)	1969	W19:251–260
In *Parenthood: Its Psychology & Psychopathology* ed. Anthony & Benedek [1970]		
Nagera, Humberto: Letter to [Feb. 15th]	1965	W17:147–148
Needs of the Under-Fives in a Changing Society	1954	W5:3–13
Nursery Journal 44/396:15		
New Light on Children's Thinking	1965	W19:152–157
Nelson, Gillian: Letter to [Oct. 6th]	1967	W17:170–171
Neonate and His Mother (The)	1964	***
Acta Paediatrica Latina Vol. 17		
Newborn and His Mother (The)	1964	W16:35–49
Acta Pediatrica Latina Vol. 17 under title "The Neonate & His Mother"		
New Society: Letter to [March 23rd]	1964	W17:140–142
Niffle (The)	n.d.	W21:104–109
Non-Human Environment in Normal Development and in Schizophrenia (The) by H. F. Searles, 1960 (Review of)	1963	W19:478–481
IJP 44		
Non-Pharmacological Treatment of Psychosis in Childhood (The)	1968	***
Concilium Paedopsychiatricum [Proc. 3rd Eur. Cong. Pedopsychiat.]		
Normality and Anxiety (A Note on)	1931	W1:98–121
Normality and Anxiety (A Note on)	1931	W6:3–21
Nose and Throat (The)	1931	W1:38–41
Note of Contribution to Symposium on Child Analysis and Paediatrics	1968	***
IJP 49:279		
Notes Made on a Train, Part 2	1965	W19:231–233
Notes on a Little Boy	1938	W21:102–103
New Era in Home & School 19		
Notes on the Time Factor in Treatment [preparation for lecture to West Sussex County Council Children's Dept.]	1961	W21:231–234
Nothing at the Centre	1959	W19:49–52
Now They Are Five [B.B.C. radio broadcast, June]	1962	W20:111–120
Originally published under title "The Five-Year Old" in W8 [*q. v.*]		
Observation of Infants in a Set Situation (The)	1941	W6:52–69
IJP 22:229		
Observer (The): Letter to [Oct. 12th]	1964	W17:142–144
Observer (The): Letter to [Nov. 5th]	1964	W17:146
Obsessional Neurosis and "Frankie" (Comment on)	1965	W19:158–160
Ocular Psychoneuroses of Childhood	1944	W6:85–90
Transactions of the Ophthalmological Society 64		
On Not Being Able to Paint by Marion Milner (Critical Notice of) [originally written under the name of Joanna Field, 1950]	1951	W19:390–392

On the Concept of the Superego [paper by J. Sandler, *PSC* 15]
    (Comments on)   1960   W19:465–473
On Transference   1956   ***
    IJP 37:386
Only Child (The) [B.B.C. radio broadcast]   1945   W4:107–111
Ordinary Devoted Mother (The)   1966   W16:3–14
Ordinary Devoted Mother and Her Baby (The) [Intro.] [B.B.C.
    radio broadcast]   1949   W3:3–6
Out of the Mouths of Adolescents [review of E. M. & M. Eppel:
    Adolescents and Morality]   1966   W21:48–49
    New Society [Sept.]
Paediatrics and Childhood Neurosis   1956   W6:316–321
Paediatrics and Psychiatry   1948   W6:157–173
    Brit. J. Med. Psychol. 21
Papular Urticaria and the Dynamics of Skin Sensation   1934   W21:157–169
    Brit. J. Children's Diseases 31:5–16
Parent-Infant Relationship (The Theory of the)   1960   W9:37–55
    IJP 41:585
Parent-Infant Relationship (Further Remarks on the Theory of
    the)   1961   W19:73–75
    IJP 43 [1962]:238
Parfitt, D. N.: Letter to [Dec. 22nd]   1966   W17:162–163
Patient (A): Letter to [Dec. 13th]   1966   W17:162
Payne, Sylvia: Letter to [Oct. 7th]   1953   W17:52–53
Payne, Sylvia: Letter to [May 26th]   1966   W17:157
Peller, Lili E.: Letter to [April 15th]   1966   W17:156–157
Persecution That Wasn't (The) [review of *A Home from a Home*
    by S. Stewart]   1967   W13:200–201
    New Society [May]
Perversions and Pregenital Fantasy   1963   W19:79–80
Physical and Emotional Disturbances in an Adolescent Girl   1968   W19:369–374
Physical Examination   1931   W1:22–31
Physical Therapy of Mental Disorder   1947   W19:534–541
    Brit. Med. J. [May 1947]
Physiotherapy and Human Relations   1969   W19:561–568
    Physiotherapy [June 1969]
    In *A Survey of Child Psychiatry* ed. R. G. Gordon [pp. 28–44]
Piggle (The): An Account of the Psychoanalytic Treatment of a
    Little Girl   1977   W12:1–201
Pill and the Moon (The)   1969   W14:195–209
Pitfalls in Adoption   1954   W5:45–51
    Medical Press 232/6031
Pitfalls in Adoption   1954   W21:128–135
Place of the Monarchy (The)   1970   W14:260–268
Place Where We Live (The)   1971   W10:104–110
Play in the Analytic Situation   1954   W19:28–29
Play Therapy by V. Axline, 1947 (A Commentary on)
    [transcript from tape recording: unfinished & unedited
    by D.W.W.; probably mid-1960s]   n.d.   W19:495–498
Play (Notes on)   n.d.   W19:59–63

Psychoses and Child Care	1952	W6:219–228
Brit. J. Med. Psychol. 26 [1953]		
Psycho-Somatic Disorder (Additional Note on)	1969	W19:115–118
Psycho-Somatic Illness in Its Positive and Negative Aspects	1964	W19:103–114
IJP 47 [1966]:510		
Psychotherapeutic Consultation in Child Psychiatry (A)	1970	
In *The World Biennial of Psychiatry & Psychotherapy* ed. S.		
Arieti		
Also appears as Case XII in:		W11:194–215
Psychotherapy of Character Disorders	1963	W9:203–216
Psychotherapy of Character Disorders	1963	W13:241–255
Punishment in Prisons and Borstals (Comments on the Report		
of the Committee on)	1961	W13:202–208
Raison, Timothy: Letter to [April 9th]	1963	W17:139–140
Rapaport, David: Letter to [Oct. 9th]	1953	W17:53–54
Regression as Therapy *Brit. J. Med. Psychol.* 36:1.		
Appears as Case XIV in:	1963	W11:240–269
Relationship of a Mother to Her Baby at the Beginning (The)		
[rewritten 1964]	1960	W8:15–20
Reparation in Respect of Mother's Organized Defence against		
Depression [revised August 1954]	1948	W6:91–96
Residential Care as Therapy	1970	W13:220–228
Residential Management as Treatment for Difficult Children		
[with Claire Britton]	1947	W5:98–116
Human Relations 1/1:87		
Residential Management as Treatment for Difficult Children		
[with Claire Britton]	1947	W13:54–72
Return of the Evacuated Child (The) [B.B.C. radio broadcast]	1945	W5:88–92
Return of the Evacuated Child (The)	1945	W13:44–48
Rheumatic Clinic (The)	1931	W1:64–68
Rheumatic Fever	1931	W1:58–63
Ries, Hannah: Letter to [Nov. 27th]	1953	W17:54–55
Riviere, Joan: Letter to [Feb. 3rd]	1956	W17:94–97
Riviere, Joan: Letter to [June 13th]	1958	W17:118–119
Rodman, F. Robert: Letter to [Jan. 10th]	1969	W17:180–182
Rodrigue, Emilio: Letter to [March 17th]	1955	W17:86–87
Roots of Aggression	1964	W7:232–239
Roots of Aggression	1968	W19:458–461
Rosenfeld, Herbert: Letter to [Jan. 22nd]	1953	W17:43–46
Rosenfeld, Herbert: Letter to [Oct. 16th]	1958	W17:120
Rosenfeld, Herbert: Letter to [March 17th]	1966	W17:153–154
Rycroft, Charles E.: Letter to [April 21st]	1955	W17:87
Sargant, William W.: Letter to [June 24th]	1969	W17:192–194
Saying "No" [three B.B.C. radio broadcasts, Jan./Feb.]	1960	W20:21–39
Schizophrénie Infantile en Termes d'Echec d'Adaptation (La)	1968	***
Recherches (Special Issue: Enfance alienée) II		
Scott, P. D.: Letter to [May 11th]	1950	W17:22–23
Scott, W. Clifford M.: Letter to [March 19th]	1953	W17:48–50
Scott, W. Clifford M.: Letter to [Jan. 27th]	1954	W17:56–57
Scott, W. Clifford M.: Letter to [Feb. 26th]	1954	W17:57–58
Scott, W. Clifford M.: Letter to [April 13th]	1954	W17:60–63

Security [B.B.C. radio broadcasts, April]	1960	W20:87–93
Also published under title "Security (On)"	1960	W8:30–33
Segal, Hanna: Letter to [Feb. 21st]	1952	W17:25–27
Segal, Hanna: Letter to [Jan. 22nd]	1953	W17:47
Segal, Hanna: Letter to [Oct. 6th]	1955	W17:89
Sex Education in Schools	1949	W5:40–44
Medical Press 222/5761		
Also in *The Case against Pornography* ed. David Holbrook [1972]		
Shared Fate by H. David Kirk [review]	1965	***
New Society [Sept. 9]		
Sharpe, Ella: Letter to [Nov. 13th]	1946	W17:10
Shock Therapy [letter]	1944	W19:523–525
Brit. Med. J. [Dec.]		
Shock Treatment of Mental Disorder [letter]	1943	W19:522–523
Brit. Med. J. [Dec.]		
Short Communication on Enuresis	1930	W21:170–175
St. Bartholomew's Hospital Journal 37		
Shyness and Nervous Disorders in Children	1938	W5:35–39
New Era in Home & School 19/7:189		
Sleep Refusal in Children	1968	W21:42–45
Medical News Magazine (Paediatrics) [July]		
Smirnoff, Victor: Letter to [Nov. 19th]	1958	W17:120–124
Some Psychological Aspects of Juvenile Delinquency	1946	W5:181–187
New Era in Home & School 27/10:295 & *Delinquency Research* 24/5		
Some Psychological Aspects of Juvenile Delinquency	1946	W13:113–119
Some Thoughts on the Meaning of the Word "Democracy"	1950	W8:155–169
Human Relations 3/2		
Some Thoughts on the Meaning of the Word "Democracy"	1950	W14:239–259
Speech Disorders	1931	W1:191–200
Spence, Marjorie: Letter to [Nov. 23rd]	1967	W17:172–173
Spence, Marjorie: Letter to [Nov. 27th]	1967	W17:173–174
Split-Off Male and Female Elements to Be Found in Men and Women (The)	1966	W19:169–183
Clinical Material [1959–1963]		W19:183–188
Answers to Comments [1968–1969]		W19:189–192
Split-off Male and Female Elements (On the) [Editors' Note]	1989	W19:168
Spock, Benjamin: Letter to [April 9th]	1962	W17:133–138
Squiggle Game (The) [an amalgamation of two papers: one unpublished, written in 1964, the other published 1968]	1968	W19:299–317
Voices: The Art & Science of Psychotherapy 4/1		
Also appears as Case III in:		W11:42–63
Stealing and Telling Lies	1949	W4:117–120
Stierlin, Helm: Letter to [July 31st]	1969	W17:195–196
Stone, L. Joseph: Letter to [June 18th]	1968	W17:177–178
Stone, Marjorie: Letter to [Feb. 14th]	1949	W17:14–15
Storr, Charles Anthony: Letter to [Sept. 30th]	1965	W17:151
Strachey, James: Letter to [May 1st]	1951	W17:24
Strachey (James): Obituary	1969	W19:506–510
IJP 50 [1969]		

String: A Technique of Communication   1960   W9:153–157
  Journal of Child Psychology & Psychiatry 4:85
Struggling through the Doldrums   1963   W13:145–155
  New Society [April]
Study of Three Pairs of Identical Twins (A) by D. Burlingham
  (Review of)   1953   W19:408–412
  New Era in Home & School [March]
Successful Step-parent (The) by Helen Thomson [review] 1967 ***
  New Society 13/4
Sum, I Am   1968   W14:55–64
  Mathematics Teaching [March 1984]
Support for Normal Parents [B.B.C. radio broadcast; published
  as "Postscript"]   1945   W2:25–27
  New Era in Home & School 26/1:16
Support for Normal Parents   1945   W4:137–140
Susan Isaacs by D. E. M. Gardner (Foreword to) 1969 W19:387–389
Susan Isaacs: Obituary   1948   W19:385–387
  Nature [Dec.]
Symptom Tolerance in Paediatrics: A Case History 1953 W6:101–117
  Proceedings of the Royal Society of Medicine 46/8
Szasz, Thomas: Letter to [Nov. 19th]   1959   W17:126–127
Teacher, the Parent, and the Doctor (The) [read before the
  Ideals in Education Conference]   1936   W21:77–93
Temperature and the Importance of Charts (A Note on) 1931 W1:32–37
Their Standards and Yours [B.B.C. radio broadcast] 1945 W2:21–24
  New Era in Home & School 26/1:13
Their Standards and Yours   1945   W4:87–91
Theme of the Mother's Unconscious as Discovered in Psycho-
  Analytic Practice (Development of the) 1969 W19:247–250
Theoretical Statement of the Field of Child Psychiatry 1958 W8:97–105
  Modern Trends in Paediatrics [Second Series]
Therapy in Child Care: Collected Papers by B. Docker-Drysdale
  (Foreword to)   1968 ***
  Longmans' Papers on Residential Work Vol. 3
Thinking and Symbol-Formation [probably 1968] n.d. W19:213–216
Thinking and the Unconscious   1945   W14:169–171
  The Liberal Magazine [March]
This Feminism   1964   W14:183–194
Thorner, Hans: Letter to [March 17th]   1966   W17:154
Times (The): Letter to [Nov. 6th]   1946   W17:9
Times (The): Letter to [Aug. 10th]   1949   W17:15–16
Times (The): Letter to [probably May]   1950   W17:21
Times (The): Letter to [July 21st]   1954   W17:76–77
Times (The): Letter to [Nov. 1st]   1954   W17:82–83
Times (The): Letter to [March 3rd]   1966   W17:152–153
Tizard, J. P. M.: Letter to [Oct. 23rd]   1956   W17:103–107
Tod, Robert: Letter to [Nov. 6th]   1969   W17:196–197
Torrie, Margaret: Letter to [Sept. 4th]   1967   W17:166–167
Torrie, Margaret: Letter to [Sept. 5th]   1967   W17:167–169
Towards an Objective Study of Human Nature 1945 W5:125–133

New Era in Home & School 26/8:179 under title "Talking about Psychology"

New Era in Home & School 33/3 [1952]:55 under title "What Is Psycho-Analysis?"

Towards an Objective Study of Human Nature	1945	W21:3–12
Training for Child Psychiatry: The Paediatric Department of Psychology	1961	W21:227–230

In *St. Mary's Hospital Gazette* [Sept.] under title "The Paediatric Department of Psychology"

Training for Child Psychiatry	1963	W9:193–202

Journal of Child Psychology & Psychiatry 4:85

Transitional Objects and Transitional Phenomena	1951	W6:229–242

IJP 34 [1953]:89

Transitional Objects and Transitional Phenomena	1953	W10:1–25
Trauma in Relation to the Development of the Individual within the Family (The Concept of)	1965	W19:130–148
Treatment of Mental Disease by Induction of Fits	1943	W19:516–521
Tribute on the Occasion of W. Hoffer's 70th Birthday (A)	1967	W19:499–505

Psyche [in German]

Twins [B.B.C. radio broadcast]	1945	W4:112–116
Two Adopted Children	1953	W5:52–65

Case Conference [Dec.]

Two Adopted Children	1953	W21:113–127
Two Notes on the Use of Silence	1963	W19:81–86
Use of an Object and Relating through Identifications (The)	1968	W19:218–227
Use of an Object and Relating through Identifications (The)	1971	W10:86–94

Based on *IJP* 50 [1969]:711

"Use of an Object (The)" (On) [Editors' Note]	1989	W19:217–218
Use of an Object in the Context of *Moses and Monotheism* (The)	1969	W19:240–246
Use of the Word "Use" (The)	1968	W19:233–235
Value of Depression (The)	1963	W14:71–79

Brit. J. Psychiatric Social Work 7/3 [1964]:123–127

Value of the Therapeutic Consultation (The)	1965	W19:318–324

In *Foundations of Child Psychiatry* ed. E. Miller

Varicella Encephalitis and Vaccinia Encephalitis [with Nancy Gibbs]	1926	***

Brit. J. Children's Diseases 23:107–127

Varieties of Clinical Confusion (Fragments Concerning)	1956	W19:30–33
Varieties of Psychotherapy	1961	W13:232–240
Varieties of Psychotherapy	1961	W14:101–111
Verbindung zwischen Kinderheilkunde und Kinderpsychologie, klinische Betrachtungen (Eine) [translation of: "A Link between Paediatrics and Child Psychology"]	1969	***

Dynam. Psychiat. 2

Verso una teoria sulla psicoterapia: il suo rapporto col gioco [translation of "Towards a Theory of Psychotherapy: The Link with Playing". Lecture given to PsA. Soc., Rome]	1969	***

Psyche 6:1

Very Early Roots of Aggression	1955	W6:210–218

Visiting Children in Hospital [B.B.C. radio broadcast]	1951	W4:121–126
Vulnerable Children by Lindy Burton [review]	1968	***
New Society 25/4		
Walking	1931	W1:143–151
Weaning [B.B.C. radio broadcast]	1949	W3:43–47
Weaning	1949	W4:64–68
What about Father? [B.B.C. radio broadcast]	1945	W2:16–21
New Era in Home & School 26/1:11		
What about Father?	1945	W4:81–86
What Do We Mean by a Normal Child?	1946	W4:100–106
New Era in Home & School 27/3:61		
What Do We Know about Babies as Clothes Suckers? [B.B.C.		
radio broadcast, Jan. 31]	1956	W20:15–20
What Irks? [three B.B.C. radio broadcasts, March]	1960	W20:65–86
Where the Food Goes [B.B.C. radio broadcast]	1949	W3:12–16
Where the Food Goes	1949	W4:23–27
Why Children Play	1942	W5:149–152
New Era in Home & School 23/1:12		
Why Do Babies Cry? [B.B.C. radio broadcast]	1945	W2:5–12
New Era in Home & School 26/1:3–11		
Why Do Babies Cry?	1945	W4:43–52
Widow's Child (The) by Margaret Torrie (Foreword to)	1964	***
Wilkinson, Agnes: Letter to [June 9th]	1969	W17:192
Winnicott, Violet: Letter to [Nov. 15th]	1919	W17:1–4
Wisdom, John O.: Letter to [Oct. 26th]	1964	W17:144–146
Withdrawal and Regression	1954	W6:255–261
Revue Française de Psychanalyse XIX/1–2 [1955]		
Psyche Heft X [1956–1957]		
Withdrawal and Regression (Notes on)	1965	W19:149–151
World in Small Doses (The) [B.B.C. radio broadcast]	1949	W3:32–37
World in Small Doses (The)	1949	W4:53–58
Yes, But How Do We Know It's True? [talk given at the		
London School of Economics]	1950	W21:13–18
Young Children and Other People	1949	W4:92–99
Young Children 1/3:36		
Your Child Is a Person by Chess, Thomas, Birch [review]	1966	***
Medical News [Oct.]		
Youth Will Not Sleep	1964	W13:156–158
New Society [May 1964]		

Chronological list

*** Indicates that the entry does not appear in volumes W1 to W21.

1936 Mental Hygiene of the Pre-school Child [talk given to the
      Nursery School Association]   W21:59–76
1936 Contribution to a Discussion on Enuresis   W21:151–156
        Proceedings of the Royal Society of Medicine 29
1936 Appetite and Emotional Disorder [read before the Medical
      Section, British Psychological Society]   W6:33–51
1936 Teacher, the Parent, and the Doctor (The) [read before the
      Ideals in Education Conference]   W21:77–93
1938 Shyness and Nervous Disorders in Children   W5:35–39
        New Era in Home & School 19/7:189
1938 Chamberlain, Mrs. Neville: Letter to [Nov. 10th]   W17:4
1938 *Child Psychiatry* by Leo Kanner, 1937 [review]   W21:191–193
        IJP 19
1938 Notes on a Little Boy   W21:102–103
        New Era in Home & School 19
1939 Early Disillusion   W19:21–23
1939 Evacuation of Small Children [letter: with J. Bowlby & E.
      Miller]   W13:13–14
        Brit. Med. J.
1939 Deprived Mother (The) [B.B.C. radio broadcast]   W5:75–82
        New Era in Home & School 221/3 [1940]:64
1939 Deprived Mother (The)   W13:31–38
1939 Aggression   W5:167–175
1939 Psychology of Juvenile Rheumatism (The)   ***
        In *A Survey of Child Psychiatry* ed. R. G. Gordon [pp. 28–44]
1940 Friedlander, Kate: Letter to [Jan. 8th]   W17:5–6
1940 Children and Their Mothers   W13:14–21
        New Era in Home & School 21
1940 Children in the War   W5:69–74
        New Era in Home & School 21/9:229
1940 Children in the War   W13:25–30
1940 Discussion of War Aims   W14:210–220
1941 Influencing and Being Influenced (On)   W5:24–28
        New Era in Home & School 22/6:118
1941 *Cambridge Education Survey (The)* ed. S. Isaacs (Review of)   W13:22–24
        New Era in Home & School 22
1941 Observation of Infants in a Set Situation (The)   W6:52–69
        IJP 22:229
1941 *Moral Paradox of Peace and War* (The) by J. C. Flugel [review] ***
        New Era in Home and School 22:183
1942 Child Department Consultations   W6:70–84
        IJP 23:139
1942 Why Children Play   W5:149–152
        New Era in Home & School 23/1:12
1943 Prefrontal Leucotomy [letter]   W19:542–543
        The Lancet [April 1943]
1943 Shock Treatment of Mental Disorder [letter]   W19:522–523
        Brit. Med. J. [Dec.]
1943 Treatment of Mental Disease by Induction of Fits   W19:516–521
1943 Delinquency Research   ***
        New Era in Home and School 24:65–67

1946 Beveridge, Lord: Letter to [Oct. 15th]   W17:8
1946 *Times (The)*: Letter to [Nov. 6th]   W17:9
1946 Sharpe, Ella: Letter to [Nov. 13th]   W17:10
1946 Educational Diagnosis   W5:29–34
          National Froebel Foundation Bulletin 41:3
1946 Some Psychological Aspects of Juvenile Delinquency   W5:181–187
          New Era in Home & School 27/10:295 & *Delinquency Research*
          24/5
1946 Some Psychological Aspects of Juvenile Delinquency   W13:113–119
1946 What Do We Mean by a Normal Child?   W4:100–106
          New Era in Home & School 27/3:61
1947 Babies as Persons (Further Thoughts on)   W5:134–140
          New Era in Home & School 28/10:199 under title "Babies are
          Persons"
1947 Hate in the Countertransference   W6:194–203
          IJP 30 [1949]:69
1947 Physical Therapy of Mental Disorder   W19:534–541
          Brit. Med. J. [May 1947]
1947 Residential Management as Treatment for Difficult Children
          [with Claire Britton]   W5:98–116
          Human Relations 1/1:87
1947 Residential Management as Treatment for Difficult Children   W13:54–72
1947 Child and Sex (The)   W5:153–166
1948 Freud, Anna: Letter to [July 6th]   W17:10–12
1948 Children's Hostels in War and Peace   W5:117–121
          Brit. J. Med. Psychol. 21/3:175
1948 Children's Hostels in War and Peace   W13:73–77
1948 Paediatrics and Psychiatry   W6:157–173
          Brit. J. Med. Psychol. 21
1948 Reparation in Respect of Mother's Organized Defence against
          Depression [revised Aug. 1954]   W6:91–96
1948 Susan Isaacs: Obituary   W19:385–387
          Nature [Dec.]
1948 Primary Introduction to External Reality: The Early Stages [talk
          given at the London School of Economics]   W21:21–28
1948 Environmental Needs; The Early Stages; Total Dependence and
          Essential Independence [talk given at The Institute of
          Education, Univ. of London]   W21:29–36
1949 Federn, Paul: Letter to [Jan. 3rd]   W17:12
1949 *British Medical Journal*: Letter to [Jan. 6th]   W17:13–14
1949 Stone, Marjorie: Letter to [Feb. 14th]   W17:14–15
1949 *Times (The)*: Letter to [Aug. 10th]   W17:15–16
1949 Hazlehurst, R. S.: Letter to [Sept. 1st]   W17:17
1949 Hodge, S. H.: Letter to [Sept. 1st]   W17:17–19
1949 Man Looks at Motherhood (A) [B.B.C. radio broadcast]   W4:3–6
1949 Birth Memories, Birth Trauma, and Anxiety [rewritten, in part,
          1954]   W6:174–193
1949 Close-Up of Mother Feeding Baby [B.B.C. radio broadcast]   W3:27–31
1949 Close-Up of Mother Feeding Baby   W4:38–42
1949 Leucotomy   W19:543–547
          Brit. Medical Students' Journal 3

Brit. Med. J. [June]
1951 Transitional Objects and Transitional Phenomena   W6:229–242
       IJP 34 [1953]:89
1951 Visiting Children in Hospital [B.B.C. radio broadcast]   W4:121–126
1952 Segal, Hanna: Letter to [Feb. 21st]   W17:25–27
1952 Bonnard, Augusta: Letter to [April 3rd]   W17:28–29
1952 Hoffer, Willi: Letter to [April 4th]   W17:29–30
1952 Ezriel, H.: Letter to [June 20th]   W17:31–32
1952 Jones, Ernest: Letter to [July 22nd]   W17:33
1952 Klein, Melanie: Letter to [Nov. 17th]   W17:33–38
1952 Money-Kyrle, Roger: Letter to [Nov. 27th]   W17:38–43
1952 Anxiety Associated with Insecurity   W6:97–100
1952 Psychoses and Child Care   W6:219–228
       Brit. J. Med. Psychol. 26 [1953]
1953 Rosenfeld, Herbert: Letter to [Jan. 22nd]   W17:43–46
1953 Segal, Hanna: Letter to [Jan. 22nd]   W17:47
1953 Scott, W. Clifford M.: Letter to [March 19th]   W17:48–50
1953 Bick, Esther: Letter to [June 11th]   W17:50–52
1953 Payne, Sylvia: Letter to [Oct. 7th]   W17:52–53
1953 Rapaport, David: Letter to [Oct. 9th]   W17:53–54
1953 Ries, Hannah: Letter to [Nov. 27th]   W17:54–55
1953 *Grief and Mourning in Infancy* by J. Bowlby (Discussion on)   W19:426–432
       PSC 15 [1960]
1953 *Study of Three Pairs of Identical Twins (A)* by D. Burlingham
       (Review of)   W19:408–412
       New Era in Home & School [March]
1953 *Maternal Care and Mental Health* by John Bowlby, 1951 (Review
       of)   W19:423–426
       Brit. J. Med. Psychol. 26
1953 *Psychoanalytic Studies of the Personality* by W. R. D. Fairbairn,
       1952 (Review of) [written with M. Masud R. Khan]   W19:413–422
       IJP 34
1953 Symptom Tolerance in Paediatrics: A Case History   W6:101–117
       Proceedings of the Royal Society of Medicine 46/8
1953 Child's Needs and the Rôle of the Mother in the Early Stages
       (The)   W5:13–23
       [An excerpt] published in series *Problems in Education*
1953 Transitional Objects and Transitional Phenomena   W10:1–25
       IJP 34:89
1953 Two Adopted Children   W5:52–65
       Case Conference [Dec.]
1953 Two Adopted Children   W21:113–127
1954 Scott, W. Clifford M.: Letter to [Jan. 27th]   W17:56–57
1954 Scott, W. Clifford M.: Letter to [Feb. 26th]   W17:57–58
1954 Freud, Anna: Letter to [March 18th]   W17:58
1954 Joseph, Betty: Letter to [April 13th]   W17:59–60
1954 Scott, W. Clifford M.: Letter to [April 13th]   W17:60–63
1954 Henderson, Sir David K.: Letter to [May 10th]   W17:63–65
1954 Bowlby, John: Letter to [May 11th]   W17:65–66
1954 Frank, Klara: Letter to [May 20th]   W17:67–68

1956 Balint, Enid: Letter to [March 22nd]   W17:97–98
1956 Casuso, Gabriel: Letter to [July 4th]   W17:98–100
1956 Lowry, Oliver H.: Letter to [July 5th]   W17:100–103
1956 Tizard, J. P. M.: Letter to [Oct. 23rd]   W17:103–107
1956 Lantos, Barbara: Letter to [Nov. 8th]   W17:107–110
1956 Varieties of Clinical Confusion (Fragments Concerning)   W19:30–33
1956 Paediatrics and Childhood Neurosis   W6:316–321
1956 Prefrontal Leucotomy [letter]   W19:553–554
         Brit. Med. J. [Jan.]
1956 Primary Maternal Preoccupation   W6:300–305
1956 Antisocial Tendency (The)   W13:120–131
1956 Antisocial Tendency (The)   W6:306–315
1956 What Do We Know about Babies as Clothes Suckers? [B.B.C.
         radio broadcast, Jan. 31st]   W20:15–20
1956 On Transference   ***
         IJP 37:386
1957 Kulka, Anna M.: Letter to [Jan. 15th]   W17:110–112
1957 Main, Thomas: Letter to [Feb. 25th]   W17:112–114
1957 Klein, Melanie: Letter to [March 7th]   W17:114–115
1957 James, Martin: Letter to [April 17th]   W17:115–116
1957 Bonnard, Augusta: Letter to [Oct. 1st]   W17:116–117
1957 Bonnard, Augusta: Letter to [Nov. 7th]   W17:117
1957 Advising Parents   W8:114–120
1957 Excitement in the Aetiology of Coronary Thrombosis   W19:34–38
1957 Hallucination and Dehallucination   W19:39–42
1957 Integrative and Disruptive Factors in Family Life   W8:40–49
         Canadian Medical Association Journal [1961]
1957 Contribution of Direct Child Observation to Psycho-Analysis
         (On the)   W9:109–114
         First published in Revue française de Psychanalyse 22:205 [in
         French]
1957 Contribution of Psycho-Analysis to Midwifery (The)   W8:106–113
         Nursing Times [May 1957]
1957 Contribution of Psycho-Analysis to Midwifery (The)   W16:69–81
1957 Mother's Contribution to Society (The) [published as Postscript] W4:141–144
1957 Mother's Contribution to Society (The)   W14:123–127
1957 Health Education through Broadcasting   W20:1–6
         Mother and Child 28
1958 Riviere, Joan: Letter to [June 13th]   W17:118–119
1958 Laing, R. D.: Letter to [July 18th]   W17:119
1958 Rosenfeld, Herbert: Letter to [Oct. 16th]   W17:120
1958 Smirnoff, Victor: Letter to [Nov. 19th]   W17:120–124
1958 Child Analysis in the Latency Period   W9:115–123
         A Criança Portuguesa 17:219
1958 Ernest Jones: Obituary & Funeral Address   W19:393–407
         IJP 39
1958 Psychogenesis of a Beating Fantasy   W19:45–48
1958 Psycho-Analysis and the Sense of Guilt   W9:15–28
         In Psycho-Analysis & Contemporary Thought ed. J. D.
         Sutherland

1960 Jealousy [four B.B.C. radio broadcasts, Feb./March]   W20:41–64
1960 What Irks? [three B.B.C. radio broadcasts, March]   W20:65–86
1961 Khan, Masud: Letter to [March 7th]   W17:114–115
1961 Khan, Masud: Letter to [June 26th]   W17:132
1961 Bion, Wilfred R.: Letter to [Nov. 16th]   W17:133
1961 Adolescence: Struggling through the Doldrums   W8:79–87
        New Era in Home & School [1962]
        Also in an altered form entitled "Struggling through the
          Doldrums" New Society [1963]
1961 Punishment in Prisons and Borstals (Comments on the Report
        of the Committee on)   W13:202–208
1961 Psychoanalysis and Science: Friends or Relations?   W14:13–18
1961 Psycho-Neurosis in Childhood   W19:64–72
1961 Varieties of Psychotherapy   W13:232–240
1961 Varieties of Psychotherapy   W14:101–111
1961 Feeling Guilty: Discussion with Claire Rayner [B.B.C. radio
        broadcast, March 1960]   W20:95–103
1961 Training for Child Psychiatry: The Paediatric Department of
        Psychology   W21:227–230
        In St. Mary's Hospital Gazette [Sept.] under the title "The
          Paediatric Department of Psychology"
1961 Notes on the Time Factor in Treatment [preparation for lecture
        to West Sussex County Council Children's Dept.]   W21:231–234
1961 Parent–Infant Relationship (Further Remarks on the Theory of
        the)   W19:73–75
        IJP 43 [1962]:238
1962 Spock, Benjamin: Letter to [April 9th]   W17:133–138
1962 Kleinian Contribution (A Personal View of the)   W9:171–178
1962 Ego Integration in Child Development   W9:56–63
1962 Providing for the Child in Health and in Crisis   W9:64–72
1962 Letters of Sigmund Freud 1873–1939, 1961 (Review of)   W19:474–477
        Brit. J. Psychology 53
1962 Aims of Psycho-Analytical Treatment (The)   W9:166–170
1962 Beginnings of a Formulation of an Appreciation and Criticism
        of Klein's Envy Statement (The)   W19:447–457
1962 Now They Are Five [B.B.C. radio broadcast, June]   W20:111–120
        Originally published under the title "The Five-Year Old" in
          W8 [q. v.]   W8:34–39
1962 Development of a Child's Sense of Right and Wrong (The)
        [B.B.C. radio broadcast, June]   W20:105–110
1962 Anti-Social Tendency Illustrated by a Case (The)
        A Criança Portuguesa Vol. 21
        Also appears as Case VII in: W11:110–126
1962 Child Psychiatry Interview (A)
        St. Mary's Hospital Gazette [Jan./Feb.]
        Appears as Case VI in: W11:105–109
1963 McKeith, Ronald: Letter to [Jan. 31st]   W17:138–139
1963 Raison, Timothy: Letter to [April 9th]   W17:139–140
1963 Case Involving Envy (A Note on a)   W19:76–78
1963 Communicating and Not Communicating Leading to a Study
        of Certain Opposites   W9:179–192

1964 Roots of Aggression   W7:232–239
1964 Concept of the False Self (The)   W14:65–70
1964 Importance of the Setting in Meeting Regression in Psycho-
        Analysis (The)   W19:96–102
1964 Newborn and His Mother (The)   W16:35–49
        Acta Pediatrica Latina Vol. 17 under title "The Neonate & His
        Mother"
1964 This Feminism   W14:183–194
1964 Youth Will Not Sleep   W13:156–158
        New Society [May 1964]
1964 *Widow's Child (The)* by Margaret Torrie (Foreword to)   ***
1964 Neonate and His Mother (The)   ***
        Acta Paediatrica Latina Vol. 17
1965 Nagera, Humberto: Letter to [Feb. 15th]   W17:147–148
1965 Fordham, Michael: Letter to [June 24th]   W17:148–150
1965 Fordham, Michael: Letter to [July 15th]   W17:150–151
1965 Storr, Charles Anthony: Letter to [Sept. 30th]   W17:151
1965 Child Psychiatry Case Illustrating Delayed Reaction to Loss (A)   W19:341–368
        In *Drives, Affects, Behavior* Vol. 2 ed. M. Schur
1965 Obsessional Neurosis and "Frankie" (Comment on)   W19:158–160
1965 Dissociation Revealed in a Therapeutic Consultation   W13:256–282
        In *Crime, Law and Corrections* ed. R. Slovenko [1966]
        Also published as Case XIII in: W11:220–238
1965 Do Progressive Schools Give Too Much Freedom to the Child?   W13:209–219
        In *Who Are the Progressives Now?* ed. M. Ash [1969]
1965 New Light on Children's Thinking   W19:152–157
1965 Notes Made on a Train, Part 2   W19:231–233
1965 Withdrawal and Regression (Notes on)   W19:149–151
1965 *Childhood and Society* by E. H. Erikson, 1965 (Review of)   W19:493–494
        New Society [Sept.]
1965 Trauma in Relation to the Development of the Individual
        within the Family (The Concept of)   W19:130–148
1965 Price of Disregarding Psychoanalytic Research (The)   W14:172–182
        *The Price of Mental Health: Report of N.A.M.H. Annual
        Conference*
1965 Psychology of Madness (The): A Contribution from Psycho-
        Analysis   W19:119–129
1965 Value of the Therapeutic Consultation (The)   W19:318–324
        In *Foundations of Child Psychiatry* ed. E. Miller
1965 *Shared Fate* by H. David Kirk [review]   ***
        New Society [Sept. 9]
1965 Child Therapy: A Case of Anti-Social Behaviour
        In *Perspectives on Child Psychiatry* ed. J. Howells
        Appears also as Case XV in: W11:270–295
1965 Clinical Study of the Effect of a Failure of the Average
        Expectable Environment on a Child's Mental Functioning (A)
        IJP 46:81
        Appears also as Case IV in: W11:64–88
1966 *Times (The)*: Letter to [March 3rd]   W17:152–153
1966 Rosenfeld, Herbert: Letter to [March 17th]   W17:153–154

1966 Becoming Deprived as a Fact: A Psychotherapeutic
      Consultation
        J. Child Psychother. 1.
        Appears as Case XVII in: W11:315–331
1966 Cardiac Neurosis in Children (On) [paper given at A. G. M. of
      Association of European Paediatric Cardiologists]   W21:179–188
1967 Aitken, Mrs. P.: Letter to [Jan. 13th]   W17:163–164
1967 Colleague (A): Letter to [Sept. 4th]   W17:165
1967 Torrie, Margaret: Letter to [Sept. 4th]   W17:166–167
1967 Torrie, Margaret: Letter to [Sept. 5th]   W17:167–169
1967 Bion, Wilfred R.: Letter to [Oct. 5th]   W17:169–170
1967 Nelson, Gillian: Letter to [Oct. 6th]   W17:170–171
1967 Dahlberg, Charles Clay: Letter to [Oct. 24th]   W17:171–172
1967 Spence, Marjorie: Letter to [Nov. 23rd]   W17:172–173
1967 Spence, Marjorie: Letter to [Nov. 27th]   W17:173–174
1967 Dowling, R. S. W.: Letter to [Dec. 8th]   W17:174–175
1967 Tribute on the Occasion of W. Hoffer's 70th Birthday (A)   W19:499–505
        Psyche [in German]
1967 "Location of Cultural Experience (The)" (Addendum to)   W19:200–202
        (The Location of Cultural Experience)   W10:95–103
1967 Delinquency as a Sign of Hope   W14:90–100
        Prison Service Journal 7/27 [1968]
1967 D.W.W. on D.W.W.   W19:569–582
1967 Environmental Health in Infancy   W16:59–68
        Portions published in *Maternal & Child Care*
1967 Healthy Individual (The Concept of a)   W14:22–38
        In *Towards Community Health* ed. J. D. Sutherland [1971]
1967 Clinical Regression Compared with That of Defence
      Organisation (The Concept of)   W19:193–199
        In *Psychotherapy in the Designed Therapeutic Milieu* ed.
        Eldred & Vanderpol [1968]
1967 Persecution That Wasn't (The): Review of *A Home from a Home*
      by S. Stewart   W13:200–201
        New Society [May]
1967 Collection of children's books reviewed under the title "Small
      Things for Small People" (A)   ***
        New Society 7/12
1967 *Kinderbeobachtung (Eine)* [A Child Observation]   ***
        Psyche 21
1967 Hobgoblins and Good Habits   ***
        Parents 22:9
1967 How a Baby Begins to Feel Sorry and to Make Amends   ***
        Parents 22:7
1967 *How to Survive Parenthood* by Edna J. LeShan [review]   ***
        New Society 26/10
1967 Meaning of Mother Love (The)   ***
        Parents 22:6
1967 *Successful Step-parent (The)* by Helen Thomson [review]   ***
        New Society 13/4
1967 Bearing of Emotional Development on Feeding Problems (The)

1968 *Children in Distress* by Alec Clegg & Barbara Megson [review]   ***
      New Society 7/11
1968 *Human Aggression* by Anthony Storr [review]   ***
      New Statesman 5/7
1968 *Psychology of Childhood and Adolescence* by C. I. Sandstrom
      [review]   ***
      National Marriage Guidance Council Journal 11/3
1968 *Vulnerable Children* by Lindy Burton [review]   ***
      New Society 25/4
1968 *Psychoanalytic Study of the Child* Vol. 22 [review]   ***
      New Society 16/5
1968 Effect of Loss on the Young (The) [talk written for the Cruse
      Club]   W21:46–47
1968 Link between Paediatrics and Child Psychology (A): Clinical
      Observations [Catherine Chisholm Memorial Lecture,
      Manchester]   W21:255–276
1969 Rodman, F. Robert: Letter to [Jan. 10th]   W17:180–182
1969 American Correspondent (An): Letter to [Jan. 14th]   W17:183–185
1969 Freud, Anna: Letter to [Jan. 20th]   W17:185
1969 Collinson, J. D.: Letter to [March 10th]   W17:186–188
1969 Conran, M. B.: Letter to [May 8th]   W17:188–191
1969 Wilkinson, Agnes: Letter to [June 9th]   W17:192
1969 Sargant, William W.: Letter to [June 24th]   W17:192–194
1969 Stierlin, Helm: Letter to [July 31st]   W17:195–196
1969 Tod, Robert: Letter to [Nov. 6th]   W17:196–197
1969 Psycho-Somatic Disorder (Additional Note on)   W19:115–118
1969 Behaviour Therapy [letter]   W19:558–560
      Child Care News [June]
1969 Berlin Walls   W14:221–227
1969 Envy and Jealousy (Contribution to a Symposium on)   W19:462–464
1969 Theme of the Mother's Unconscious as Discovered in Psycho-
      Analytic Practice (Development of the)   W19:247–250
1969 *Susan Isaacs* by D. E. M. Gardner (Foreword to)   W19:387–389
1969 Freedom   W14:228–238
      Nouvelle Revue de Psychanalyse 30 [1984] [in French]
1969 Strachey (James): Obituary   W19:506–510
      IJP 50 [1969]
1969 Mother's Madness Appearing in the Clinical Material as an
      Ego-Alien Factor   W19:375–382
      In *Tactics & Techniques in Psychoanalytic Therapy* ed. P.
      Giovacchini [1972]
1969 Physiotherapy and Human Relations   W19:561–568
      Physiotherapy [June 1969]
1969 *Indications for Child Analysis & Other Papers* by A. Freud
      (Review of)   W19:511–512
      New Society [Aug. 1969]
1969 Mother-Infant Experience of Mutuality (The)   W19:251–260
      In *Parenthood: Its Psychology & Psychopathology* ed. Anthony
      & Benedek [1970]
1969 Pill and the Moon (The)   W14:195–209

1971 Location of Cultural Experience (The)   W10:95–103
         IJP 48 [1967]:368
1971 Place Where We Live (The)   W10:104–110
1971 Use of an Object and Relating through Identifications (The)   W10:86–94
         Based on *IJP* 50 [1969]:711
1971 Adopted Children in Adolescence   ***
         In *Social Work in Adoption* ed. Robert Tod
1977 Piggle (The): An Account of the Psychoanalytic Treatment of a
         Little Girl   W12:1–201
1984 Aggression and Its Roots   W13:84–99
         See W5: pp. 167–175 ["Aggresssion" ca. 1939]
         See also W7: pp. 232–239 ["Roots of Aggression" 1964]
1986 Holding and Interpretation: Fragment of an Analysis   W15:1–202
         An earlier version published in *Tactics and Techniques in*
            Psychoanalytic Therapy ed. P. L. Giovacchini [1972]
1988 Human Nature   W18:1–189
1989 Split-off Male and Female Elements (On the) [Editors' Note]   W19:168
1989 "Use of an Object (The)" (On) [Editors' Note]   W19:217–218
n.d. Knowing and Not-Knowing: A Clinical Example   W19:24–25
n.d. Niffle (The)   W21:104–109
n.d. Play (Notes on)   W19:59–63
n.d. Point in Technique (A)   W19:26–27
n.d. Delinquent and Habitual Offender (The) [probably early 1940s]   W21:51–53
n.d. Ideas and Definitions [probably early 1950s]   W19:43–44
n.d. Absence and Presence of a Sense of Guilt Illustrated in Two
         Patients [probably 1966]   W19:163–167
n.d. *Play Therapy* by V. Axline, 1947 (A Commentary on) [transcript
         from tape recording, unfinished & unedited by D.W.W.;
         probably mid-1960s]   W19:495–498
n.d. Mother-Foetus Relationship (A Note on the) [probably mid-
         1960s]   W19:161–162
n.d. Thinking and Symbol-Formation [probably 1968]   W19:213–216

INDEX

D. W. Winnicott

DONALD WOODS WINNICOTT [1896–1971] was born into a prosperous Plymouth family with a Methodist background and political interests. He had two older sisters. His family lived across the road from his father's brother, with his family of three boys and two girls. Winnicott was the youngest of all the children, who were brought up almost as one family.

Winnicott went to boarding school at the age of 14 years, then on to Cambridge to read for a degree in Biology and subsequently to study Medicine. The 1914–18 War intervened, however, and he joined the Navy and served as a surgeon probationer and medical officer on a destroyer. He lost many friends in the War.

In 1923 he was appointed to The Queen's Hospital for Children and also to the Paddington Green Hospital for Children, where he stayed for the next forty years, practising as a paediatrician, child psychiatrist, and psychoanalyst.

His first book, on clinical disorders in children, was published in 1931 and was the first of many. Winnicott was a prolific contributor to medical, psychiatric, and psychoanalytic journals, and he wrote also for magazines for the general reader in which he discussed children and family problems; in addition to his published books, he left over 100 published and unpublished papers. Winnicott was a great individual, speaking and writing not only with great courage but also with a poetic and imaginative quality that gives a unique voice to his theoretical and practical work.

3821906R00209

Printed in Great Britain
by Amazon.co.uk, Ltd.,
Marston Gate.